CONTENTS

FOREWORD 2

INTRODUCTION 3

ACKNOWLEDGEMENTS 6

1857-1879 : IN THE BEGINNING 7

1880-1899 : THE BIRTH OF THE UNIONS AND COMPETITION 17

1900-1913 : LULL BEFORE THE STORM 29

1914-1918 : THE FIRST WORLD WAR 43

1919-1938 : BETWEEN THE WARS…WHAT DEPRESSION! 51

1939-1945 : THE WAR YEARS 73

1946-1968 : 'HOW ARE THE MIGHTY FALLEN' 81

1969-1979 : THE ROLLER COASTER YEARS 95

1980-1997 : BACK IN THE BIG TIME 111

1998-2007 : THE THIRD GOLDEN ERA 131

2007 : THE SESQUICENTENARY YEAR 153

APPENDICES 163

FOREWORD

Having reached 150 a few times in my career I fully appreciate the effort and dedication required to get there. Congratulations North Down Cricket Club on a marvelous achievement and I'm very proud to have been asked to write this short foreword.

My first introduction to North Down was meeting a young man called Miller O'Prey in the Umpires Inn that I partially owned in Barbados over ten years ago. Like all Irishmen his tongue wasn't tied, but he was an endearing conversationalist and over the years I got to know him and his family very well. A short time later I met another North Down man Clarence Hiles, and we have been close friends ever since. When Clarence and Pamela moved to live in Barbados it started a long series of dinners and parties with many Irish visitors, so I've become well versed on Irish cricket and its personalities.

I have been to Ireland a number of times dating back to 1954 when I played at Holywood in a special match to mark the opening of their new pavilion. I returned in 1995 for a very memorable celebration to mark my knighthood organized by my dear friends Malcolm Brodie, Cecil Walker, Billy Boyd and Robin Walsh. That same year I visited The Green for the first time and met a lot of happy people, not least

because your team had just won the Irish Cup by one run.

What a great game I recall and you certainly know how to celebrate!

The North Down/Barbados connection is not solely reserved for the Hiles household as last year I met the Shields family and their friends when your captain Peter and his lovely young bride Claire were married on the island. I had a great night in the company of some old and some new friends from Comber.

I'd also like to congratulate Ian on completing this fine history, a labour of love and dedication.

Cricket is changing all over the world and I'd like to encourage the next generation of North Down members to ensure that your fine club goes from strength to strength in the future.

I've read a lot about Northern Ireland over the past thirty years and I'm very pleased to see that peace appears to have returned after so many years of terrible hardship. I hope the next generation never sees those times again. I also hope the younger North Down players draw inspiration from the great displays by Ireland in the West Indies at the Cricket World Cup. The Irish players showed great spirit and teamwork and I'm sure those same qualities have been shown by the North Down members down the years to get your club to such an historic milestone and in such a strong position.

Enjoy your celebration, enjoy your cricket, and above all play the game in the spirit it was intended.

Well done North Down Cricket Club, 150 not out and still at the crease!

SIR EVERTON DE COURCEY WEEKES
Barbados, September 2007

INTRODUCTION

'What goes round comes round' and what a good feeling it is to be writing the history of North Down Cricket Club as we reach a landmark sesquicentenary celebration, and with it, the knowledge that success on and off the field of play has come round yet again.

The greatness of a club can be measured by its ability to deal with the good times and the bad times in equal measure, and while it is easy to bask in the glory, it is much more difficult to persevere when the going gets tough. Rudyard Kipling has given us a benchmark with the lines:

"If you can meet with Triumph and Disaster
And treat those two impostors just the same
....then you'll be a man, my son"

It is often said that cricket 'is a great leveller' and how true it is that from season to season, individuals and their teams' performances have fluctuated between the sublime and the awful, mirroring our trials and tribulations over 150 years.

The story of the club highlights the impact of the people who made it what it is today; cricketers of all abilities, administrators, some of whom never played the game, and seasoned occupants of the 'critics' bench', the loyal supporters who bask or suffer accordingly, but are always there in the good times and the bad.

Only those directly involved in the game really appreciate the time and effort needed to run a club efficiently, and the sacrifices that are made by players and administrators to fulfil their commitments to the game. From ground staff, bar staff, entertainment organisers, commercial committees and catering, to the selection committee, youth development officers and especially the captains of the various XIs, the short summer time frame is packed with activity.

In his excellent book, 'A History of Senior Cricket in Ulster', Clarence Hiles, himself a dyed in the wool North Down man, has given us a great insight into our club over the years and I have drawn on these references and customised them to our requirements.

I remember running to the ground with bat in hand, turning into Castle Lane and along the footpath with the old stone wall and in through the little gate that opened on to The Green.

To me, still in short trousers, it was fascinating when there was a match in progress, to see the array of multicoloured caps and hear the sounds unique to the game; the sound of willow on leather, the bowlers' appeals, muted applause and the clink of china as the teas were prepared.

I wanted the job of turning the knobs on the old scoreboard and swinging it round to allow the few elderly critics at the gate to see how the game was progressing. This was no easy task as the numbers on the rotating drums usually stuck at some point.

Even as a boy I thought there was something special about the place, but during a match, the sign that hung on the railings round the pavilion made it quite clear that I could proceed no further. PLAYERS, MEMBERS and OFFICIALS ONLY.

The pavilion was an intriguing place, with the old stain glass windows and photographs dangling from twisted, dust covered wires. It had a lingering aroma; a blend of old pads and bats, ancient leather cricket bags and linseed oil. It had its sacred places, like the tall man's dressing room and the lockers that doubled as seats in the changing areas and held stumps and old bats way past their best, discarded cricket clothing and balls that had lost their seams and leather casing in the journey from the 1st XI match, where they were treated with respect, to the thrashing in the nets.

I was too young to make selection on the strong under 15 side with Wilmer McKibbin, Denis Artt, Jim Moreland, Don Shields, Tom Savage and Co., under the direction of Jimmy Boucher, who even then seemed to have been our coach for years.

My parents were keen sporting people, my mother loved her tennis and played at Comber Tennis Club, while my father played football with Comber Rangers and senior cricket and hockey from boyhood at The Green. One of the hockey players at the foundation of the club was Sammy Caughey from my mother's side of the family, and uncle Jackie Shields was a renowned cricketer and hockey player in the all conquering sides of the late Twenties and Thirties.

Uncle James Caughey organised a team, known as Ballydrain, to play in the Dundonald League and although too young to be a regular, I made up the team that included some of the North Down veterans like Willie Watt DFC, Gerry Spence and my father and youngsters like Sammy Alexander, now a well known umpire in the NCU, Ronnie McBurney and brother Don. It was an enriching experience played by lovers of the game on the worst imaginable wickets.

Sister Christine played hockey at the Ulster College of Physical Education, then for Pegasus and Ulster, before returning to her home club at North Down in her twilight years, to join husband Robin Mitchell and daughters Cathy and Karen.

Brother Don was adept at most ball games, was a skilful footballer at Trinity College Dublin, Leytonstone and Comber Recreation and played senior hockey and cricket at The Green, playing his fiftieth cricket season in 2007. We have shared many cricketing experiences, from our early 'test matches' in the yard at home, where rules were changed during the game and frequent rows caused regular postponements, to the triumphant opening partnerships in the senior league. As we opened the innings in our twilight years with our names and numbers on our backs, the young Instonians' cricketer, who suggested that at 43 and 46 we were rather old to be playing the game, didn't realise that those numbers indicated our year of birth!

I played tennis at the Andrews Memorial Hall during the long summer holidays and I had the honour, though I didn't fully appreciate it at the time, of captaining the tennis club in my teenage years. I took my tennis seriously, played in junior tournaments, won a few junior club trophies and played alongside the seniors in the Belfast and District League.

I played and enjoyed my cricket at Regent House School, was coached by Alf Chapman at the nets and was selected for Ulster Schools.

Roy Thompson, secretary and player at North Down encouraged me, on an evening visit to the tennis courts, that cricket was the sporting path to take. It didn't take all that much encouragement, as I always felt drawn to The Green, the history of the place, and my family's part in the 'good old days'.

My father died suddenly when I was seventeen and left a huge void in our family and a vacuum at North Down where he had returned, after a senior cricketing career, to captain the 3rd XI.

As the cricketing father of two sons, I took my turn with coaching and arranging Boys XI matches, and remember the visit to The Lawn at Waringstown, when Peter made his first appearance with brother Kevin and cousins Karen and Cathy Mitchell in the team.

The game has given me many great memories.

The hope of travelling to Sri Lanka for the Youth World Cup in January 2000 was realised, when my Chairman of Governors at Ballynahinch Primary School, Dr Hadden Wilson, gave me 'the green light', and my good friend and vice principal at the time, John Knaggs, carried out his and my duties with the co-operation of a wonderful staff. I flew to Columbo to see my son Peter, and his three North Down teammates play at the highest level. It was an unforgetable experience.

The opening partnership with Raman Lamba on the new wicket at Upritchard Park was one of those great days. I had 'cried off' to captain Robin Haire in the morning, but played with the promise of a runner. It wasn't needed, as Raman and I put on 237 for the first wicket. Former international opener and adversary Con McCall made a point of shaking my hand and saying with a glint in his eye and a nod to the dressing room, that it was a better century than his!

As captain, the 1975 hammering by Waringstown in the Senior Challenge Cup final and relegation to Section 2 in that same year was bitterly disappointing. The Waringstown captain's remark on the steps at Ormeau were truly prophetic.

"You might win it when we retire".

My part in the 1991 cup final against Woodvale was minimal, but it was one of the most exciting matches in the twilight of my career. After two days of competitive cricket in the scorching sunshine the game was decided in the last over, and the euphoria when Billy Adams bowled the last ball to give a 7 run win, was palpable.

I have enjoyed captaining the 1st XI and 3rd XI at the club and playing representative cricket for Ulster Country and later Ulster Town and was honoured to have been the club's President from 2002-2004 and the Vice President of the NCU in 2005.

When I look at the great cricketers who have played for the club through the years I marvel, and take great pride, at holding the record for the player who has won the 1st XI batting award more than any other.

Forty-four years of cricket at 'The Green' have passed very quickly and the last sixteen of them have been even more enjoyable playing in the junior ranks.

I am thankful that I have had the opportunity to play for the junior teams 'on the way down' before retiring, as the richness and rewards from the game know no boundaries.

WI SHIELDS
Comber, November 2007

"MR W SHIELDS WAS A FINE ALL ROUND SENIOR CRICKETER WHO, WITH CHARACTERISTIC LOYALTY AND INTEREST, ACCEPTED TOWARDS THE END OF LAST SEASON, THE POSITION OF 3RD XI CAPTAIN, AND WAS LOOKING FORWARD, BEFORE HIS SUDDEN DEATH, TO CARRYING ON THIS SEASON THE WORK BEGUN SO WELL AT THE END OF LAST."

WILLIAM ANDREWS 1963.

THIS BOOK IS DEDICATED TO MY LATE FATHER, BILLY, WHO LOVED HIS SPORT AND WHOSE INNINGS IN LIFE WAS MUCH TOO SHORT, AND TO DEL WHO WAS SIMPLY A WONDERFUL MOTHER.

ACKNOWLEDGEMENTS

This history has been a pleasure to research and write and the associated pressures of meeting deadlines have been greatly eased by the assistance and encouragement of those around me.

Constant promptings and support from my family has kept me going. My wife Brenda, in particular, has assisted in every conceivable way. No surprise, as her support during my lifetime of cricket, has been given wholeheartedly and without conditions.

I thank the Chairman, Executive Committee and members, past and present of North Down Cricket Club, who gave me permission, information and encouragement to write the history of our great club.

Clarence Hiles who has provided information for this book through his 'History of Senior Cricket in Ulster' and with his passion for North Down Cricket Club has kept me focused to the task. He has assisted greatly in all aspects of its production, and has brought his wealth of experience in sports journalism and publishing to ensure that the book was completed in the club's sesquicentenary year.

The proof readers – Brenda Shields, Peter Shields, Robin Haire, Ian Carser.

Sir Everton De Courcey Weekes for his foreword; Ian Callender for his editorial expertise; Roy Melvin at printers Graham & Heslip Ltd.; Alistair Reddick for his book design and enthusiasm for the project; the staff at the Newspaper Library, Belfast Central Library for their help; Mary Bradley at Ballynahinch Central Library for the SEELB; Stephen Dunwoody, Bob Torrens and Jonathan Coates at the Newtownards Chronicle; Robert Patton, Jim Montgomery, Charlie Black, Sammy Burgess, Ben Brundle, Paul McLaughlin, Lester Morrow, Margaret Thompson, Leslie Thompson, Ralph Smyth, Desmond Rainey, Gordon Hull, the Coulter family, Wilmer Baxter, Susan Seymour, Norman Beck, the Campbell family, Stanley Glover, Bertie Frazer.

Photographs from: Rowland White, Jessica Homer, Roy Clements, Tara McMillan, The Ulster Cricketer, Newtownards Chronicle, Stevenson's Studios, the late Billy McLeod, Ian Shields, Richard Finlay, Peter Shields, David Irvine and a host of others who gave us great images from the early days in the club's history.

The following members and friends of North Down Cricket Club who have eased the financial burden of production through their generous contributions:
Alan Foley, Billy Artt, Roger Scott, Clarence & Pamela Hiles, Wesley Graham, Don Shields, Kevin Shields, Peter & Claire Shields, Derriaghy Cricket Club, John Boomer, Raymond Moreland, Cyril Peake, Sammy Haire, Robin Haire, Ryan Haire, Andrew Haire, John & Jill Russell, Neil Russell, Joan Russell (in memory of Christopher), Gavin Rodgers, the late Brian Rodgers, Bob & Donna Sharpe, Sam & Anne Wallace, John & Anne Knaggs, Robin & Christine Mitchell, Jimmy Patterson, Ian Carser, Tom & Hilary Mills, Michael Quinn, Leslie Quinn, Cairns Boyd, Jessica Homer, Terry Ritchie & Family, Sam Magill, David & Frances McVeigh, Jason McCullough, Alistair Shields, Ken Boucher, Alan Stevenson & Family, Peter Eakin, Norman Mawhinney, Scott & Craig Irvine, Roy Thompson, Peter Artt, La Mon Hotel, James Campbell, Paul Davidson, Sue Seymour, The Napier Family, Beth & Darcy McLaughlin, Jonathan Montgomery, John & Pat Montgomery, Bill Brundle, North Down Glentoran Supporters' Club, John Patton, The Elliott Family, Richard Johnston, Ivan McCombe, Stephen & Hazel Barry, Bobby McGorman, Walter Wishart, John Hiles, JD Gamble, Gary Patterson, Colin McCaughey & Family, Billy, Shelley & Matthew Adams.

CHAPTER 1
1857 – 1879 : IN THE BEGINNING

"TO THOSE THAT MARVEL AT THE PROFICIENCY OF THE COMBER MEN AT CRICKET, IT SHOULD BE SAID THAT THE TRADITIONS OF THE GAME HAVE BEEN HANDED DOWN IN THE RIGHT MANNER, PRINCIPALLY THROUGH THE CARE AND GENEROSITY OF THE ANDREWS FAMILY, SINCE 1857. THEN AGAIN, EVERY WELL-CONSTITUTED COMBER LAD 'DREAMS' CRICKET FROM HIS CRADLE UPWARDS. DURING THE SUMMER MONTHS THE STREETS AND SQUARE OF THE TOWN SWARM WITH BOYS ENGAGED IN THE FASCINATING GAME; AND HAPPY IS THE MAN WHO GOES ROUND A CORNER WITHOUT RECEIVING A CRICKET BALL IN HIS EYE."

BELFAST NEWSLETTER 1878

> *The day being fine, an immense concourse of people was assembled to witness the contest as the Newtownards club, having been defeated at Comber, intended putting forth their full strength on this occasion.*
>
> MATCH PLAYED IN A LARGE MEADOW AT MOUNTSTEWART 1858

COMBER IN 1857

Local historian Desmond Rainey, in his address to the Comber Historical Society in November 2004, stated that St. Patrick visited Comber in the fifth century and that a son of the local chieftain, Conla, offered him a field called the Plain of Glone to build a monastery. 'It is thought to have stood where North Down Cricket Club is today.' This comes as no surprise to those who have witnessed miraculous events on this 'holy ground' over the years.

Possibly the same monastery disappeared under the decree of Henry VIII and was hardly likely to have been used in a sporting context during Cromwell's influential period.

On the site where a duel had resolved a question of honour a generation before, the statue of Robert Rollo Gillespie was erected in 1845 to honour his courage and achievements in battle and his heroic death at Kalunga in 1814. His famous last words, 'One shot more for the honour of Down' give credence to his attitude, determination and never-say-die approach, characteristics shown throughout our 150 years on and off the field.

John Andrews (1721-1808) had established a flourishing wash mill and bleaching green from around 1745 and a new flourmill was built in 1771 and these, with the spinning industry, gave employment to most of our townspeople. In 1823 the flax was officially reported to be 'the best in Ireland and the Netherlands'.

In 1824 George Johnston and John Miller opened the Upper Distillery and by 1830 Comber was described as a small but busy industrial town that also included John Ward's paper mill on the Newtownards Road, soon to be converted into the Lower Distillery under William Byrne.

Interestingly, by 1836 over 100 people per year were leaving Comber for North America, chiefly Canada, although the population of the town, recorded at around two thousand in 1841, remained static until the turn of the century. By then the Market House had been established and the quarterly fairs instituted, the Grain Store built and street lighting was in place via the new Comber Gas Company, bringing some respite for the drivers of the four-wheeled coaches that made their journey through the town from Belfast to Downpatrick. The major transport in the pre-train era depended on the horse and cart and often on 'Shanks' Mare', and this limited cricket matches to the local area where real hardship, in terms of work and living conditions, made it difficult to imagine any form of recreation time.

The creation of the first Bank in the town reflected the level of business activity and promoting this was John Andrews, known as 'John the Great', whose business acumen ensured that nothing in the trading world stood still. The famous 'Piggery', situated close to The Green, was completed in December 1863, built as a grain store at a cost of £1,750. More important in the history of our club was the building of the Comber Spinning Mill in the same year. Until the modern era, managers at the Mill were synonymous with the leaders at North Down. It gave its name to a cricket team, was the building where many of the club records were archived and where committee meetings were held. James Combe & Co., who also supplied most of the machinery, drew up the plans for the mill, but sadly John Andrews didn't see it in action, as he died the same year.

Some of the names associated with the early cricket club occupied the pulpit from time to time and this tradition, established early in the club's history, continued into modern times.

The church communities in Comber were active in their building programmes and had leaders who gave commitment to the town and its development, and were well prepared for the 'Great Revival' of 1859. At this time a Reverend Killen was at the helm in the First Presbyterian Church in High Street, and a generation later EB Killen was to become a 1st XI player of distinction. St Mary's Parish Church received a major facelift in 1840, as did the Unitarian Church in 1859 with a new manse being built. This church had a major connection with North Down as it was the church of the Andrews family, so it seems likely that when selecting the new clergyman, knowledge of the game and the candidate's attitude to it would come under close scrutiny! The Reverend John Orr was installed in 1850 and in 1878 the Reverend Thomas Dunkerly took over. Both were early members of the Club.

The spread of Orangeism throughout the Province saw club members involved, in one way or another, and the Andrews family had close connections with the Order. In 1875 the White Flag (LOL 244) received its warrant and many mill workers became members, but earlier the Goldsprings (LOL 103) was warranted in 1861 by Mr. Thomas Drennan, the warrant passing to Mr. Alexander Bell in 1875 and Mr. Andrew Dickson in 1893, the former being connected to the Andrews family and the latter also being a club member.

Memorial Junior (LOL 139) had displayed on its banner a picture of Dr Robert Henry, another club member who visited his patients on his fine black stallion, and pictures of the heroic Bruce, De Wind and McRoberts, famous North Down cricketers and soldiers, fluttered proudly on the banner of the Comber Ulster Defenders, (LOL 100) that was unfurled on the 1st July 1925.

'THE GREEN'

A field called 'The Lines' was the first home of Comber Cricket Club. We believe this was a field between the Old and New Ballygowan Roads close to the flour mill and beside the new railway line, opened in 1850. Cricket was played here for the first 17 years before the move to 'The Green'.

DR ROBERT HENRY

The earliest book of the Comber Linen business which has survived is the *Green Book* of 1763. From this we learn that the field on which the linen was spread for bleaching was known as 'The Green' and the bleaching season lasted for nine months. From the middle of February, six men were employed, and the number was increased to 12 in the summer at a rate of eight pence per day. In 1839 'The Green' turned out a massive 20,000 pieces of flax.

Robbing bleach greens was one of the commonest offences around 1800 and punishable by hanging. The *News Letter* of 1767 reported such an offence at 'The Green' where three armed men, having 'feloniously entered', stole 11 pieces of linen cloth, were chased by Thomas Andrews and the watchman of 'The Green' and in pursuit dropped the articles but made their escape. A more successful raid occurred in 1778 when the 'pieces' were removed by 'professionals' and not recovered. From the spring of 1797, due to civil unrest, bleaching at 'The Green' was suspended

...Eleven) and North Down C.C. on 20 June 1868

The Analysis of the Bowling   First Innings

Bowler's Name	No Balls	Wide Balls	The number of 'overs' and the 'runs' made from Bowlers &c.
Rogers			
Braithwaite	11	113	
Frame	1		
Tucker			

| | Total no Balls | Total wide Balls | Total Balls | Total Runs | Total Maiden overs | Total Wickets | Bowler's Names cont.d | Total no Balls | Total wide Balls | Total Balls | Total Runs | Total Maiden overs | Total Wickets |

By all means then let the gallopers have their riding place; but let us have a large cricket ground where we could really enjoy the game as, at present, there is not a place at all adapted for such healthy, harmless and now fashionable amusement within some miles of Belfast.

LETTER TO THE WHIG 1858

until the conclusion of a series of battles, culminating in the famous Battle of Ballynahinch in 1798.

In 1872 the linen bleach works at 'The Green' were closed down and work began to convert it into the cricket ground.

When the club moved to the bleach green the pitch wasn't always in favour of the batsmen or the outfield to the satisfaction of the fielders. We know that the levelling process to eradicate the ridges and furrows was gradually brought about and that the bats used were made out of staves from puncheons obtained from the distillery, the shapes being fashioned by the coopers.

Scrabo Tower, the most famous landmark seen from the ground, was built in 1857 and so shares our sesquicentenary, and remains to this day an indicator of the weather forecast, a vital ingredient in any cricket game. When the Tower can't be seen it is raining. When it can be seen the rain is on its way!

EARLY CRICKET IN ULSTER

The 19th century was a time of the 'haves' and 'have nots', the rich owning the land and the poor working for a pittance for their landlords, but a number of well-to-do patrons developed cricketing interests largely from the Garrisons and the early English and Scottish planters. A lot of crude cricket was played around 1800 but the organisation of clubs began with the Belfast Cricket Club being formed in 1830, Lisburn CC (1836), Ulster CC (1839) and Downpatrick CC (1849). From 1850 onwards many clubs came into existence and some thrived due to the patronage of the landowners and mill proprietors. Factories and schools had their own elevens and many villages and towns had teams, initially playing within their own areas, but progressively venturing out to challenge teams from other areas. Ballymena was playing Ballymoney in 1855; a lot of cricket was also being played in the Armagh area with teams like Banbridge, Monaghan, Markethill, Portadown and the Royal School Dungannon playing matches on a regular basis. The steam trains on the newly installed lines greatly aided the spread of the game and clubs like Cookstown, Larne, Carrickfergus, Strabane, Omagh, Limavady and others came into existence. As chairman of the Belfast and County Down Railway, Thomas Andrews Senior may have had some influence in regard to the concessionary fares and season tickets that were available for the travelling North Down supporters!

Three of the clubs that were later to dominate cricket in the Province were founded in the 1850s, namely Waringstown, North of Ireland and North Down. Our club was particularly fortunate to have a strategic placing on the Belfast and County Down line and the patronage of the Andrews family, associated with the Spinning Mill. We were not alone on that count as Sion Mills and Donacloney, the latter playing at the 'Factory Ground', were two of many Ulster clubs built around factories and places of work.

In a rapidly expanding and increasingly prosperous Belfast, the North of Ireland club was founded in 1859 and in that era no club did more to spread and popularise the game in Ulster. All the top touring sides came to Ormeau, amongst them an All Ireland XI, the nomadic club 'I Zingari', the Irish equivalent 'Na Shuler', an All England XI and culminating in a visit by the Australians in 1880, only the second Aussie side to visit the British Isles. With most of the top clubs visiting from the south, Ormeau became the 'Headquarters' of cricket in the North, and the rapidly expanding game soon found its way into the far corners of rural Ulster. Belfast had many clubs, none making a contribution more than Ulster CC, founded in 1873, and whose ground at Ballynafeigh was second only to Ormeau and hosted many important games.

The Belfast Newsletter in 1828 makes reference to a cricket match at Killinchy and within the North Down area cricket was soon being played at Newtownards, Donaghadee, Saintfield, Bangor and Dundonald, with Comber at the core. More than a decade before the founding of North Down Cricket Club, or Comber Cricket Club as it was known in 1857, there were many examples of cricket matches in the locality.

NORTH DOWN CRICKET CLUB

The original founders of North Down Cricket Club were two Inland Revenue men, Braithwaite and Knowles who presumably established the club on a firm financial footing, and Robert Braithewaite Senior was

ROBERT WITHERS

the first captain from 1857 to 1861. Mr Robert Withers held the office until 1868, being succeeded by Mr RJ Braithwaite, son of the founder, who led the side the following year. Dr John Frame then captained the side until the return from England of John Andrews Junior in 1876.

The Northern Whig records a match played between Newtownards and Comber in September 1858, being a return match at Mountstewart, courtesy of the Marquis of Londonderry's agent John Andrews. Comber had won the first encounter and when the home team 'borrowed' a Mr Despard from Downpatrick and Mr McMinn from Donaghadee, it was quite clear they wanted to win! The North Down founding members, Knowles (31 runs and 10 wickets) and Braithwaite (3 catches) made their contribution, but it was to no avail as Newtownards won by four runs in an exciting, low-scoring game.

The earliest reference from club records dates from the 1860 scorebooks between North Down and North of Ireland.

The Comber CC team that played North of Ireland 2nd XI at Ormeau in 1860 had Braithwaite at the helm and Withers, a future captain, in the team, and won by ten wickets. In the days when 'double figures' was recognised as a major contribution, McCarten's 33 runs won the day after Heron had taken 12 North wickets in their two innings.

Lord Massereene's XI were regular opponents at Comber and Antrim Castle, but Comber CC won in 1867 even though the Lord had acquired the North of Ireland professional, Rosebuck, for his team.

One of the earliest recorded games against North of Ireland 1st XI was played at Ormeau in July 1867 when the inimitable Charles Stelfox showed his class for the Belfast club with an undefeated 80, leaving the 17 players of North Down soundly beaten by an innings and 21 runs.

Within the '17' were the names of leading figures in the club, cricketers who would oversee the development of the Ground with its new pavilion and outfield; men who would also have influence as the idea of a union unfolded, and as competitive cricket drew near. The 17 were: RJ Tucker, R Menagh, C Finlay, EH Clarke, J Frame, RJ Braithwaite, R Withers, T Rogers, J McGowan, J McDowell, R Heaney, CJ Andrews, A Malet, TJ Andrews, S Rogers, J Andrews and JH Montgomery.

In 1873 the Comber Spinning Mill team, soon to be absorbed by the 'new' North Down Club, lost to Wolfhill CC and by 1876 the original Comber CC had taken the name of North Down, moved to The Green and continued to play matches against the Spinning Mill, one record showing that Sixteen of the mill were considered a match against Eleven from North Down and proved more than a match with a resounding innings victory based on the 'destructive' bowling of Bennett and Johnston and the batting of Hiles and Wilson.

The Andrews family influence was strong at this time, as their business interests and political interests had established the family in many areas of Comber and in Ulster society and not least in the linen industry. The first wages were paid in Comber Spinning Mill in June 1864 and the drudgery of the doffers, machine boys and hacklers with the long hours and poor conditions were somewhat offset by the recreation time afforded to them by the new boss at the mill, John Andrews Jnr. Having returned from the Lancashire Mills with cricket 'in his blood' he was to play a dominant role in local cricket for many years to come. Mr. John began at the mill and encouraged his employees to play the game during their break times. Comber Spinning Mill CC was thus born and played regular two innings matches against North Down. Mr. John led by example captaining his club from 1876 until 1901, missing only 1892 when his brother, and owner of the Bleach Green, Thomas James, was at the helm.

Thomas James Andrews was born in 1847, son of Isaac Andrews of Flour milling fame and was to become the owner of the ground in 1895. With his

THOMAS JAMES ANDREWS

brother John he was responsible for the continued development of the bleach green into the marvellous ground that we have and building a splendid wooden pavilion. No decision was made about the ground without 'approval' from TJ Andrews.

He was a capable and enthusiastic cricketer, playing as a youngster in the sides of the 1860s and a regular with the 1st XI, earning seven Senior Challenge Cup winning badges from the first eight Finals played. In 1892 he captained the 1st XI to their fifth Senior Cup win.

JOHN ANDREWS JNR

John Andrews Jnr was born in 1849, son of Isaac Andrews. He was educated at the Royal Academical Institution and afterwards spent three years at Queen's College, Belfast, where Engineering and Arts' classes occupied his attention. Towards the end of 1868 he went to Liverpool to learn the business of flour milling at the extensive North Shore Mills. His business capabilities were quickly nourished as he rose to become foreman, then sub manager and afterwards manager of the entire works. In 1876 he returned from Liverpool and took over the management of his father's business at Comber. He lived at Knock for some time before moving to Greenville, between Orangefield and Bloomfield, and although married in 1872 he became a widower in 1885.

Mr John was a fervent believer in an Irish Cricket Union and worked hard to bring this about. An all Ireland interprovincial series had begun in 1890 and although the cricket lacked a few high profile cricketers and was plagued by poor weather, it did sow the seeds of union.

The political situation across the country didn't

help in the drive towards the goal of cricketing unity, but Mr John was instrumental in bringing the case before the Northern Cricket Union (NCU) and beyond, addressing well attended and well received meetings as far afield as Rathmines and Phoenix. The wave of euphoria that swept through cricketing circles was quickly quelled as the NCU officially declined to recognise the new Irish Cricket Union (ICU) much to the disappointment of Mr John.

He played a lot of midweek cricket at North of Ireland and had close associations with that renowned club, but even though he moved to live in Belfast where his business interests lay, Mr John continued to play his 'serious' cricket at The Green.

North Down Cricket Club became his great love and as an early club historian he was able, in an interview for 'The Irish Athletic and Cycling Record' in January 1897, to give a detailed account of the club's origins and administrators.

'I myself', he said, 'think that there was more excitement in the matches we played in the old days before the introduction of the Cup ties, than there is

I was talking to a prominent cricketer in Liverpool a few days ago and he told me that golf had done the game a lot of harm.

JOHN ANDREWS JNR 1874

now. For instance we used to go to Antrim Castle every year to play off a fixture with Lord Massereene's XI, and the excitement at those matches was almost greater than that which prevails at a cup tie now-a-days. Lord Massereene very often brought the whole cream of the North to play against us; and we have had opposed to us such well known cricketers as James and Charles Stelfox, the brothers Orr and Ned Henderson, and yet succeeded in bringing off victory.'

John remembered playing on the old North of Ireland ground that stood on the site of the Gas Works and witnessing a match between an All England XI and the North of Ireland played in September 1860 at Botanic Gardens.

He was a great scholar of the game and was not short of opinion on the Irish weaknesses in batting and bowling techniques, of the misuse of the 'net' practice for slogging and the preoccupation of the bowlers sacrificing accuracy for pace. He was a great believer in the art of slow bowling and referred to the success of WT Graham at North Down and RH Lambert of Leinster. His desire to take teams to the mainland and

Early days Andrews family at The Green with owner TJ Andrews and John Jnr in hooped caps.

have sides from England and Scotland visit Comber was rarely realised and it was left to his nephew William, a generation later, to make these dreams a reality.

John was confident in the future of cricket even though the game had come under serious opposition from lawn tennis, cycling and *'the most formidable game that ever came to the front to contest summer honours with cricket (is) golf; and to all intents and purposes golf has come to stay.'* The good news was that seemingly golf was seen as a game for older men!!

Cricket was healthy with Cliftonville fielding four teams and North Down, North of Ireland and Ulster putting two teams each in the field.

North Down may have been Mr John's first love but he was a man of many talents. He was a devotee of hunting and trained horses and, in 1897, held a record of having won a steeplechase carrying 16 stone four pounds. He held several cups for his riding in the point-to-points to add to his prize cricket bats presented on the occasion of having made consecutive annual centuries. His clay pigeon trophies and his football and rugby exploits underline what a remarkable character John Andrews Jnr was and his legacy to the cricket world would include his three sons, Oscar, Sidney and Earnest, the former being the 'pick of the crop' throughout the wider Andrews family.

Later to become His Excellency Lord Lieutenant, John captained the North Down side to eight Senior Cup wins.

WT 'TOMMY' GRAHAM

Tommy Graham was a remarkable man. He was North Down Cricket Club secretary from 1875 to 1898 and one of the team's finest all rounders in an era when they dominated Ulster cricket. He was a top class player and regularly opened the batting and bowling for the 1st XI. Above all he was a lovely person with a genial personality that endeared him far beyond his cricket interests. And those interests were just as varied as the range of shots he played because WT 'Tommy' Graham was one of the finest administrators in the history of Irish sport and played prominent roles in the early development of organized cricket and hockey.

TOMMY GRAHAM

Tommy was a Comber man born and bred who remained a bachelor all his life. This probably explains why he had the time to take on so many roles because throughout his life he was a busy man. He loved sport and was particularly good at cricket, hockey and rugby. He trained and qualified as an accountant and for many years ran a successful practice in Belfast before joining Harland and Wolff. He was a staunch member of both the Orange and the Masonic Orders and he was a popular member of the congregation at First Comber Presbyterian Church.

One of the biggest landmarks in Tommy's life was his retirement as club secretary although it didn't curtail his playing involvement nor hinder the many other responsibilities he either held or was about to undertake. Quite simply Tommy had discovered there were only 24 hours in a day and seven days in a week!

To mark the 'retirement' the club presented their esteemed secretary with a magnificent photo album of all the playing members of the club, a beautiful archive that remains one of North Down's most treasured antiques thanks to its custodian Ralph Smyth. In making the presentation, club captain John Andrews Jnr. was fulsome in his praise of his popular colleague:

"For more than 20 years you have acted as honorary secretary to our club, and you have been ungrudging and unsparing in the sacrifice in time and means in furthering its welfare. The high position that it holds at present is largely due to your unwearying exertions on its behalf. By your care and attention the membership of the club has increased, the grounds have been improved, and the players have been better trained, until at present it holds the premier position among the cricket clubs in Ulster."

If anyone felt Tommy Graham was taking a sabbatical then they were greatly mistaken. Tommy was secretary of the Northern Cricket Union from 1891 to 1920, president from 1909 to 1914, president of the Ulster Branch of the Irish Hockey Union from 1903 to 1906, honorary treasurer from 1897 to 1919, president of the Irish Hockey Union from 1906 to 1920, and secretary/treasurer of the North Down Hockey Club during its inaugural year.

He was also a prominent hockey umpire who officiated at interprovincial and international matches. By any standards this is an amazing sporting CV and a measure of the man's commitment and popularity throughout Ireland.

But cricket was Tommy Graham's first love and throughout his long playing career he was a prolific performer with bat and ball. He was a steady opening bat for a long time but, in later years, moved down the order to facilitate the younger players coming into the team. Tommy was always a team player, but just as popular with opponents who found his wily off spin extremely difficult to read. In tandem with the legendary Willie Turner they were a formidable attack and in later years he was just as damaging alongside the younger Oscar Andrews. Tommy is credited with nine Senior Challenge Cup wins from 1887 to 1909 and

The ground which was re-laid last winter, was in capital order; and, although owing to the long continued drought, it played 'fast' yet it played quite true, and we may congratulate the North Down club on now having a pitch they need not be ashamed to invite any club to play on.

BELFAST NEWSLETTER 1874

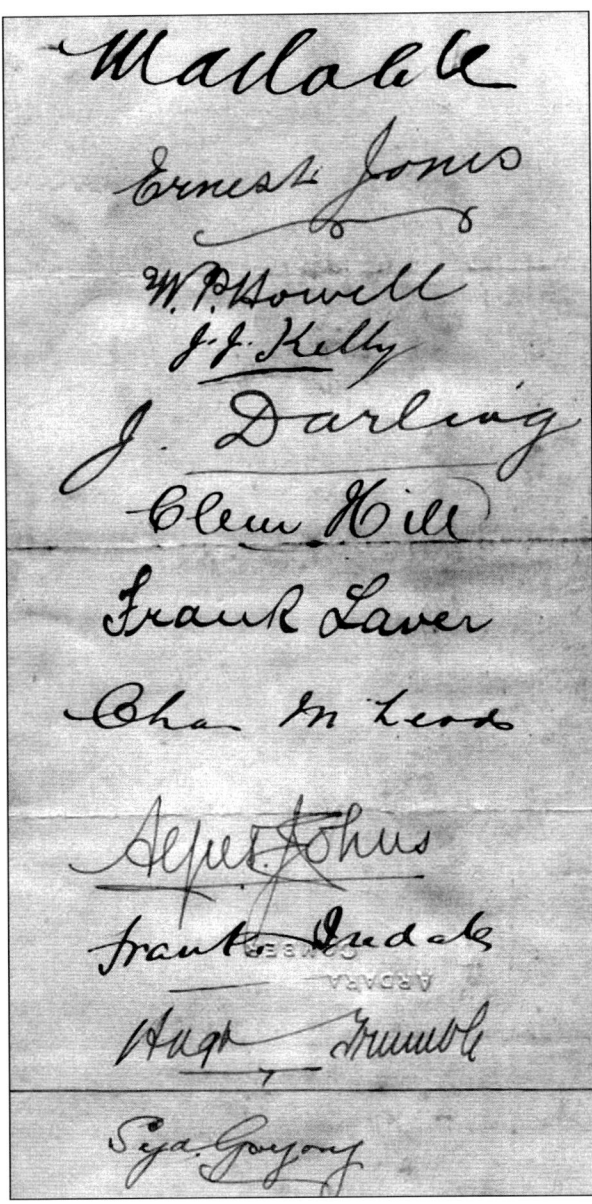

One of the very early Australian teams to visit England (from the Wm. Andrews Collection)

figured in two infamous cup finals that never took place. He was a member of the North Down team that was awarded the 1890 cup win when Armagh refused to play on the date proscribed by the NCU and a member of the North Down team that suffered the same ignominious default in 1901 when they displayed similar intransigence. Both stances would have pained this great administrator, but he set the 1901 disappointment behind him and played in five more finals before easing out of the team in the pre war years.

Amongst Tommy's long list of outstanding personal milestones are match figures of 11 for 57 in the 1898 cup final win over Ulster and his 6 for 21 against Ballymoney in 1892. He scored a number of centuries including 116 against Carrickfergus in 1889, another 100 in a record stand with his captain John Andrews (Jun) in the 1891 match against Whiterock and 106 against Ulster in the 1897 cup semi-final. He played a number of times for the province of Ulster, including the inaugural interprovincials in Dublin in 1890 and the famous historical match County Down versus County Antrim in 1885 that is accepted as the first NCU representative game. He also played in the first match of the NCU Senior League in 1896 when North Down played Lisburn and marked the occasion with a superb eight for 17 bowling performance.

In the history of Irish sport there are very few individuals who performed at the highest level on and off the pitch to match Tommy Graham. He was a remarkable man, one of North Down's true all time greats.

A BEGINNING RICH IN PROMISE

At the end of the 1879 season the North Down members could reflect on two decades of club formation that had seen them established as one of the leading cricket clubs in the Province, and while the game was still in its embryonic stage, it was a beginning that was rich in promise. Not only had the club established cricket as the premier recreational activity in Comber, it had good playing facilities, a strong membership, and the benevolent patronage of the Andrews family and the Comber community in general. It was to prove the springboard of greater things to follow as the 1880s saw the advent of organized cricket and not only did North Down Cricket Club assert its dominance on the field, but some of its members played leading roles in the development of sport throughout Ireland.

CHAPTER 2
1880 – 1899 : THE BIRTH OF THE UNIONS AND COMPETITION

"THERE IS NO PLACE IN IRELAND, FOR THAT MATTER IN THE KINGDOM, WHERE THE ENTHUSIASM FOR CRICKET IS AT SUCH A HIGH POINT AS THE LITTLE VILLAGE OF COMBER WHEREIN THE FAMOUS NORTH DOWN CLUB HAVE THEIR GROUNDS. BUT THE CLUB REQUIRES NO DESCRIPTION; IT IS TOO WELL KNOWN TO NEED ANY COMMENT FROM OUR PEN REGARDING THE LENGTHENED PERIOD THEY HELD THE CHALLENGE CUP OR THE MANY BATSMEN AND BOWLERS THE VILLAGE HAS PRODUCED. IT IS NOT SURPRISING THEREFORE THAT COMBER IS THE FIRST IN THE FIELD WITH A REGULAR MATCH."

BELFAST NEWSLETTER 1896

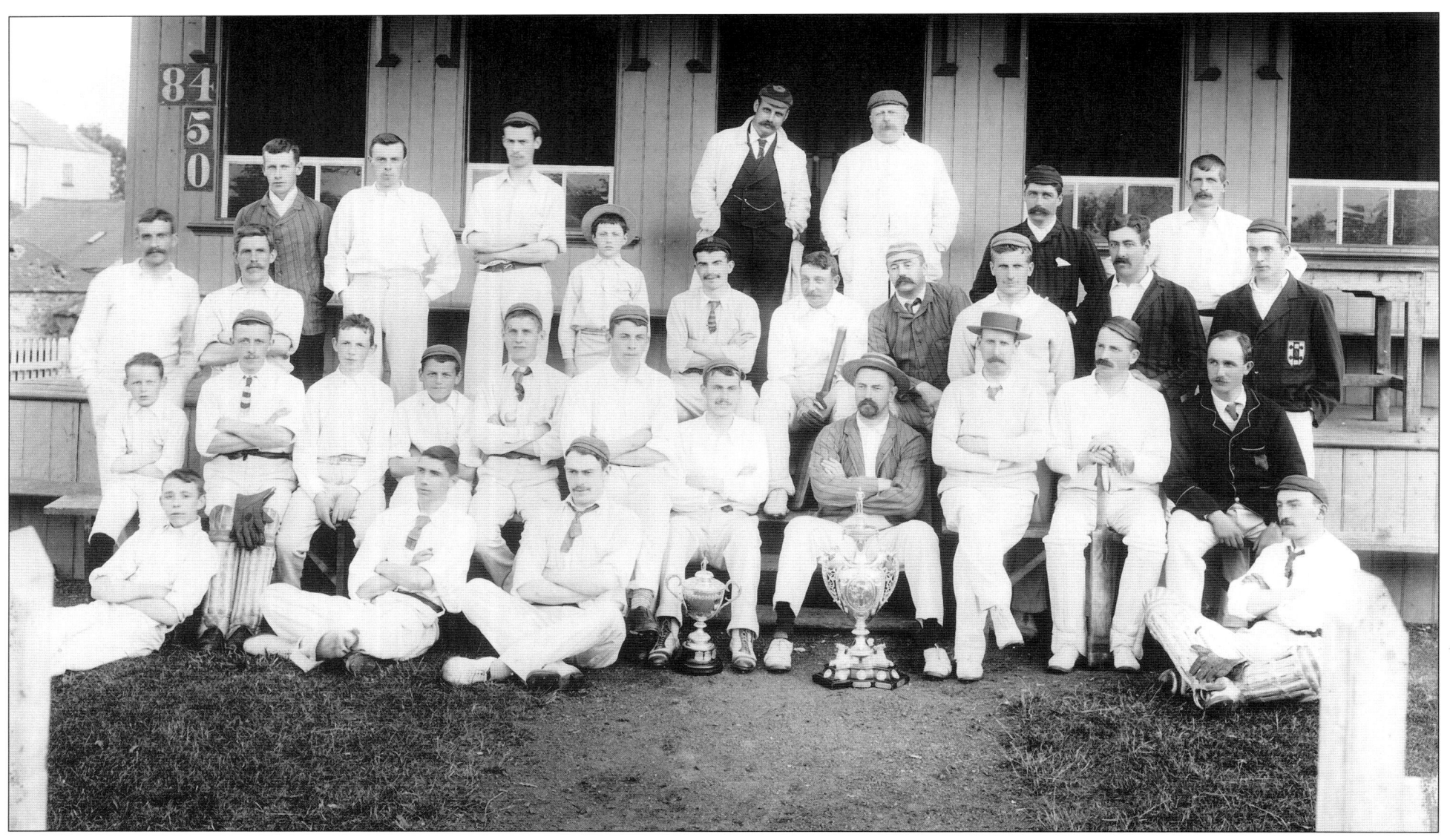

1894 Senior Cup and Junior Cup winning teams: John Andrews Jnr. 'guards' the Senior Cup and John Miller Andrews is pictured behind the Junior Cup. To John Miller's right sits James Andrews and in front of James sits Thomas of Titanic fame.

COMBER IN 1880

This was a period of stability for the town, with its population now around 1,700 after the earlier emigration rush. Big changes occurred in land ownership, with large portions of the vast estates of the aristocracy sold off, and this emancipation carried with it a 'feel good factor' which in turn led to further expansion of trade in the Comber district.

The town had an abundance and variety of traders; the main industries of spinning and distilling were in full swing with the Distilleries, united in 1860 under John Miller, taking over the Market House in 1886 and producing vast quantities of 'Old Comber Whiskey'. The town boasted a pawnbroker, watchmaker, saddler, nailer, letter carrier, auctioneer and blacksmith with at least six drinking establishments including Mrs Patton's Railway Inn in Mill Street and in 1882 the first telephone lines in Comber were in use.

The town's gentry were landowners, industrialists, clergy and professionals, distinguished by where they lived, where they worshipped, where they banked, their Loyal Orange Lodge and political allegiance.

Samuel Stone of Barn Hill, Samuel Bruce the distiller, William Berklie of Nurseryville and James Fisher of Camperdown were all regarded as Comber gentry, and our club had no shortage of patronage and support from the influential. Foremost was the Andrews family, but there were other notables from the community who were also members.

One of the most prominent citizens was James George Allen of the Square who was acclaimed for his engineering feats. He constructed steamrollers and traction engines and was accredited with owning the first car in Comber, probably the one that he crashed on the Newtownards Road!

The Reverend RJ Semple MA was the minister in Second Comber Presbyterian Church from 1897 until 1910 and was later appointed Professor of English and History at Magee College, Londonderry.

James Shean JP was a woollendraper, haberdasher and postmaster in Downpatrick Street who, in 1897, donated the beautiful rosebowl for presentation to the 1st XI batsman who scored the highest number of runs in a season.

There were also John Blair, the bookkeeper; John Caughey, secretary at the distillery; Thomas Coulter of Londonderry House, Cattogs; Edmund de Wind, war hero; Andrew N Dickson, Worshipful Master of the Goldsprings LOL in 1893; Robert Graham BA, Minister in First Comber Presbyterian Church; Frank McRoberts, veterinary surgeon; William Shean, solicitor. And so the long list went on, indicating the strength in numbers and the middle class nature of the membership. But the Andrews family was the

1887 INAUGURAL SENIOR CHALLENGE CUP FINAL, NORTH DOWN v NORTH OF IRELAND AT ORMEAU. NORTH DOWN TEAM TO THE LEFT OF THE CUP. BACK – WT GRAHAM, R MILLING, TJ ANDREWS, JOHN ANDREWS JNR. MIDDLE ROW – S TURNER, AA DE WIND, EB KILLEN, FM HARRIS. FRONT – DAH MILLING, WS TURNER, R PATTON.

dominant force within the club in the 1880s and such was their commitment to the game that they fielded an Andrews XI in an annual fixture against the Club throughout the nineties.

Members of this team were to make a huge impact and contribution within Ulster society as John Jnr had three sons, Ernest who became a partner and later Chairman of Isaac Andrews & Sons, Oscar of whom we will read more and Sydney, who in addition to his Chairmanship of Isaac Andrews & Sons in 1956, was Governor at the Linenhall Library and author of 'Nine Generations – A History of the Andrews Family'.

John Jnr's cousin Thomas Andrews senior had four sons; John Miller captained the 2nd XI, was four times a Junior Cup winner, played regularly on the 1st XI and was destined to become Prime Minister of Northern Ireland during the war years; Thomas Jnr played for the 2nd XI, rarely for the 'firsts', designed and 'went down with' the Titanic in 1912; and James, captained the 1st XI for seven seasons at the turn of the century and became President of the NCU in 1927 under the title of Lord Justice Andrews. The other son, William, a future High Sheriff of Down, was too young to be selected for the family side, but he, more than any other player in Ulster, dominated the NCU administration for many years.

Herbert, the grandson of John who built the Spinning Mill, was the first president of the Ulster Branch of the Irish Hockey Union and was North Down Hockey Club president from 1908 until 1925. He played for North Down in the first ever hockey game played at The Green along with cousins Oscar and Sydney. Younger brother Arthur was a Belfast solicitor who emigrated to Toronto and Cecil served in the Boer War with the Irish Imperial Yeomanry and farmed in Canada before returning to Comber.

We are pleased to learn the Juveniles in Comber are being well looked after by Mr Shean, who is a retired player of the NDCC, but who, nevertheless, takes a keen interest in the game. He has arranged evening matches, and generally has about 30 boys taking part, many of whom make a creditable show and so long as there are gentlemen of the stamp of Mr Shean to encourage the boys, cricket will flourish in Comber and the North Down cricket will not lack rising players.

NORTHERN WHIG 1892

THE ANDREWS FAMILY 1895: (FROM BACK) – THOMAS, THOMAS JAMES, JOHN JNR., JAMES, JOHN MILLER, OSCAR, CECIL, ERNEST, SIDNEY, ARTHUR, HERBERT

CHAPTER 2 : 1880 – 1899 : THE BIRTH OF THE UNIONS AND COMPETITION

FORMATION OF UNIONS

This was the most formative period in Ulster cricket, with numerous clubs being joined under the banner of the newly formed Northern Cricket Union and the County Derry Cricket Union (1888). Cup competition was started and the idea of Interprovincial competition taken a step further under the direction of a proposed Irish Cricket Union. The Irish Rugby Union was formed in 1880 and later in the year the Irish Football Association came into being followed in 1884 by the Gaelic Athletic Association. A Golfing Union and Hockey Union followed in 1891 and 1893 respectively. It was the era of organised sport and cricketers were much to the fore in the development of the rugby, football and hockey unions.

The NCU had its first secretary in 1884 but lists 1886 as its inaugural year, when plans were drawn up for the Senior Challenge Cup competition the following year. The funds to pay for the magnificent trophy were raised by the clubs through a committee convened by John Andrews, although some clubs refused to acknowledge the benefit of competing and didn't enter the fray. Although John Andrews was to lead his North Down side to many cup victories, he was far from convinced of the benefits of this competition. However, Armagh, Bessbrook, Carrickfergus, Clarence, Cliftonville, Milford, Whiterock, Holywood, Banbridge, Ulster, North Down and North of Ireland participated.

The winning of the NCU Senior Challenge Cup became the ultimate goal for clubs and, as John Andrews had feared, its winning and losing led inevitably to times of friction. In 1888, big guns North of Ireland failed to field anything like their strongest eleven, the reason being that the opposition were infamous for their aggressive and argumentative style on the field of play, and subsequently lost their first round encounter.

North Down knew all about the East End Club's abrasiveness on the field and the Newtownards Chronicle reporter, earlier in the season, vividly and dramatically gave the reason for it, blaming "a lot of cantankerous Yorkshire men who look with contempt on Irish cricketers" as the root cause of the problem.

Prior to the advent of competitive cricket in 1887, North of Ireland had no equal, but from then to the turn of the century North Down was the team that was often quoted as 'hard to bate'.

Only twice in the history of the NCU has the same club won the Senior Challenge Cup in five consecutive seasons and it was from 1890 until 1894 by North Down and later from 1900 until 1904 by North of Ireland.

GOLDEN YEARS

The period 1887 to 1899 produced phenomenal success for the club and is regarded as our first 'Golden Era'. The Senior Challenge Cup was the premier competition and it was won a remarkable nine times in 1887, 1888, 1890, 1891, 1892, 1893, 1894, 1897 and 1898. The first Senior Challenge Cup match involving North Down was played at The Green against Carrickfergus with WT 'Tommy' Graham and the Turner brothers, Sam and Willie, taking all the Carrick wickets.

When the Senior League was first played in 1896 it was won three years in succession, the inaugural win being shared with Cliftonville. In the same period the 2nd XI won the Junior Cup twice in 1894 and 1897.

As one of the most successful North Down captains, it is remarkable that John Andrews told of his lack of confidence in the success of the Senior Challenge Cup competition from its inception in 1887. His attitude to the Senior League Cup was different, indicating that the league cup holders quite clearly demonstrated that a lot of hard work had been put into the season.

John was in the habit, when business permitted, of leading his staff out to the Bleach Green for practice. This kept the Spinning Mill team in shape and was good preparation for the regular encounters with the North Down side.

With victories against Banbridge and Armagh, North Down and North of Ireland met in the final at Ormeau in 1887 and surprisingly the visitors won by an innings and five runs and the Senior Challenge Cup was on its way to Comber for the first time, a journey it would make many times in the years to follow.

The visitors recorded 65 and 85 in their two innings leaving North Down requiring 10 runs to win from their second spell at the wicket. EB Killen, who had scored 22 not out batting at number eleven first time around, was given the honour of opening the batting and scoring the winning runs.

The secret of Comber being 'hard to bate' lies in their all round excellence at the game. In batting, in bowling and particularly in fielding they are superior to any local eleven. This success has not been attained without hard work, though in the case of the Combermen it has been a labour of love.

BELFAST NEWSLETTER 1895

The side had in its ranks some of our more interesting personalities. Sam Turner with his 'lob' or 'grub' bowling style was a major wicket-taker and one of a unique group of 'grub' bowlers in Ulster cricket, a style of underarm bowling where the bowler used exaggerated wrist action to curve or spin the ball. It is hard to imagine such an action being effective in the modern game, but it had its time and place, and it wasn't until the turn of the century that the round arm or overarm code replaced it.

These were the days of big crowds and detailed press coverage with the Belfast Telegraph, Northern Whig, Belfast Newsletter and Ireland's Saturday Night giving full reports, not only of senior games, but also of many junior and friendly matches. The local papers were not to be outdone and in Lisburn, Downpatrick and Comber early versions of the Ulster Star, Down Recorder and Newtownards Chronicle carried strong opinions on team performances and kept the locals well informed.

The North Down side was well balanced with the bowling of the Turner brothers and Tommy Graham's off breaks and it also had the youthful exuberance and skill of David Milling behind the stumps. David 'DAH' Milling played in the inaugural Senior Challenge Cup final at the age of 14, a record that still stands today, and went on to play in nine more, seven on the winning side. Educated at Dublin University,

now Trinity College Dublin, he played with great success in the university team alongside his North Down colleague James Andrews and it was while living in Dublin that he played for the Gentlemen of Ireland. DAH later joined the Leinster club, toured with and played alongside the legendary WG Grace on the Leinster tour where they played against WG's London County in 1903.

George Combe, a member of the family of engineers that supplied and fitted the machinery for the Spinning Mill in 1863, was also a key player in the side. His batting was of the highest calibre and he wasn't short of practice, as he was one of a number of cricketers who played midweek cricket for North of Ireland, and weekend cricket for North Down. He played in four winning cup finals scoring an impressive 93 against Ballymoney in 1892. George was one of the top batsmen in the Province and was often at the crease with JC Lindsay, noted for his cameo contributions such as his 137 runs in the Senior Challenge Cup semi-final match against Gilford in 1891.

Another high order batsman was EB Killen, who has the distinction of being the first NCU cricketer to 'carry his bat' in a Senior Cup tie. Like Combe, Killen played in four winning cup final sides and made regular all rounder contributions en route to those finals.

Add to these the class of the youthful Oscar Andrews and the experience of the professional at the time and the blend led to the domination by North Down in this first Golden Era.

During the eighties and nineties the club had a succession of professionals who coached and worked on the ground. None was more highly thought of than Arthur Clay who performed his duties so well, that even after his third and final year in 1886 the club kept in close contact with him and he assisted the North

SAM TURNER AND THE SEVEN BADGES

Down committee in their regular deliberations regarding the appointment of new professionals.

Many years later, in 1935, during the North Down innings against Ulster, Mr S Turner, son of Sam, handed over to Mr William Andrews, for the North Down Cricket Club Pavilion, a photograph of his late father, surrounded by the seven Northern Cricket Union badges he had received as a member of the North Down team which won the Senior Challenge Cup in 1887, 1888 and 1890 to 1894 inclusive.

In making the presentation, Mr Turner said his father never considered he had won these badges, and always referred to them as having been won by the team. While his family much treasured the photograph and badges, they felt that under the circumstances these should be offered to the Club. He was pleased that the old Club continued to be very successful, and that they had won the Senior Cup again that season.

Mr Willie, in replying, said the committee accepted the gift with much pleasure and gratification, and that it would be a nice remembrance of a fine gentleman who had rendered most valuable services to the club in past years. The views which the late Mr Turner held, and which his son had just expressed, were a splendid example for all cricketers, who should in a sportsmanlike way play and do everything which was for the success of the team as a whole, and not for their personal glorification.

Lord Justice James Andrews said that he had played in many matches with the late Mr Samuel Turner, who was a stylish bat, and a very successful 'grub' bowler, particularly against English touring sides, who were not accustomed to playing that kind of bowling, which had now become almost entirely extinct. He also referred to Mr Turner's good and plucky fielding at 'silly point', and the spirit that he put into the game.

The club had also a strong 2nd XI at this time, indicated by their Junior Cup successes in 1894 and 1897 and their appearance in the inaugural final in 1891. The selection of Oscar Andrews, age 15 and batting at number ten, was significant, as was John Miller Andrews, age 20 and batting one place higher. Neither made an impression in that final, but the mature Oscar was later a match winner at the highest level and John Miller would be the mainstay in a side that he would captain to four cup wins in the future.

In 1895 the 2nd XI played 15 matches, won nine, lost two and drew four with Sam Davidson, the Castle

Street draper on top of the averages and Malcolm Macdonald's 31 wickets at 6.19 top of the bowling averages. James Niblock was the workhorse bowler with 141 overs and James Andrews, John Ritchie, Joe Macdonald, Sam Davidson and James Chambers, the schoolmaster from High Street, were the regular bowlers used.

Teenager David Taylor, who was to play with distinction well into the new century and captain the 1908 Senior Challenge Cup winners, and Thomas Andrews, of Titanic fame, were well up the batting averages in this side so ably led by John Miller Andrews.

THE CREST AND THE SPADE

Our crest at this time could be found on a cap of the 1880s showing a mangle of NDCC letters in the adopted green and gold colours. The present crest is entirely different and represents a number of features intimately connected to the club.

Some are directly connected with the game like the set of wickets and the ball, the latter placed above the founding year. In 1845, thousands gathered in Comber Square, close to the house where Robert Rollo Gillespie had been born, to see the erection of his famous statue. His last words were recorded as, 'One shot more for the honour of Down'.

Scrabo Tower has stood overlooking The Green before cricket was even played there, the Distillery is another old landmark sadly out of production since the 1950s and only recently losing the chimney to a controversial and seemingly premature explosion! Its produce has been tasted throughout the decades – too often for one former groundsman who regularly slept off the effects in the pavilion!

The old Comber Spinning Mill has more recent and relevant links with the Club, not only through the Andrews family connection and their own Spinning Mill CC, but also for the many employees who played in the streets as youngsters and later represented their street at The Green in organised competition.

In our quest to unearth some of the club's treasures we have secured for our archives one of the more important links with this period. Passed down from the Andrews family to the late Jim Barry, our former patron ensured that the spade would be in safe keeping and it has been framed and displayed within the pavilion as part of our club heritage. This is the inscription on the little silver spade:

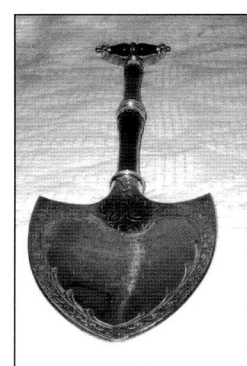

PRESENTED TO
Mrs Thomas James Andrews
COMBER

BY THE COMMITTEE
OF
North Down Cricket Club

ON THE OCCASION
OF HER
Laying the First Sod

IN CONNECTION WITH THE
Extension of the Club's Ground COMBER
20th Nov. 1893

Mrs Thomas Andrews was the wife of the original owner of the estate and her husband played in the early 1st XIs and captained the side for one year only in 1892.

FUND RAISERS

In 1892 a Christmas Concert was held in the schoolroom. This could have been the schoolroom associated with the Spinning Mill or to similar premises connected with First or Second Comber Presbyterian churches. However the schoolroom referred to was most likely the one associated with the Unitarian Church.

The rewards for attendance seemed attractive with four tons of tea distributed in one pound or half-pound packages courtesy of 'Valentine & Co.' 6 Castle Place, Belfast. The real attraction however must have been the musical entertainment itself with a menu rich in vocals and instrumentals.

The cricketing connection among the performers was evident with Mrs TJ Andrews opening the concert with a dashing 'Polonaise' by Chopin and playing four pieces; 'From Foreign Parts', 'A Curious Story', 'Too Happy' and 'Dreaming' by Schumann.

Ethel DeWind, sister of Edmund, sang 'Gondola Dreams' and Mr WS Turner of 1st XI cricketing fame sang 'Let Me Like a Soldier Fall'.

The reflective mood deepened when Miss McKisack sang 'Tears', and the Mascagni 'Intermezzo' was played on violin by Mr J Crothers.

Miss Combe, sister of the notable 1st XI batsman George Combe, sang 'Sunshine and Rain', followed by Mr Imrie's 'Honour Bids Me Speed Away', and the first half of the programme was brought to an end with a 'humorous' song from Mr JE Hind.

No doubt thankful for the ten-minute interval, the assembled would have had time to peruse the rich array of advertisements within the programme.

The Gentlemen's Outfitting Establishments in Royal Avenue, Arnotts in Bridge Street, The Comber Book Stall of Olley & Co., Robinson & Cleaver's, Lowry & Officer and the Tailoring Department of James Shean, The Square, Comber, all received space and refreshments were available from Millings Aerated Waters in The Square. Surprisingly there was no mention of the Distillery! Smoked for more than 30 years the 'Carrowdore Mixture' was a mild cool tobacco and could be purchased in Leahy, Kelly & Leahy of the Castle Tobacco Warehouse in Belfast.

Two of North Down's greatest cricketers began the second half as WS Turner, joined by his brother Sam, performed the duet 'Two Mariners Bold'. After the Mandolin solo by the versatile Mr Crothers, the Concert followed a similar pattern until the rendering of 'God Save the Queen.'

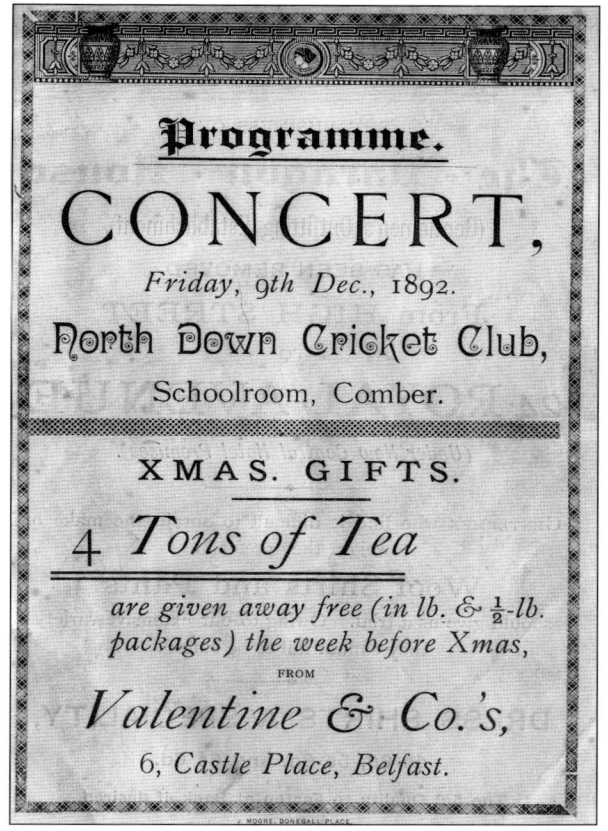

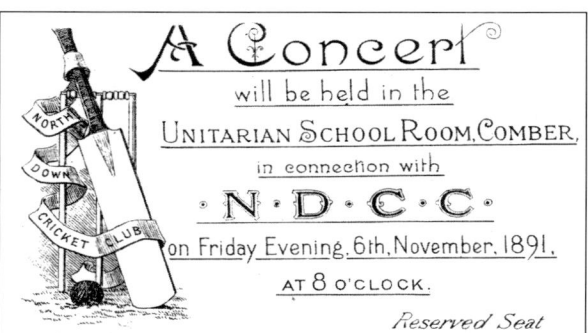

The last entry in the Programme is Valentine's advert proclaiming a forfeit of £100 if their advertisement, that claims 'The Finest Tea ever retailed in Belfast', is exaggerated.

NORTH DOWN HOCKEY CLUB

With a relatively short season, cricketers, even in the early days when September was regarded as a cricket month, have had to endure the long winter months devoid of the scent of new mown grass and the sound of leather on willow.

To maintain the comradeship and give another option to the footballers who had used the ground in the eighties, the proposal to play hockey at The Green might have been predicted. The first hockey match in Ireland was played in Dublin in 1892 and on the 24th August 1896 a meeting of North Down cricketers, with TJ Andrews in the Chair, met to discuss the formation of a hockey club. The outcome at a well-attended meeting was the unanimous decision to form North Down Hockey Club. Oscar Andrews was elected the first captain, WT Graham the secretary and four senior members of the Andrews family along with J McC Blizard and solicitor William Shean were made patrons.

The pitch was marked out on the Castle Lane side of the ground and remained in constant use until the advent of the artificial surfaces over 100 years later. The first competitive club match in Ulster was played between North Down and Cliftonville in November 1896 with at least eight of the team being members of the cricket club. For the record, North Down won 8-0 and Oscar Andrews, who scored six of them, was good enough to play for Ulster and Ireland at this time. The involvement of the Andrews family in

WILLIE S TURNER

hockey was such that they mirrored their summer extravaganza by playing an Andrews XI against the hockey club and losing 2-1 in the first season.

Sam Davidson was right back on the very successful hockey 1st XI and was captain, standing in for the indisposed HW Andrews, when North Down won the Kirk Cup for the first time in the 1899/1900 season. The two elevens in the early days were mostly made up from the cricket membership, a situation that would gradually change as the years passed.

WILLIE TURNER

Willie Turner was a prolific round-arm medium pace 'trundler' in the early North Down teams. At the height of his prowess he was described by that doyen of NCU cricket administrators JC 'Jimmy' Picken as "the best in the North, possibly in all Ireland".

There can be no greater accolade, but it was no idle boast as Willie's bowling performances set him apart from his peers and his batting contributions were huge.

Willie Turner emerged in the 1880s and for over 20 years he was the club's most prolific bowler. In tandem with his brother Sam and the peerless Tommy Graham they formed the formidable bowling attack that produced virtually every North Down victory. Willie loved the challenge of competitive cricket and the introduction of the Senior Challenge Cup in 1887 gave him a bigger stage on which to perform. He relished the opportunity so it was no surprise that in the first final the Turner brothers took 14 wickets between them. Sam was the last of the great 'grub' bowlers in Ulster cricket and on this occasion upstaged his elder brother, but it mattered little as the great seamer took a record 130 wickets that season and also scored 326 runs with the bat.

Willie played in ten cup finals winning eight times. He is also credited with a win in the walkover victory over Armagh in 1890. Some of his cup final performances remain all time NCU records and in every final he played, he made telling contributions. His best returns were match figures of eight for 28 in the 1888 final, 11 for 84 in 1891, eight for 60 in 1893, 11 for 40 in 1894 and 12 for 80 in 1897. Willie Turner and Tommy Graham bowled out most teams in their heyday and their work rate was phenomenal. In that record 1887 season Willie bowled a staggering 473 overs and he narrowly failed to hit the 100-wicket mark again in 1895 when he took 97 wickets and, for good measure, added 542 runs with the bat.

Willie Turner should have played for Ireland, but in his day the hosting clubs picked the 'national' teams so Phoenix and Dublin University players dominated the so-called Ireland teams. He played for Ulster many times and figured in the first interprovincial series that was staged at Rathmines in Dublin in 1890. In the first match against Munster, Ulster scraped home with two wickets to spare and Willie took 13 for 38 but the northerners were well hammered by the strong Leinster team in the second game. It was at this gathering that talks about forming an Irish Cricket Union first emerged, but it was another 30 years before it actually happened and, by then, Willie Turner had long since disappeared from the cricket scene.

The interprovincial matches were a great platform for Willie's talent, but clubs throughout the north saw his abilities week in week out. Willie opened the 1891 season with eight for 36, but his best performance that season was against Gilford in the semi-final

It was reported that Mr WS Turner, who had gone to reside in Dublin, was presented by some of his friends with a bag of sovereigns.

FROM THE MINUTES

of the Challenge Cup when he scored 108 not out, then took seven for four with the ball. He had a great sense of occasion and in the first game of the newly formed NCU Senior League in May 1896 he took four for 11 against Lisburn and then hit an unbeaten half-century.

It is tempting to reel out endless statistics about this amazing cricketer but Willie Turner was also a genial and popular club member. He took a full part in the club's activities and joined with brother Sam to sing the "Gendarmes Duet" at fund-raising concerts held in Comber.

So whether in concert or at the wicket, these two fine cricketers were always in full song and they have left an indelible mark on the club's history.

OSCAR ANDREWS

Born in 1876, Oscar Andrews was educated at Rossall School in Lancashire, married Amy Lyttle in 1904 and had two daughters. His career followed the path of his grandfather Isaac in whose mills he became a partner in 1894, director in 1924 and chairman in 1937.

Without question, Oscar was the most accomplished cricketer in the Andrews family.

In the late 1890s he was the best cricketer at North Down, in Ulster and possibly in Ireland, and when he switched allegiance to North of Ireland in 1900 it effectively swung the balance of power in favour of the Belfast club.

Oscar was born into cricket as father John Jnr.. and uncle TJ were at the centre of everything that happened at the North Down club. From a very early age he played in the Single v Married club games and the annual Andrews Family v North Down games. He made his senior debut aged 13 in 1889 and played in the inaugural Junior Cup final in 1891, losing to

OSCAR ANDREWS

Lavinia. Two years later he made a winning debut in the Senior Challenge Cup final and in the same year played for North of Ireland against the touring South Africans.

He was a star performer at Rossall School and many of his outstanding performances were generously reported in the Belfast press. His good friend 'Ned' Newett of Cliftonville and North of Ireland fame was at the school at the same time and they were destined to dominate Ulster cricket for many years thereafter. North Down played Rossall on their English tours at the time and the school team also visited The Green.

Like many of the Andrews family members, Oscar mixed his cricket at The Green with midweek cricket at Ormeau and in 1900 he moved permanently to Belfast. It was a poignant time for North Down as the dashing young fast bowler with an adventurous batting spirit had been the rising star at Comber during the 1890s and was destined to bring further honours to his club as his career matured.

He scored the first century in the Senior Challenge Cup final in 1897, after a first innings 73. He rarely failed with either bat or ball in cup finals and in the 1912 win against Ulster, captaining North of Ireland, he had record match figures of 14 wickets for 61 runs, including nine for 44 and a half-century. His Challenge Cup final record of 10 wins from 12 finals spanning 31 years ensures he has a lofty place in NCU archives, but it was his many outstanding individual performances that earned him the status as the best player of his era. After establishing himself at North Down he went on to excel for North of Ireland, scoring over 12,500 runs with a top score of 186. As a bowler he took over 1,500 wickets, topping 100 every season from 1901 to 1906. He totally dominated club cricket at his peak and, in addition to his individual brilliance, he was an inspirational and astute captain. His 161 run partnership with Willie Pollock in 45 minutes of blistering cricket at Phoenix Park remains one of cricket's great archives.

Strangely his international record was poor and he seemed to have little appetite for it. He was a willing tourist playing in England, the USA and Canada, but he played for Ireland only eight times from 1902 to 1909 and was not available for selection on numerous occasions. He played many times for Ulster and his 103 not out for the NCU against Leinster in 1902 was in the same year as he made his international debut against WG Grace's London County at Crystal Palace. His last match for Ireland was against Philadelphia in 1909 but he continued playing prominent fixtures including the fixture against an Indian touring side in 1911 and the North of Ireland side that played Wales in 1924. He bowed out of serious competitive club cricket in the 1920s and played in his last Challenge Cup final at the age of 49 in 1925 when his good friend Willie Pollock stole the show against Cliftonville.

Oscar was also a distinguished hockey player and a founder member of North Down Hockey Club. He was the club's first captain and went on to be capped by Ireland four times.

Oscar Andrews died in Belfast in October 1956, aged 80.

DAWN OF A NEW CENTURY

The end of the century marked the end of an era of North Down cricket dominance and it would be easy to say it largely revolved around the switch of cricket allegiance of Oscar Andrews from The Green to Ormeau but this was not the complete picture. The heroes of the 1880s and the 1890s were an ageing team and many of them were well into their forties. The old stagers had given the club magnificent service and set records that have stood for over 100 years. They were always going to be a difficult act to follow and the next generation without Oscar Andrews not only felt the loss, but the full brunt of his ability as North of Ireland took over North Down's mantle as the best club in the Province with the greatest years in their history.

A gentleman known as 'The Count of Killynether' led the local supporters in their criticism of visiting players, and in reference to a match against North at The Green the Whig relates thus: "All were caught out, with the exception of one unfortunate who was given out lbw. Albeit he made one clumsy slip, which earned for him the derision of the Count of Killynether and the other critics in the pavilion."

THE NORTHERN WHIG 1895

NORTH DOWN 2ND XI V. SPRINGFIELD IN JUNIOR CUP FINAL 1894: BACK – UMPIRE, G COUSER, M MACDONALD*, J NIVEN*, T ANDREWS*, TJ MACDONALD*, UMPIRE. MIDDLE – JAS. HAWTHORN, W CROWE, J MCCLEAN, T HAMILL, A BLACK, J HAMILL, J ANDREWS*, J SMYTH*, J NIBLOCK*, J MACDONALD*. FRONT– J STOCKMAN, T IRVINE, JOHN HAMILL, JOS. HAWTHORN, JM ANDREWS*, S DAVIDSON*, DR TAYLOR*. (*NDCC)

CHAPTER 3
1900 — 1913 : LULL BEFORE THE STORM

"EVERY LOVER OF THE NOBLE GAME IN ULSTER RECOGNISES THE GREAT SERVICES TO NORTHERN CRICKET FOR MANY YEARS PAST OF THE COMBER ORGANISATION. COMBER HAS BEEN TO ULSTER THE NURSERY OF THE BEST OF ITS YOUNG MATERIAL, THE TRAINING SCHOOL FOR THE BEST OF ITS PLAYERS AND THE HOME OF THE BEST OF ITS ENTHUSIASTS. MANY OF THE SMARTEST COLTS THE PROVINCE HAS EVER SEEN GOT THEIR EARLIEST TRAINING AT COMBER UNDER THE FATHERLY EYE OF THE LATE MR. W. SHEAN, MANY OF THE SMARTEST CRICKETERS THAT EVER FIGURED ON BELFAST GROUNDS HAVE BEEN MEMBERS OF THE NORTH DOWN ELEVEN, AND MANY OF THE STEADIEST AND MOST RELIABLE PLAYERS THAT EVER REPRESENTED THE PROVINCE AGAINST THE RIVAL TALENT OF THE SOUTH WERE WEARERS OF THE GREEN AND GOLD CAP."

THE NORTHERN WHIG 1901

COMBER AT THE TURN OF THE CENTURY

The Ordnance Survey map in 1900 described Comber as a market town in County Down, 14 miles from Downpatrick, seven ESE from Belfast, situated on the road from Belfast to Downpatrick with a population of 2,357. The Square was the focal point where fairs and markets were held on Tuesdays, and there were two extensive distilleries, corn mills, hotels, a bleachgreen and a spinning mill. The Church of Ireland was described as a neat little building and other places of worship existed for Presbyterians, Unitarians, Methodists and Roman Catholics. The educational establishments consisted of a school, founded by Viscountess Castlereagh in 1813, one under Erasmus Smith's charity and Congregational and National schools, one of the latter being attached to Second Comber Presbyterian Church, called Smith's National School. There was also an Orange Hall to facilitate the ever-strong loyalist traditions within the town.

Comber had several industries – whiskey distilleries and a large flax spinning mill to keep its population busy, while it stood at the junction of the railway lines from Belfast to Donaghadee and Newcastle. By 1900 a corn and a flourmill were already shown as disused and there was no sign of the 'aerated waters' factory mentioned in earlier references.

North of the town stood Castle House, built on the site of Mount Alexander and constructed of stone taken from the ruins of the old abbey originally founded by St Patrick in the 5th century, hence 'The Mount Alexander End' of the ground.

The vantage point on the hill provided an excellent viewing spot when the annual club fair was held, and in 1901 the Comber population flocked to the surrounds to witness what was, in effect, a major sports event. The best talent in Ireland and representatives from England were on show and although the weather was poor, the events ran to schedule and there were many spills in the cycling events and close finishes in the athletics. The patron, Mr. Justice Andrews and vice patrons were on view, and many ladies watched the races until the six o'clock deluge that brought a premature end to the last cycle race. James Coulter's catering was deemed satisfactory and the Comber Flute Band, whose music had been 'agreeable', entertained the crowd all afternoon.

The weather was delightful and the programme varied and included football, an obstacle race, schoolboys' under 14 race, 200 yards scratch, three-legged race, blindfold walk, wheelbarrow race and others. Dart gun competitions, Aunt Sally and ring-throwing added to the variety and the clay-pigeon shooting featured the Ulster Championships.

THE NORTH DOWN CRICKET CLUB FETE 1904

In the bigger world the Boer War was raging in Africa, while within a few years Queen Victoria would die, the Pope would die and William McKinley the 25th President of the United States would be assassinated. The arrival of the motorcar preceded man taking to the air but behind these great technological advances the threat of civil war loomed large in Ireland as the Home Rule campaigners grew more agitated. Little did anyone know at the time but an even greater horror lay on the horizon barely 14 years into the new century.

THE STATE OF CRICKET IN THE NCU

The administrators within the NCU ensured that organized cricket was in good shape at the turn of the century and the North Down input was strong with Thomas Andrews Jnr., Oscar and Willie Andrews on various committees and Tommy Graham the honorary secretary from 1909 until the outbreak of the Great War.

The proposed formation of the Irish Cricket Union and the antagonism with its promoters in Dublin played some part in the lack of interprovincial cricket at the time, and the co-operation within Ulster between the NCU and the North West unions was not good. Representative cricket between the two northern unions was eventually restarted and other representative games took place when the Province of Ulster played visiting teams such as Woodbrook, West of Scotland and the Philadelphians.

North Down caused considerable controversy within the NCU in 1899 and 1900. According to NCU archives, North Down won the 'first' two years of the Senior League competition in 1897 and 1898, but newspaper records show that North Down and Cliftonville shared the title the previous year in 1896! It must have seemed rather strange to the substantial cricket loving public therefore, when the holders of the 'Ireland Saturday Night Cup', as the league cup was then known, and the Senior Challenge Cup, opted out of the league competition in 1899 and 1900. This was attributed to "the absence of sport" in the competitive matches, owing to the anxiety of the clubs to win the ties, as compared to the conviviality and camaraderie of the friendly matches.

During their self imposed exile North Down continued to play against senior teams, receiving the same press coverage as the league games, but perhaps because they did not relish the absence of competitive cricket, Oscar Andrews and David Taylor played for North of Ireland in the league whilst still playing for North Down in the cup.

1908 SENIOR CUP WINNERS: BACK – AE ANDERSON, AM CRAWFORD, AJ TAYLOR, WT GRAHAM, J MCDONALD, TJ ANDREWS. FRONT – W ANDREWS, W COULTER, DR TAYLOR, S DAVIDSON, J ANDREWS, RP HOUSTON.

ONE SHOT MORE ...FOR THE HONOUR OF DOWN : A HISTORY OF NORTH DOWN CRICKET CLUB 1857 — 2007

NCU Senior Challenge Cup 1913 – North Down v Waringstown: Back– Millership (Pro)*, DR Taylor*, HB Hanna*, DR Wheeler*, WG Abernethy*, W Frier, W Scott, R Irwin, H McKenzie, J Williamson. Front – WC Coulter*, J Dearden*, James Andrews*, AE Anderson*, J Taylor*, W Andrews (Capt.)*, R Scott (Capt.), C Ferguson, T McKenzie, R Harwood, T Anderson Ground– V Benson*, J Hampton. (*NDCC)

More controversy followed in 1901 when North Down refused to play on the date set for the Challenge Cup final because it clashed with the annual fair, where they hoped to raise enough money to clear the club's debt of £70. Unfortunately, the club's intransigence was met with similar brick wall officialdom from the NCU and the club decided to withdraw from the final and gift the trophy to North of Ireland.

However, despite many challenges that the NCU administrators had to deal with, they had sound structures and finances in place and proved very capable officials.

CRICKET AT THE GREEN

The first 'Golden Era' of the club ended in 1899 and for the next 15 years the club played second fiddle to North of Ireland who won seven out of nine Senior League titles and seven from eight Senior Challenge Cups between 1900 and 1914. Changes had occurred at The Green and the heady days of the 1890s had gone and so had the old timers. Within a few years there was to be no John Andrews Jnr., DAH Milling, Willie Turner, JC Lindsay or TJ Andrews, and the 1908 Senior Cup winning side produced no less than seven new names to add to the plinth of that renowned trophy. Most notable among the debutants were Willie Coulter, Albert Anderson and Willie Andrews.

Professionals, for those clubs that could afford them, did a good job, as their playing restrictions in the Challenge Cup and for a time in the league, meant that they could concentrate their talents in groundsmanship and coaching at all levels. North Down did not support the playing of 'pros' in competitive games and in 1904 took the field under protest against Jones, the 'pro', being included in the Downpatrick side on the opening day of the season. Jones duly took six wickets and hit the winning runs, thus inviting an official protest from North Down and a counter protest from Downpatrick. The harassed NCU ordered a replay but before that match took place the sides met at Downpatrick in the second round of the Senior Challenge Cup with two sets of highly charged teams and supporters. Ironically Jones was one of the umpires.

Fleming and Cleland took four wickets each as North Down were all out for 109, with RP Houston 32 and James Andrews 25, the main run makers. The tension was 'in the air' as Downpatrick edged towards the target, but AM Crawford took four for 28 and the home side failed by four runs. North Down went on to contest the final against North of Ireland in August and the scorebook records the fact that AM Crawford, who registered four for 52 and scored 27 in the semi-final, was 'absent for the first innings'. His presence may have improved matters, as North of Ireland totalled a formidable 195 in the first innings and North Down lost by 177 runs. There would have been little sympathy at Strangford Road. In the re-arranged league game with Downpatrick later that season, North Down won comfortably much to the chagrin of Downpatrick!

I met AC Bannerman who has been to England five times and, thinking that you might like his autograph, have got him to write on your sheet of paper. Let me know of any of the old players whose autographs you would like and I will get them for you.

THE AUSTRALIAN CRICKETING ICON VICTOR TRUMPER WRITING TO MASTER WILLIAM ANDREWS, 1900

WILLIE COULTER

The 1st XI contested eight Senior Challenge Cup Finals in the period, winning two of them, the first in 1908, the side being captained by DR Taylor, the first player not belonging to the Andrews family to do so. North Down met Cliftonville in the final, and they also met in a league encounter at The Green shortly before when, amazingly, only 13 of the players in the eventual cup final sides turned out.

RT Adair, the North Down bowler, claimed seven wickets for 62. North Down looked beaten on 82 for nine but were rescued by Albert Anderson and TJ McDonald. The same 'Red' Adair had scored an undefeated 95 and taken three for 42 against Waringstown in July but, for reasons unknown, couldn't make the cup final side!

As it turned out he wasn't needed, as the North Down first innings score of 250 was too much for Cliftonville and Tommy Graham and AM Crawford shared ten wickets to see them all out for 76. However, Cliftonville put up a great performance 'following on', and their 204 ensured that North Down would have to bat again, which they did, winning easily by eight wickets.

Performances in the senior league were varied, and throughout the period the availability of key players was always an issue. Fifth, sixth and seventh final league placings from 1901 until 1903 were a reflection of continuing difficulties. Full strength teams for cup matches didn't seem to be a problem, especially when they doubled as league games!

However in 1905, in a determined bid to finish as runners-up, they fielded a strong side to play Cliftonville in the last game of the season. North Down scored 116, defying the Lancashire 'pro' Turner, with DR Taylor and R Martin the run makers, and dismissed the opposition for a paltry 41, with Tommy Graham six for 27 and James Niblock four for 10.

The league was won in 1906 and in 1910 under new captain Willie Andrews. There was also the promise of even better times ahead with the 'signing' of PF Montgomery from Campbell College, NB Graham the Queen's University bowler and Alfred Taylor the rugby international player.

The 1906 league win was duly celebrated in 'Ye Olde Castle' restaurant in Belfast with the bonus of a three shillings and sixpence profit on the evening.

JAMES NIBLOCK

Disappointment followed in the club's Jubilee year of 1907 when they lost by five runs against Holywood in the Challenge Cup semi-final, despite David Taylor's superb 102.

The second round senior cup game went well in 1910 when the side chased Ulster's 278 runs and won by five wickets, thanks to a magnificent 164 from opening batsman Willie Coulter, who followed this with 191 not out against a strong Cumberland club, Millom CC. He was admired at the club for his run making and wicket taking, and was highly respected for his great loyalty, as he regularly travelled from his home in Scotland and further afield to play for North Down.

In 1912, he topped the batting averages with 33 and took 17 wickets at 10.5 but his five for 52 wasn't good enough against Queen's University to save North Down from a first round cup exit, an unusual occurrence for the club.

A century from Willie Andrews brought the trophy 'home' in 1913.

ON HIS RETURN TO THE CLUB AFTER ILLNESS, JAMES NIBLOCK WAS PRESENTED WITH THIS CHEQUE

George Bruce, whose heroic exploits were to bring him and the club honour during the Great War, laid the foundation for the first round win against Banbridge with 66 runs and David Taylor ensured a final place with his 90 against Cliftonville in the semi-final. It was fitting that the captain and his vice-captain Albert Anderson, batting at number six and seven, scored 111 and 80 respectively and posted a first innings total of 432. Waringstown was beaten by an innings and 97 runs with Willie Coulter taking seven wickets for 100.

The 1914 cup run saw wins against Lisburn and Armagh before they met Waringstown again in the final. This time it was a battle of the bowlers and Waringstown's Tom McKenzie won the day with 12 for 66, edging out Willie Coulter's 12 for 69 and leaving the villagers winners by 71 runs.

The Junior Cup was won twice during this period; for the third time in our history in 1902 with a victory over North of Ireland by five wickets, the team being: T Macdonald, R Guiney, H Ritchie, W Coulter, J Macdonald, D Smyth, JM Andrews, T Andrews, S Gracey, C Gordon and J Watson.

It was then won for the fourth time in 1904 with most of the side being senior hockey players and including Bob Guiney, whose name is given to the 'Guiney Stones' that still sit at the entrance to the ground. James Watson and Thomas Andrews both made contributions, unaware of the tragedy that would befall them with the Titanic disaster in 1912.

The 2nd XI's strength was usually gauged on their performances against North of Ireland and in 1905 they won a league game at Comber by 19 runs, opener Joe McDonald scoring 39 and A Smyth taking five wickets in a low scoring game. They had beaten Forth River by five runs in the Junior Cup, but ran into a

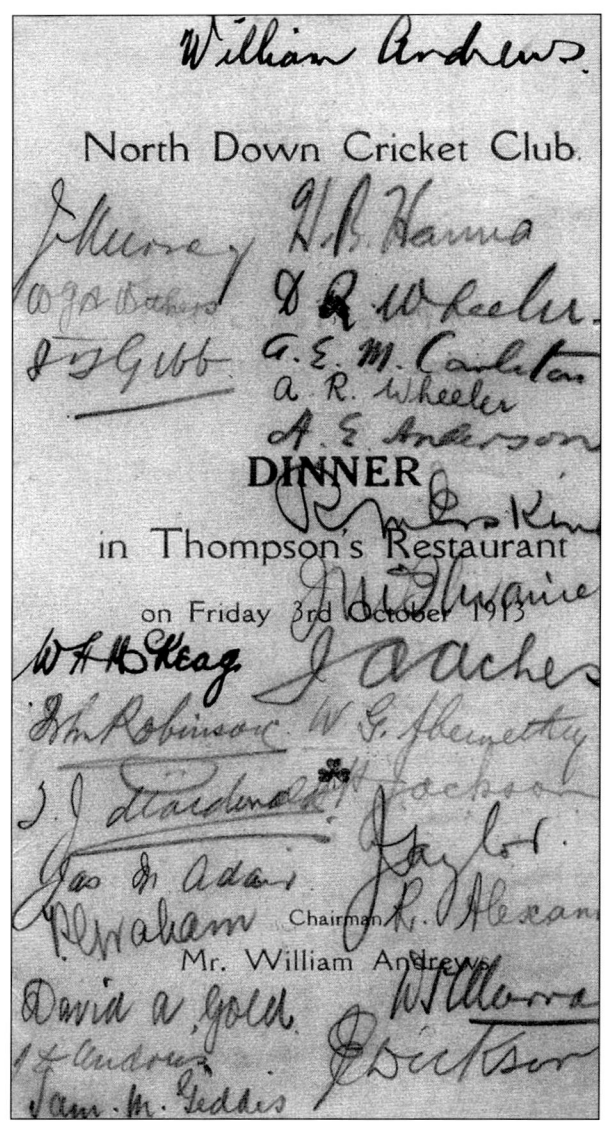

CELEBRATION DINNER MENU ON WINNING THE 1913 SENIOR CHALLENGE CUP

diplomatic row in the second round when they made the long train journey to Ballymena only to have the game called off in controversial circumstances.

'The Slogger', who was the 'Ireland Saturday Night' correspondent at the time, stated that 'the whiskey men' were not amused and claimed the tie. In compensation for not playing the cup tie a match was hastily arranged against the Spinning Mill.

However, hopes of winning the Junior Cup again in 1905 were halted in the semi-final, when North of Ireland won by six wickets.

First round Junior Cup exits in 1908 and again in 1909 to Balmoral when, in the latter year the side played 15 games and only won four, did nothing to boost morale in the side, although in 1909 they were the only team to defeat Harmony, the kingpins in the Junior league.

TJ Macdonald captained the side with TK Wheeler as his deputy and the main batting came from John Miller Andrews, WL Clarke and S Carson, with JB Prenter, W Gilmour, Eddie Wishart and the captain all scoring significant runs. James Patton, as he had done the previous season, collected the junior bowling award with 23 wickets with W Bloomer and JM Andrews supporting.

It may have looked like the club had lean years from 1900 to 1914, but that was only in comparison to the 1890s and although in the shadow of North of Ireland, North Down was in a healthy state.

JUBILEE CELEBRATIONS

Preparations to celebrate the club's 50th birthday had been ongoing for nearly a year and three events stood out as requiring special organisational skills beyond the norm.

Tommy Graham, Willie Andrews, TJ Macdonald and John Murray occupied the official positions within the club and now had a 'man management' task way beyond their normal duties. They called on the captain of the club, Mr. James Andrews, treasurer Mr. James Shean and the committee members to delegate a multitude of tasks to the many volunteers at their disposal and the response was overwhelming.

The events would be held not only from a sentimental viewpoint but also from the practical consideration of raising funds for the building of a much-needed new pavilion to replace the original wooden structure that had served the club so well. The target was to raise between £300 and £400 and the main event was a Fete or Bazaar, as it was known at the time.

The opening of the Bazaar in the spacious grounds of the Unitarian Church was a great occasion, with marquees dotted between the trees and 'furnished with decorated stalls'.

The numerous side shows, many of an original character, added to the ambience as the strains of McCormick's band drifted softly over the church grounds.

The opening ceremony was held in the large central marquee and the platform party was a 'Who's Who' of social, political and North Down personalities with the guest of honour being the Countess Annesley.

The Right Hon. Thomas Andrews, in his address to the large crowd, stated that it was a great honour to be asked to speak at this, the greatest social occasion in the club's illustrious history. He spoke with obvious affection for the little provincial town that, through its cricket, was known and respected all over the country. He spoke of the Comber people with affection, the successful offspring of the club, namely the hockey club, and the excellent ground and its management. He elaborated on the contribution of the ladies over the last year in their preparations for today and how many of them had looked on this as 'a labour of love'.

He lavished the guest of honour with praise referring to her as 'the fairest daughter of all Ireland' and in return the Countess spoke of the success of the Club and the pride that it had brought to the townspeople. After a vote of thanks the Countess declared the Bazaar open and the many features, including the Art Stall, Veteran's Stall, Provisions, Belfast Works and Maryborough Stalls, along with the ever-popular 'Aunt Sally' outdoor skittles swung into action.

In tandem with the Bazaar, a 'Go-As-You-Please', the early version of Marathon running, began at the Variety Market in Chichester Street, Belfast, with over 140 top-class local and overseas athletes. The event passed through Conway Square in Newtownards and continued into the midst of huge crowds at Comber Square.

The Belfast Newsletter recorded at the time:

"In which (the Square) were many motor cars, carts, and vehicles of every description. Mr Ritchie and some of the leading residents took charge of the arrangements in the town and did everything possible for the convenience of the competitors. The various runners were loudly cheered, Lee being especially accorded an ovation, and Mr McKinley, the Ballycastle veteran, the oldest competitor and young Shannon of Belfast a mere lad, getting great encouragement from the people".

At The Green, where the last two miles were run, the scene was one of colour and excitement, where, "a great number of ladies, dressed in the gayest of summer costumes, patronised the big enclosure and cheered home the two Ulsterville Harriers runners, Lee and Weatherall, ahead of Kennedy McArthur from the South African Constabulary".

The bazaar had been a tremendous financial success and in 1908, £209 and ten shillings along with £28 for extras, was paid to Mr Black in connection with the erection of the new pavilion.

The official opening in 1909 was a major event in the life of North Down Cricket Club and was extensively covered by the 'Ireland Saturday Night' thus:

"The pavilion attached to the North Down cricket club's ground in Comber has been enlarged at a cost of £300, and the opening ceremony was performed on Saturday afternoon by Mrs TJ Andrews, whose late husband proved himself such a warm and devoted friend of the organisation. The pavilion is, to all intents and purposes, an entirely new building, for comparatively little of the old structure has been left standing, and besides being an ornament to the ground, it should prove of inestimable benefit to the club and visiting teams on match days. The dressing rooms are commodious, excellent lavatory accommodation has been provided and there is a kitchen in which food can be cooked and arrangements made for the entertainment of visitors, so far as the supply of refreshments is concerned. A large number of special invitations had been sent out to friends residing in the district to attend the opening ceremony, and several hundred people witnessed the interesting proceedings and enjoyed the hospitality of the club, everyone on the ground being entertained to tea.

"Mr James Andrews, captain of the club, in introducing Mrs TJ Andrews, said he would like to take that opportunity of thanking all their friends who had contributed to the success of their recent bazaar, and so made it possible for them to erect the handsome pavilion of which they had now obtained possession. The success of that undertaking was assured by the harmonious manner in which the workers combined.

The committee had been unanimous in all their decisions, and especially had their unanimity been displayed in regard to the proposal to invite Mrs Andrews to open their pavilion. It was largely owing to the kindness and forethought of the late Mr TJ Andrews that they now had that splendid ground at their disposal, and they welcomed Mrs Andrews both for her own sake and for the cherished memories that they had of her late husband. (Applause)

"Mrs Andrews then unlocked the door with a silver key, which was presented to her for the purpose by the committee, and in the course of a happy little speech she said the North Down club had a glorious record, and she was sure that the present members would do all in their power to maintain the reputation that it had built up for fair play, good play, and splendid hospitality.

"An enlarged photograph of her late husband was presented by Mrs Andrews, and gratefully accepted

A matter, which was of personal knowledge to him (Thomas Andrews Snr), was the fact that Lady Annesley had refused for the present week a most tempting invitation, in order that she might come to Comber and assist the North Down Cricket Club.

NEWTOWNARDS CHRONICLE SEPTEMBER 1907 ON THE CELEBRATION OF THE CLUB'S JUBILEE.

THOMAS ANDREWS, DESIGNER OF RMS TITANIC, WAS LOST AT SEA

on behalf of the committee by Mr WT Graham, who said it was nearly thirty years ago since he was first associated with the late Mr TJ Andrews on the cricket pitch. When their ground was re-laid some years ago, Mrs Andrews turned the first sod and it was a happy coincidence that she should be with them that day to open their new pavilion. He proposed a vote of thanks to Mrs Andrews.

"*The motion was carried with great enthusiasm, and Mrs Andrews having briefly responded, the proceedings terminated.*"

THOMAS ANDREWS AND THE TITANIC DISASTER

RMS Titanic was the second of a trio of luxury superliners designed to provide an express transatlantic service for the White Star Line. She was built at Harland and Wolff shipyard in Belfast and was the largest passenger steamship in the world. Construction began in March 1909 under the watchful eyes of William Pirrie, chairman at Harland & Wolff, Thomas Andrews, the chief designer and Alexander Carlisle, the general manager, and she was launched on the 31st of May 1911, the pride and joy of her Belfast workforce.

During her maiden voyage from Southampton to Cherbourg to Queenstown, destination New York, she struck an Atlantic iceberg late on the 14th April 1912 and sank, in just under three hours, with a great loss of life.

Reports of Thomas Andrews assisting with the rescue of passengers arrived on shore with those fortunate to survive, and he went down with the ship, his body never recovered. One can only imagine the devastation felt by his widow, Helen, and at Ardara by his parents, three brothers and sister Elizabeth.

Thomas Andrews was born in Ardara House in Comber into a well to do and much respected family of long standing in the town. His brother James became Lord Chief Justice, John Miller was the Prime Minister of Northern Ireland during the Second World War and William became High Sheriff of Down, managing director in Comber Spinning Mill and held a great many honorary positions in society.

Thomas was educated at the Royal Belfast Academical Institution and from there worked his way from the 'shop floor' through the ranks to become the chief designer at Harland and Wolff. He was the inspiration behind the design of the magnificent 'Titanic'.

He was brought up surrounded by cricket at his home in Ardara and as a boy he accompanied his elders to matches and enjoyed the wide-open spaces at 'The Green'.

'The Admiral' as he was known, played for the 2nd XI, a number four or five batsman who occasionally bowled and was frequently run out, 'thrown out' or recorded in the scorebook as 'duck'.

His best bowling performance was one that he would have treasured, as his five wickets for 17 runs was recorded against the Comber Spinning Mill in 1892. In 1893 he played in the annual Andrews XI versus North Down match and scored a 'duck' in both innings for the family.

The following year he played for Queen's Island, his employer, against North Down at Comber, and was bowled by his close friend John Macdonald for two runs and the next week he hit a swashbuckling 31 against the Spinning Mill before he was clean bowled by brother James.

His invaluable 22 not out in the 1894 Junior Cup Final ensured that the trophy came to 'The Green' for the first time and by 1897 he was at the peak of his involvement at the club and, together with brother John Miller, he donated a rose bowl to be presented annually to the 2nd XI bowler who took the most wickets during the season.

Saturday April 20th 1912 was noted in the North Down fixture book as a General Practice. It was cancelled, to be replaced by a much more sombre meeting by the cricket and hockey club members, who drew up the following resolution.

"At a joint meeting of the members of the North Down Cricket and Hockey Clubs held in the Pavilion on Saty 20th April 1912, the following resolution of sympathy was unanimously passed and copies forwarded to the Right Hon. Thos Andrews & Mrs Andrews, Ardara, Comber.

"We, a number of the members of the North Down Cricket and Hockey Clubs meeting voluntarily and spontaneously, desire to give expression to our sincere sorrow & regret at the irreparable calamity which has overtaken you and the members of your family through the loss of your noble, loved and devoted son, and we as fellow members, many of us acquainted with him from boyhood days, desire to offer our sincere sympathy in this your hour of darkness & distress".

Such was the volume of mail received by Thomas Andrews Snr. that the reply was posted a month later to David Gold, the club secretary:

"Will you kindly convey to the members of the North Down Cricket & Hockey Clubs the sincere thanks of Mrs Andrews and myself & our family for the very kind resolution of sympathy with us in our great sorrow which they have been good enough to adopt & forward to us. The heroism of our son up to his last moment & the sympathy of so many kind friends are our comfort. I trust I shall be excused for the delay in replying as I have had a very large correspondence to deal with of late".

Similar letters were sent from the club to Thomas's widow, Helen, and addressed to her parents' home in Dunmurry. She replied thanking the club:

"For their kind resolution of deep sympathy and sorrow for me and my family in our great loss, and also for the well deserved attributes expressed to a noble life that was heroically self-sacrificed in accomplishing the rescue of others"

The nine-man Guarantee Group was a very select group of workers headed by Thomas Andrews, who accompanied Titanic on her maiden voyage, to attend to any unfinished work or problems that might appear on the voyage to New York and back. It was a great honour, especially for an apprentice, to be asked to make the trip.

There would have been much excitement and pride in the Watson family at Madrid Street in Belfast when son Ennis was included.

Ennis Hastings Watson was an apprentice electrician at Harland and Wolff who studied successfully at the Belfast Municipal Technical Institute for five years and had a promising future ahead of him with Harlands, until he lost his life on the fateful voyage with 'Titanic'.

Great sadness was felt at North Down Cricket Club for his father, a loyal club member, and his reply to the North Down letter of condolence showed great strength of character under terrible circumstances.

"Please convey to the members of North Down Cricket Club the heartfelt gratitude of my wife, family and myself for their kind and sincere sympathy in our very sad bereavement.

It is hard to say 'thy will be done' but we find consolation in the thought that he died doing his duty by the side of so many brave men. It is our earnest prayer that the Great Consoler may send comfort to the hearts of those who are likewise stricken".

DR DAVID R TAYLOR

Davy Taylor was a fine all round sportsman who graduated through the Boys' XI in the early 1890s and went on to be capped by Ireland at both cricket and rugby. His North Down career spanned over 40 years, although he was also a member at North of Ireland at the same time. A doctor by profession, he was the son of the Moderator of the General Assembly of the Presbyterian Church and attended the Royal Belfast Academical Institution before going on to study at Queen's College, Cambridge and Edinburgh Universities. David learned his early cricket under the guidance of William Shean, one of the founder members of the club, and benefited greatly from the tutelage of the wily professional Harry Baines, both at Ormeau and at The Green. The Northern Whig

DAVID TAYLOR

Leinster Cricket Club Tour London 1903: Back Row – SD Lambert, DAH Milling (North Down CC), WM Butler, HS Kelly, Cockcroft (Pro). Middle Row – CR Fausset, WG Grace, RH Lambert, N Peterson, EJ Donovan Front Row – AA Abraham, F Wood (Scorer), FW Taylor.

earmarked him for greatness as early as 1892 in a report on the North Down Juniors' match against Ulster Juniors:

"Master Taylor played well for his 19 runs and we have no doubt he will be learned of later to greater advantage."

Wise words indeed as "DR" made his senior league debut in 1896 as a 15 year-old, in a strong North Down team that included the Turner brothers, Tommy Graham, Oscar, John Jnr. and Herbert Andrews, JC Lindsay and James Niblock. Batting number 11 he scored seven not out in a comfortable win over Ulster. It was the start of an illustrious cricket career and barely two years later David was fully established in the team and scored a fine 61 in the Senior Challenge Cup final win over Ulster. He also scored 99 against Cliftonville that same season. He was a solid orthodox batman and difficult to dislodge. He started his career as a wicketkeeper but became an outstanding athletic fielder specializing at cover point. He was also a useful change bowler who "bowled a capital length with a bit of spin". In 1899 he scored 21 and 73 in the freshman's match for Cambridge and a few years later he also figured in the Edinburgh University team. He had fond memories of his university cricket and wore Edinburgh's traditional blue cap for many years thereafter. He had a very special year in 1903 when he scored 117 not out against Lisburn, his best innings in senior cricket, and followed it up during the autumn with a rugby international debut against England. Ireland won that game 6-0 but it was to be his only international rugby appearance despite his glowing reputation as a dashing wing-three-quarter. Ironically he was only capped once by Ireland at cricket as well, being one of seven Ulster players selected against Wales in an historic match at Ormeau in 1924. David played for Ulster many times including another historic match in 1908 against the touring Philadelphians, the famous American cricket club that included the legendary JB "Bart" King. All the top players in the province were selected for this game including Oscar Andrews, Willie Andrews, and Willie Pollock.

David Taylor was a mainstay in the North Down team for nearly 35 years and at 50 years of age was still deemed good enough to win selection for the 1931 Challenge Cup final team. In total he played in 18 Challenge Cup finals, winning on 12 occasions, including 1902 when he played at North of Ireland for a season. He was very consistent and while he didn't go on to make many centuries he was a prolific half-century batsman. One exception however was in 1907 when he scored 102 against Holywood in the cup semi-final thriller that North Down narrowly lost by five runs. Another memorable innings was his 55 not out in the 1926 Challenge Cup final although in his last few cup final appearances he batted low in the order as the younger players took precedence. He was very popular with the new generation at The Green and his experience and wise counsel was the hallmark of his legacy to them.

David Taylor also served with the Medical Corps in France during the Great War.

JAMES ANDREWS

James Andrews was born in 1877 and after attending "Inst" he was accepted at Trinity College Dublin in 1896 to study law. He was an outstanding legal student who rose to the lofty status of Lord Chief Justice in 1937 and was awarded a Baronet in 1942. Born and reared at Ardara, James Andrews was indoctrinated into North Down Cricket Club from an early age and shared his brothers' passion for sport, especially cricket. He was an enthusiastic member of the Andrews XI that annually played against the club and throughout his life was particularly close to his brother John Miller, later to be Prime Minister of Northern Ireland. In addition to cricket he was a keen rugby player, hockey player, golfer and sailor. He loved sport and law and excelled at both. He played regularly in the North Down teams of the 1890s and emerged as a senior cricketer in the 1897 Senior Cup final victory over North of Ireland. In total he played in ten senior cup finals for the club, winning on four occasions and captaining the side several times. He was a modest performer with the bat but scored a brilliant 97 against Ulster in the 1909 final, a match North Down lost by the massive margin of an innings and 89 runs. As an administrator he took an active part in the administration of the unions, firstly while serving on the NCU junior committee, then as NCU president in 1927/8, and then as Irish Cricket Union president in 1929. With his brother Willie, he is credited with having

JAMES ANDREWS

re-written the constitution of the NCU in the mid-twenties. For many years he mixed business and pleasure between Dublin and Belfast. He was in Dublin at the time of the Easter Rising in 1916 when his uncle Willie (Judge William Drennan Andrews) was lucky to escape with his life after the rebels forcibly took over his house. James Andrews became one of the original members of the Supreme Court when the state of Northern Ireland was established in 1921 and he was made Lord Justice in the Court of Appeal. He was regarded as an excellent judge and in 1937 the ailing Prime Minister, Viscount Craigavon, appointed him Lord Chief Justice in succession to Sir William Moore. For most of his adult life he lived at Eusemere on the Killinchy Road where, in 1941, two escaped German prisoners-of-war were discovered taking refuge in the garage and were returned to their camp by the B Specials who guarded the house. His long-term faithful driver and close friend was Jack McGreeghan who for many years lived in Castle Lane and regularly attended North Down home games. James Andrews never forgot his cricket roots despite the demands of his prominent position and his brother Willie kept him abreast of everything that was happening at both the club and the union. After his playing days were over he made occasional visits to The Green to watch games but that became increasingly more difficult when war broke out.

He was a popular Comber citizen and his death in 1951, at the age of 73, was met with great sorrow in the local community and none more so than amongst the members of North Down Cricket Club.

THE STORM ARRIVES

The Home Rule issue reached a peak in the period 1900 to 1914 and in the years preceding the Great War it looked likely Ireland would be plunged into a civil war. Preparations were well under way all over Ulster and several cricket grounds had already been taken over by the Ulster Volunteer Force for training purposes. Comber was a staunch unionist town and many of the members were already committed to the cause, but just as battle stations were about to be taken, a greater threat erupted on the continent and Britain was plunged into the Great War, a war of huge and tragic human loss.

The irony of the civil conflict in Ireland was that two sides which were about to engage in violence could, just as quickly, take up arms together to face an even greater threat. Ireland could wait for another day because from 4th August 1914 Ulster was at war and, throughout the Province, many young cricketers were answering the call of King and Country.

PHILADELPHIANS V PROVINCE OF ULSTER 1908: BACK – FS WHITE, AD ADAMS, NUTTER, HV HORDERN, JH CRANE, CC MORRIS, EM KRUGER, DR TAYLOR*. CENTRE REAR – JDM MCCALLUM, JB KING, AM WOOD, JA LESTER (CAPT), FH BOHLEN, O ANDREWS (CAPT)*. CENTRE FRONT – AN MCCLINTON, NZ GRAVES. FRONT – NA MOORE, FA GREEN, CH WINTER, J FLEMING, WP NEWHALL, W POLLOCK, W ANDREWS*. (*NDCC)

CHAPTER 4
1914 – 1918 : THE FIRST WORLD WAR

"THEY ALL KNEW HOW SPLENDIDLY ULSTER DID IN THE WAR; WHAT A MAGNIFICENT RESPONSE SHE MADE TO THE APPEAL OF KING AND COUNTRY, AND IT COULD BE SAID, WITHOUT THE SLIGHTEST FEAR OF CONTRADICTION, THAT NO TOWN OF ITS SIZE OR POPULATION DID BETTER THAN AND FEW DID AS WELL AS THE TOWN OF COMBER."

THE NORTHERN WHIG 1919

COMBER AT THE OUTBREAK OF THE GREAT WAR

Comber's population had increased in the period 1900 to 1914 from just over 2,000 to around 2,700 and from their midst 426 men answered the call, 79 of whom were destined to make the supreme sacrifice. It says little for the general quality of life in Ulster at the time that many young men and women saw war as a break from the drudgery of everyday life and enlisted. The call to arms was spontaneously received throughout the Province and the response from towns and villages was huge. Within weeks young soldiers were being drilled and trained and almost as quickly they were on the trains and boats to the green fields of France, where they faced horror and death on a scale they could never have imagined.

Comber was a sombre place after 1914. The fairs and the markets stopped, there was virtually no organized recreation and families hid behind closed doors, dreading the delivery of a telegram from the War Office. The tragedy of the Titanic had barely sunk in before the Great War started, and although the Andrews Memorial Hall was officially opened in 1915, it was some time before it became functional as a social and community centre for the town. Work was scarce, a development that had been happening for some years as the agricultural industry declined and local people sought work in Belfast at either the shipyard or the Ropeworks factory.

War took precedence over everything. Comber Distillery general manager and well-known cricketer George Bruce had been training his UVF recruits for civil action, but after war broke out they were drafted into the British Army as the 36th (Ulster) Division. Local ministers, the Reverend Manning of St. Mary's

THE VENERABLE CC MANNING

Parish Church and the Reverend McConnell of 2nd Comber Presbyterian Church enlisted, and they were joined by hundreds of others, including over 60 members of the cricket club.

The War Memorials erected in many towns and villages throughout the Province are witness to how disastrous this war was for local communities and Comber was no exception.

CRICKET IN IRELAND CLOSES DOWN

When war broke out in early August 1914 the cricket season was almost finished, but it still took a strong letter from the great WG Grace to 'The Sportsman' several weeks later to bring a complete cessation of games. It took some time for the reality of this war to sink in, as many so-called experts felt it would be over by Christmas, but when news of the heavy losses became known, sport gradually closed down. The NCU senior committee met in September and Captain William Andrews suggested that a charity match should be arranged for the War Fund and it was immediately passed. However, all competitions were dropped for the duration of the hostilities and NCU president Fred Warden praised the patriotism of Ulster cricketers on active service. Only two committee meetings were held at North Down in 1915 as virtually all local cricket had ceased, although Captain Andrews still found time to take the Ulster Schools team to Dublin to play Leinster Schools. It was a similar situation for the next three years although special charity matches continued to be played for the War Fund and wounded soldiers were invited to the games. When news of the horrific losses at the Somme was received back home, even the charity matches were cancelled. Ulster was at war and cricket seemed a long way from home for those brave young North Down men at 'the Front.'

JIM BAXTER

On Saturday 18th June when we played Cliftonville, the 'box' money of three pounds, eleven shillings and eight pence ha'penny went to St Dunstan's hospital for the blind.

FROM THE MINUTES

Few towns were spared and clubs like Holywood, Muckamore, Downpatrick, Lisburn, Waringstown, North, North Down and others suffered badly as their members were either killed or wounded in action.

The Belfast Cricket League was more directly affected, as many of the players were employed at the Harland and Wolff shipyard in Queen's Island, and with their workload increased considerably, their matches were scrapped.

NORTH DOWN GOES TO WAR

An idyllic afternoon's cricket at The Green was enjoyed by many of our young men before the call to war and the green fields of France became the venue for horrendous war games. How often would the thoughts of those in the trenches have returned to home, family, friends and the pastimes enjoyed at The Green or elsewhere?

David Smyth, who served with the Auckland New Zealand Reserve, played for the 2nd XI against North of Ireland 2nd XI under the captaincy of John Miller Andrews.

Wallace B Gilmour, 2nd Battalion of the South Staffordshire Regiment, played for the 1st XI against Instonians and W Coulter, Honourable Artillery Company, played against the Royal Academical Institution. Lieutenant Colonel Lawrence A. Hind of the 7th territorial Battalion Sherwood Forresters, who was wounded twice, mentioned in despatches and killed in action, played against Woodvale, and scored a 'duck'.

David Gold was the club's only Prisoner of War and was held in Kriegefenenlagar near Minden. He was club secretary from 1908 until 1912 and played against Queen's College as a middle order batsman.

Tom McRoberts bowled for the 2nd XI against Oakleigh and a year later died in action with the 17th Battalion, Royal Irish Rifles.

In 1913 the 3rd XI team that played against Harland & Wolff in June and lost by 42 runs had the following batting order:

TJ Macdonald, J Spence, (13th Service Battalion Royal Irish Rifles, killed in action), W Morrow, G

TOM McROBERTS

Murray, (13th Service Battalion Royal Irish Rifles), RF Kerr, (18th Reserve Battalion Royal Irish Rifles, killed in action), W Galbraith, T Morrow, (North Irish Horse), J Patton, D Young (Military Medal), W Savage, S Geddis, (1st Service Battalion Leicestershire Regiment & Army Cycling Corps, killed in action).

The 3rd XI that lost by two runs to UPS had JR Wheeler, (Royal Field Artillery), in the side and when they played Campbell College later in the season, included was EB Cinnamond, (13th Service Battalion West Yorks Regiment), who distinguished himself on the field with runs and wickets, was wounded three times and received the Military Cross.

Matches played during the war were often against Forces teams based at Thiepval or Palace Barracks, or against sides based at Ballykinler when many enduring friendships were established. The outbreak of the Great War in 1914 caused a temporary curtailment of the league, and when it was resumed in 1919 the 'Big Two' of North Down and North of Ireland finished at the top of the table, the former being awarded the title on the most slender of margins to complete the 'double' for the third time. The focus wasn't always on senior cricket, and for many years after the war, the Northern Ireland District Army Cup Final was played at 'The Green', yet another of the many military matches played in Comber that preserved and strengthened a tradition that lasted into the Seventies.

North Down had seventy members or ex-members who served with the Colours, sixteen of them making the supreme sacrifice. There was no organized recruitment as everyone was left to do what they felt was the right thing. It is amazing where each member eventually took up service and a miracle that so many of them returned home alive after the horrors of this war.

We should never forget the sacrifices these brave members made and their place in the history of North Down Cricket Club is, rightfully, at the top of our tributes to those who have gone to a greater calling.

In December 1919 the club secretary Edward Wishart wrote to the people of Comber and beyond, indicating that the North Down Committee had contracted for a War Memorial for the pavilion that would record not only those members who gave their lives in the Great War, but also those who served with the forces.

"I have no doubt you will esteem it a privilege to subscribe to such a worthy object"

In April 1924 Mr Willie wrote to copper and brass engravers in Leicester:

"I have just been informed that you engrave copper and brass in a manner which is very much cheaper than embossed lettering …we have nothing like sufficient money to do one with the usual brass or copper lettering."

A letter from John Robinson & Son, Monumental Sculptors from York Street in Belfast, was sent to North Down in July 1933, indicating that the club's dilemma was solved and that their proposal for green marble with lettering in gold, the club colours, would be perfect for the tablet. The tablet in Chatillion Green with gold lettering would cost thirty pounds.

And so it was no real surprise that in August 1933, the year when Adolf Hitler became German Chancellor and preparations began in Germany for the Second World War, North Down still hadn't sorted out the First World War memorial and sadly it never materialised.

This chapter is our permanent memorial to the fifty four who fought for us and returned home to live with the horrors they had witnessed and, sadly, to the sixteen who made the supreme sacrifice.

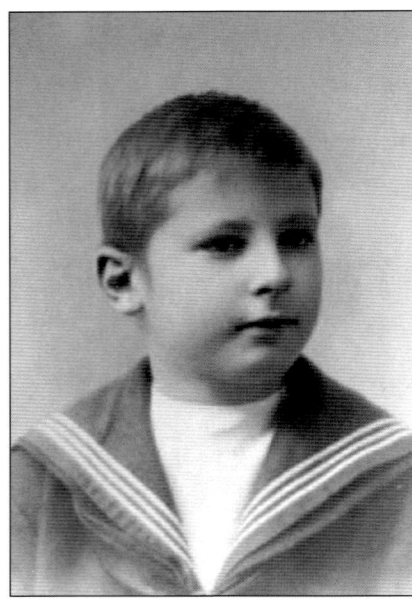
JS Culverwell

JL Galway

Chief PO James G Allen

HD Ritchie

North Down Cricket Club Members who served with the Colours during the Great War 1914-1918

Chief PO James G Allen *Royal Naval Yacht Patrol, ML Section who became a Justice of the Peace and a prominent citizen of Comber.*
James John Cullamore Allen, RASC *Mechanical Transport.*
Lieut. William Andrews *Royal Garrison Artillery & Royal Army Ordnance Corps.*
Major C Blakiston-Houston *RASC, was a Major in the Ulster Division and was 'Mentioned in Dispatches'. He also served as Church Warden in St Mary's Parish Church.*
David M Byers *Royal Canadian Regiment was wounded in action.*
Lieut. HP Cinnamond *1st Battalion West Yorkshire Regiment. Thrice wounded. Awarded the Military Cross.*
Private L'Isle Cinnamond *3rd Battalion of the Canadian Machine Gun Corps was twice wounded.*
WL Clarke
Capt. Francis EP Cowan *Artillery Captain at the North Antrim Garrison and was wounded in action.*
Col. RG Sharman-Crawford *18th (Reserve) Battalion Royal Irish Rifles.*
WC Coulter *Honourable Artillery Company.*
Major GH Culverwell MD *RAMC.*
A Davis
R Gailey *7th (Service) Battalion East Lancs. Regiment.*
GL Gibson *Chartered Accountant BEF.*
Lieut. Wallace D Gilmour *2nd Battalion of the South Staffordshire Regiment.*
Sergt. Robert Webster Glass *Royal Inniskilling Fusiliers. Mentioned in dispatches. Awarded the 'Medaille Militaire.'*

Lce/Corpl. DA Gold *14th (Service) Battalion RIR. Wounded Prisoner of War.*
Capt. NB Graham MD *RAMC. Wounded. Awarded the Military Cross.*
Major DS Graham MD *North Irish Horse and RAMC, Field Ambulance.*
Capt. LD Graham MD *RAMC.*
Capt. RF Henry *15th (Service) Battalion Royal Irish Rifles and Headquarters Staff 36th Ulster Division and Royal Field Artillery.*
JW Hicklin
Lieut. JE Hill-Dickson *13th Royal Irish Regiment. 1st and 2nd Gn. Battalion RIF.*
CB Houston *RASC Ulster Division, 36th Reserve Pack.*
Capt. RT Jamison MD *South African Medical Corp Botha's SW African Force.*
D Keith
WA Miller *4th (Territorial) Battalion Royal Scots Fusiliers and the 2nd King Edwards Horse and Tank Corps.*
Capt. WN Montgomery MD *3rd Reserve Battalion Royal Irish Fusiliers and RAMC. Mons Star, Order of the Nile, Order of 'Nahda' Twice mentioned in despatches.*
Capt. FP Montgomery MD *RAMC. Awarded the Military Cross and the French Croix de Guerre & Bar.*
Col. JS Moore *Royal Army Service Corps. Wounded.*
K Moran
2nd Lieut. TH Morrow *3rd Hussars Cavalry Regiment.*
Lieut. NB Munn *19th (Reserve) Battalion Royal Irish Rifles. Awarded the Military Cross.*
WJ Murphy

Lieut. DJ Murray *3rd Battalion King's Liverpool Regiment.*
2nd Lieut. Geo L Murray *13th (Service) Battalion Royal Irish Rifles.*
Capt. AN McClinton *10th (Service) Battalion Royal Irish Rifles.*
DL McGarrson
Sergt. JT McIntyre *18th Battalion Royal Irish Rifles.*
Capt. W McWilliam *2nd Battalion Connaught Rangers.*
GH Nicholson *5th (Reserve) Battalion Royal Irish Rifles. Wounded.*
T Prenter *Canadian 72nd Scottish Seaforth Highlanders. Wounded.*
Prentice
2nd Lieut. JA Ritchie *Royal Army Service Corps Mechanical Transport.*
David Smyth *Auckland New Zealand Contingent.*
JM Spence *13th (Service) Battalion Royal Irish Rifles.*
N Stouppe *14th (Service) Battalion Royal Irish Rifles.*
Lieut. DR Taylor MD *RAMC.*
WT Turnbull *Engine Room Artificer with the Australian Navy. HMS 'Sydney'.*
Capt. A Wallace *10th (Service) Batt. Royal Irish Rifles. Shell Shocked. French Croix de Guerre.*
Lt. Col. SH Withers MD *RAMC. CMG.*
WGA Withers *North Irish Horse. Meritorious Service Medal.*
Lieut. DR Wheeler *RAMC and Army Service Corps Ulster Divisional Train.*
Lieut. JR Wheeler *B/46 Brigade Royal Field Artillery. Twice wounded. Mentioned in Despatches.*
Lieut. AR Wheeler *15th Battalion Royal Irish Rifles. Twice wounded.*

North Down Cricket Club members who were killed in action during the Great War 1914-1918

MJ Alexander *North Irish Horse. Trooper.*

AE Baxter *3rd South Lancashire Regiment. Lieutenant.*

JE Drake *79th Battalion of the Canadian Expeditionary Force. Private.*

LA Hind *7th Territorial Battalion (Robin Hood) of the Sherwood Forresters, wounded, twice mentioned in despatches and awarded the Military Cross. Lieutenant Colonel.*

W Carruthers *Royal Engineers. 2nd Lieutenant. 3rd Reserve Battalion RIR.*

RD Niblock *8th Battalion Australian Contingent. Private.*

JS Culverwell *59th Royal Scinde Rifles FF. Captain. Mentioned in Despatches.*

HD Ritchie *2nd Scottish South West African Infantry Force. Private.*

AS Taylor MD *Royal Army Medical Corp.*

E de Wind *31st Service Battalion, 2nd Canadian Contingent and 17th Battalion of the Royal Irish Rifles. 2nd Lieutenant. Victoria Cross.*

T McRoberts *15th Battalion of the Royal Irish Rifles. 2nd Lieutenant.*

JM Spence *13th Battalion of the Royal Irish Rifles. Lance Corporal.*

GJ Bruce *13th Service Battalion of the Royal Irish Rifles and Staff at the 107th Brigade. DSO. Military Cross and Bar. Captain.*

SM Geddis *1st Battalion of the Leicestershire Regiment and Army Cyclist Corp. Lieutenant.*

JL Galway Jnr *31st Battalion Canadian Infantry died of wounds received in battle. Private.*

RF Kerr *18th (Reserve) Battalion Royal Irish Rifles.*

In Memory of
Second Lieutenant EDMUND DE WIND
VC

15th Bn., Royal Irish Rifles
who died age 34
on 21 March 1918
Son of the late Arthur Hughes De Wind, C.E., and Margaret Jane
De Wind, of "Kinvara", Comber, Co. Down.
Remembered with honour
POZIERES MEMORIAL

Commemorated in perpetuity by
the Commonwealth War Graves Commission

In Memory of
Lieutenant Colonel LAWRENCE ARTHUR HIND
MC

1st/7th Bn., Sherwood Foresters (Notts and Derby Regiment)
who died age 38
on 01 July 1916
Son of Jesse and Eliza Hind, of Edwalton, Nottingham husband of
Eliza Montgomery Andrews, of Ardara, Comber, Co. Down.
Remembered with honour
THIEPVAL MEMORIAL

  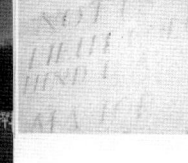

Commemorated in perpetuity by
the Commonwealth War Graves Commission

EDMUND DE WIND

The name Edmund de Wind doesn't feature too highly in the North Down teams of the late 1890s or early 1900s, although the de Wind family had several players at the club. However, the 15-year-old Edmund was included in the historic photo album of members that was presented to Tommy Graham in 1898 when he retired as club secretary. Despite his frail build, the young de Wind would certainly have been a keen cricketer, as his family was very friendly with the Andrews and Stone families, and he would have been a willing participant in games at Ardara and Barnhill when the families got together. He was also a pupil at Campbell College from 1895 to 1900 so cricket would obviously have been one of his regular summer sports.

Edmund de Wind may have been a very ordinary cricketer, but he was certainly not an ordinary man, and his name is immortalized in Comber history as our only recipient of the Victoria Cross. On the green fields of France, far from Castle Lane, he brought great honour to North Down Cricket Club through his heroic acts.

Edmund was born in Comber in 1883, the son of Arthur de Wind, chief engineer for the Belfast and County Down Railway. His mother was Margaret Jane Stone, and the Stone family lived at Barnhill on the Belfast Road, although the de Winds eventually settled on the Killinchy Road at 'Kinvara', a house that Arthur built himself. Young Edmund worked with the Bank of Ireland in Cavan following school, before emigrating to Canada in 1910, where he joined the Bank of Commerce. When war broke out he immediately enlisted with the 31st. Battalion (Calgary Regiment) of the Canadian Expedition Force and served in the machine-gun section in France from 1915 to 1917. He kept in close contact with his family in Comber and, it was said, he used his Andrews connections to gain the commission that led to his posting to the 36th (Ulster) Division in late 1917. He joined the Royal Irish Rifles and was in the frontline in France on 21st March, 1918 at 4.40am when the Germans launched a major offensive called Operation Michael, with a deluge of heavy artillery on the Allied positions.

The German onslaught was horrific and within a few hours their barrage of shells and gas had decimated virtually all the Allied frontline trenches. The 36th (Ulster) Division was hit at 9.40am and within minutes was almost completely overrun with heavy losses. Two positions bravely held out until late afternoon, and the third at Racecourse Redoubt near Groagie was where Second-Lieutenant Edmund de Wind of 15th Irish Rifles was pinned down. It was to prove a bitter end for this brave young Comber man who was wounded twice in the onslaught, but held his position for seven hours before another section came in support. He made several sorties into enemy trenches despite the heavy machine-gun fire but was eventually fatally wounded.

For his 'conspicuous bravery and self-sacrifice', Edmund de Wind was awarded the Victoria Cross posthumously, and the medal was received from King George V by his proud mother at Buckingham Palace on 21st June, 1919. His burial place is not known, but Mount de Wind was named in his honour in Canada and De Wind Drive was later named in his memory in his home town of Comber. After the war an old German field gun was presented to the Comber people and positioned in the Square in his memory, but it was later used for scrap metal in the munitions build-up to the Second World War. The metal engravings were saved and remain in nearby St. Mary's Parish Church where there is also an engraved plaque in his honour.

Every year the Comber fallen are remembered with special services on 1st July and Remembrance Day. It is a poignant moment to pay tribute to the brave young Comber men who made the supreme sacrifice, none more so that Second-Lieutenant Edmund de Wind, VC.

GEORGE J BRUCE

George Bruce joined North Down in 1905 and made a useful debut for the 2nd XI against Corinthians, taking two wickets. He was promoted to the 1st XI the following week for a league game against Lisburn that was won easily, but his finest performance in his debut season was his six for 23 in the Senior Challenge Cup semi-final win over Ulster. Unfortunately, due to work commitments, George was unavailable for many matches including the final, but he did play in the final in the following year losing to North of Ireland.

EDMUND DE WIND

GEORGE J BRUCE

Like many of his peers, George was a member of both clubs, North Down and North of Ireland and, ironically, played for the Ormeau team in their 1907 win over Holywood. George's match figures of 12 for 80 remain one of the best cup final performances in the history of the competition.

An old Winchester boy, George Bruce was born in Gloucestershire in 1880, the eldest son of a Scotsman, Samuel Bruce. His mother was from the famous Cork cricketing family Colthurst, so he had strong cricketing roots from the outset of his sporting career. And what a talented all rounder he was at sport. In addition to cricket, George was a two-handicap golfer, an excellent shot, and a fine tennis and billiards player.

When he moved to live and work in Comber, he took up the position of managing director at the Comber Distilleries Company where his father was chairman, but his busy job played havoc with his availability, so he played only sporadically for both 1st and 2nd XIs in the pre-Great War period. But George's claim to fame in this North Down history is not just for his fine cricketing achievements, but in the bigger world for his brave action in France.

George was a staunch unionist and in the volatile 1912 Home Rule period he prepared for civil war, as commander of a company of the Ulster Volunteers, by drilling his men in the Lower Distillery yard on the Newtownards Road. The war in Europe eventually shelved the threat of civil war in Ireland and, amazingly, both sides answered the call of king and country and joined together to fight the common enemy. On the formation of the Ulster Division, George obtained a commission in the 1st County Down Battalion and was promoted to the rank of Captain in September 1914. He trained his men at Clandeboye and was known as a popular and efficient officer. He then went with the battalion to Ballykinler for rifle practice before moving to Seaford in Sussex in preparation for action. Within a few weeks his battalion crossed the English Channel and the horrors of the Great War became reality for his young soldiers, many of them from Comber and some from the cricket club. A Comber man, Willie Humphries, was his groom and they fought and survived many horrific battles in the 13th Battalion of the Royal Irish Rifles, including the Battle of the Somme, at Thiepval on 1st July, 1916.

George became Brigade Major of the 109th Infantry Brigade, much to the chagrin of his men in the 13th Battalion who regretted losing such a popular leader, but tragedy was just around the corner and the brave old Winchester boy was killed in action on 2nd October, 1918 at Dadizelle in Flanders. He was 38 years old, and his death came just six weeks before the Armistice was signed.

The brave and courageous George Bruce is remembered not only in North Down archives, but also on the war memorial in Comber Square, on a stone tablet in St Mary's Parish Church, on a street called Bruce Avenue in the town, and on a special war memorial tribute at North of Ireland Cricket Club.

Gone but not forgotten.

THE LIFE THEREAFTER

Despite the huge loss of life there was a life thereafter and while it took many people a long time to get back to any semblance of normal life, for others it was simply a question of getting on with it. When the NCU senior committee met in the spring of 1919 to discuss cricket for the new season, it was unanimously agreed to re-commence competitions. On that committee were Willie Andrews and TJ Macdonald, while former member Oscar Andrews was an Ulster selector. Many old faces had disappeared both from the committees and from the playing ranks, but life had to go on and for North Down it was a case of getting back to the top of Ulster cricket.

Willie Andrews was at the helm and there was no better man to bring back the golden years to the club.

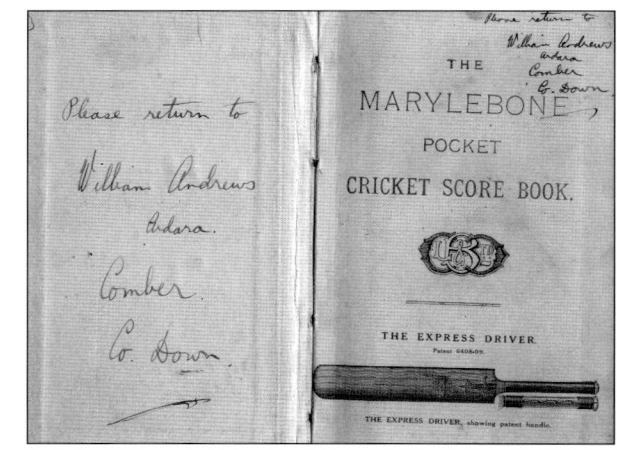

CHAPTER 5
1919 — 1938 : BETWEEN THE WARS — WHAT DEPRESSION!

"TRA LA LA, TRA LA LEE, THE BEST TEAM IN IRELAND IS NORTH DOWN CC, DEAR LADIES AND GENTLEMEN GATHERED TONIGHT WE WELCOME YOU ALL WITH THE GREATEST DELIGHT; YOU'VE COME HERE TO HONOUR THE MEN OF NORTH DOWN, WHO ONCE MORE HAVE BROUGHT THE CUP TO THE TOWN"

MR. A HUNTER, TO THE TUNE OF 'SIX MILES FROM BANGOR TO DONAGHADEE'.
HE SANG ALL EIGHTEEN VERSES AT THE CLUB DINNER HELD
IN THE ANDREWS MEMORIAL HALL OCTOBER 1926.

COMBER IN THE AFTERMATH OF WAR

The human cost of the Great War was counted by many Comber families but life had to go on after 1918. Sadly the lessons of self-destruction had not been learned in an Ireland that returned to the old Home Rule argument, with violence on the streets, anti-British campaigns and a future of great uncertainty. Economically, the traditional industries were struggling and, in a changed world, unemployment gathered pace to create even more hardship for most families.

Comber escaped virtually all the civil disturbances of the 1920s and forged ahead in those depressing times with a new Albion stitching factory, and a new Nut & Bolt factory and Gas Company. Miss Patterson's Post Office was established in Mill Street and the Upper Distillery was rebuilt in 1920. Comber was, in the words of Jack Drain, one of our most loyal supporters, 'the best in Ireland!'

The Andrews family continued to have a huge presence in the community and, according to the Belfast and Ulster Directory farmed over 1,000 acres and employed 535 workers in their Comber Spinning Mill at the time. The mill offered employment and security in tough times and was to be the major economic heartbeat of Comber for many years to follow. The Andrews connection with the cricket club opened economic doors to its members and over the next few decades a number of them found employment through the good offices of Mr. Willie.

The physical face of Comber didn't change much although a War Memorial was unveiled in the Square in 1923 and a captured German field gun was placed on the other side of Gillespie's statue.

The formation, in 1925 of LOL 100, Comber Ulster Defenders, the ex-serviceman's Orange Lodge, saw the images of three North Down men, Bruce, De Wind and McRoberts, unfurled on the new banner. Silent movies were shown in the Andrews Memorial Hall before a cinema was opened in 1934 with the showing of "King Kong". The five schools were amalgamated in 1938 when Lord Chief Justice Sir James Andrews, our former 1st XI captain and esteemed member, officially opened Comber Elementary School on Darragh Road.

CRICKET IN THE NCU

It was difficult for any sport to prosper against a background of civil disturbance, but cricket got its act together much quicker than its contemporaries. The NCU made a few changes but it had good men at the helm like Stanley Jackson, Bob Erskine, Sam Clarke and Jimmy Picken. Willie Andrews was on the committee and his brother James was a vice-president. The interprovincial matches were re-started in 1920 and Oscar Andrews captained the team against Leinster with North Down wicketkeeper Jack Dearden also in the side. It is noted in the NCU minutes that Dearden's request for 'lost wages' was declined, as it would have made him a professional!

International matches were also re-started in 1920 after a six-year absence and the northerners finally agreed to the formation of an Irish Cricket Union, ironically in the wake of the partition of Ireland and the establishment of the Irish Free State and Northern Ireland. History was made in 1924 when Ireland played Wales at Ormeau.

Seven Ulster players were selected for the game and, almost at one fell swoop, the selectorial injustices of the past were remedied!

SAMUEL DAVIDSON

North Down had a strong presence at the NCU in the towering presence of Mr. Willie, and with brother James he was largely responsible for re-writing the rules of the union in the mid 1920s. He also moved into Irish cricket circles and was a principal negotiator in discussions with the North West, Munster and Leinster Cricket Unions on the future of Irish cricket. At the invitation of the NCU, he captained and selected the Ulster teams to go to Munster in 1925, and in 1928 played his only game for the Gentlemen of Ireland at the ripe old age of 42.

James Andrews was elected president of the NCU in 1926, although his duties as Lord Justice hindered his attendance at meetings, but Mr. Willie was omnipresent and kept him well informed. North Down's representation in the NCU was also strong on the field and, as they dominated club cricket, many of the leading players were selected for Ulster and, later, Ireland.

CRICKET AT THE GREEN

Between the wars North Down enjoyed their second 'Golden Era' following the emergence of some very special players who would eventually dominate the NCU scene and go on to distinguish themselves at the highest level. A few of the pre-war stalwarts remained in 1919, and they helped the club re-build and recover from the devastations of the Great War.

In his 'History of Senior Cricket in Ulster' Clarence Hiles describes how the clubs reformed and rebuilt in this period and highlighted North Down's plight:

"How appropriate this was in the case of North Down, a club that had suffered more than most during the Great War, but had bounced back with resilience and character to dominate the Twenties and Thirties"

The North Down general committee of 16 members was ably led by chairman William Andrews, undoubtedly the driving force behind everything that happened, and Samuel Davidson, 'one of the finest batsmen the province ever possessed', taking on the vital role as secretary which continued until 1925. A Hunter captured him in song:

"The County Down Railway kicked up a great fuss,
The time Sammy Davidson started the bus
And Sam says he'll soon kill the railway outright,
If you don't believe me ask Robert James White." *
Tra la la. Tra la lee,
The best team in Ireland is North Down CC."

John Murray, who fought to hold the senior playing subscriptions at one pound ten shillings in 1920, continued as treasurer until 1930 when WJ Taylor, Willie Morrow and James Macdonald performed this important role until the outbreak of the Second World War in 1939. John Murray JP died in 1934. Never a player, he had been treasurer from 1909 until 1930, during which time his work was characterised by outstanding ability, energy and tact, strengths he also brought to his role as team secretary to the 1st and 2nd XIs in 1906 and 1907.

"In our friend Mr Murray you've a treasurer rare
When subscriptions are due he is sure to be there,
But I'm sorry to hear about poor Davy Wherry, †
Since the motors came on he has no bags to carry"
Tra la la. Tra la lee,
The best team in Ireland is North Down CC."

With the senior league and cup double achieved in 1919 there was a great optimism at the club, based not only on the 1st XI playing strength but also the fact that more new members than usual had joined the ranks, some with good reputations. The hope was that the bowling, indicated as the weaker part of the side, would be considerably strengthened.

The prospect that the 1st XI would play about 30 matches was encouraging, but there was still a great disappointment felt that no teams from Dublin, England or Scotland would travel here to play, the reason being the political turmoil and violence in other parts of the country at that time.

The fixture lists were becoming demanding and in addition to the league and cup games, friendlies had been arranged with the Railway & Steam Packet Union CC at home and in Dublin, North of Ireland, Cliftonville, Ulster, Queen's University, Woodvale, St Mary's and several of the regiments. Add to this the Lancashire Tour of four games and the demands on the players' commitment were obvious.

JOHN MURRAY

Player turnover was no different than the present day with the usual winter rumour mill in full swing and Fred Willis, who had been a Senior Challenge Cup winner in 1920, departed in 1922, compensated somewhat with the arrival of RJE Cadogan. He played in the 1924 senior cup winning side and also had time from his military duties to play golf in the meadow adjoining the ground, and donate a penny a ball to the retrieving youngsters!

It was also significant at this time that the English players based here during the war years had returned home and this deprived the club of players such as CAA Hiatt, Capt RE Dewar, Walter Lea, CPR Johnston and Colonel WN White.

The Macdonald family created a record in 1926 by winning all four of the handsome silver rose bowls.

---

* ROBERT JAMES WHITE, AKA, 'MICKEY' HAD A CONFECTIONERS SHOP IN MILL STREET AND WAS THE CLUB CATERER.
† DAVY WHERRY WAS A PORTER AT COMBER RAILWAY STATION.

GEORGE, JAMES AND TOM (TJ) MACDONALD

James won the 1st XI batting and bowling, George the batting on the 2nd XI and 'TJ' for his bowling on the 2nd XI. One might have thought that this feat would not be repeated but they did it again the following year!

In addition to the annual English tour, where they won all four games against good opposition, 1927 was to see a mini tour to the North West where matches against Strabane and Sion Mills were played and won.

It had been eight years since the last 'double' at The Green, but it was won in style in 1927 for the fourth time in the club's history and by a side that won 23 games of the 34 played that season.

Statistics are a present day fixation, so it is worth noting that this 1st XI side scored 5,843 runs for the loss of 212 wickets at 158 runs per match more than their opponents. Such was the pursuit of excellence that the North Down season 'Review' commented:

"All that is required to make the team a great club side is another fast bowler, a 'free' bat capable of going in early in the batting order, and a good second slip fielder."

Jack Dearden's wicket keeping was singled out for special mention, having surpassed his previous season's 46 dismissals with an incredible tally of 54, which at that time was a record for a wicketkeeper in Irish senior cricket.

As the club entered the Thirties the prospects looked good, even with the loss of top administrator John Murray. Thomas Johnston, captain of the 2nd XI, had gone to Scotland but the main post remained intact with Willie Andrews as chairman.

The only resignation came from Willie Cannavan, but this was offset by a number of new members including the promising local schoolboys, George Moore and Andrew Hogg. The Lurgan Mail printed

170 annual fixture cards so we can assume there was a healthy membership at the time.

The great military cricket tradition continued with games against the Belfast Garrison, the 1st Battalion Royal Inniskilling Fusiliers, the 2nd Battalion Gordon Highlanders and the 1st Battalion Royal Ulster Rifles and others; a tradition that was to help greatly with the sustaining of the game in Comber during and immediately after both World Wars.

In 1932 the 1st XI played 37 matches, with James and TJ Macdonald coming top of the batting averages. Other major run makers were HC Graham, Jackie Shields, Albert Anderson, Teddy Bebe, Stanley Morgan and Harry Morgan. Tom Pearson, the 'pro', topped the bowling averages with 76 wickets but James Macdonald took 90, Harry Morgan 52, Jackie Shields 39 and TJ Macdonald 28.

North Down entertained the team from HMS Rodney at The Green on the 28th June, 1933, unaware of the historic part the ship would play eight years later in the sinking of the German Battleship 'Bismarck', and the following year the annual pre-season's 'newsletter' indicated that Victor Metcalfe (ex North of Ireland) and D Wolseley (ex Rossall School) had joined the club and it was hoped that Donald (EDR) Shearer, who had joined a year earlier, would be available to play.

It was the custom at this time that every batsman should have an innings during a game and it caused quite a stir within the NCU when a side batting first and finishing with a low total, refused to continue the match after the team batting second had passed their score. The North Down representatives at this time, namely William Andrews and Albert Anderson, had definite views on the situation and it was left to the great upholder of the status quo, North Down chairman and powerhouse of the NCU, Mr. Willie, to make his

It was proposed and unanimously agreed that a notice reading: 'Children to be neither seen nor heard near to the pavilion', should be erected on entrance to the ground.

FROM THE CLUB MINUTES

and North Down's view clear in a reply to Mr. Loughrey who had raised the issue at an NCU meeting:

"*Our view is, that not only should a team be willing and pleased to give, if possible, all their opponents an innings, but the best test possible of the esprit-de-corps and sportsmanship of a side is how they play after they have been defeated. Everyone can play a winning game, but a man is seen at his true value, both in sport and in life by how he takes his defeat.*"

Our Supporters' Club epitomised the enthusiasm at this time and by 1935 it had 80 members who organised functions and filled the buses for the away matches.

There was always a constant lookout for new recruits to join the club and in 1938, under a little pressure from Mr. Willie, Captain Miller of the Royal Ulster Constabulary ensured that a list was drawn up at the Commissioner's Office, and sent to North Down, listing members within the Belfast area who had played cricket.

The list included personnel based in Musgrave Street, Brown Square, York Street, Cullingtree Road and Glenravel Street, amongst others. All, with the exception of Sergeant JV McFadden who had played in Downpatrick and Dundonald, were Constables, including G McLean who had played at Regent House School, V Jones at Bangor and a bowler, appropriately named SA Over, who played for Ophir based in Newtownards.

As the decade moved on, the club went from strength to strength. It would appear that regular practice was taken for granted and the Boots 'Scribbling Diary' of 1939 confirms that players booked their practice slots well in advance. Frank Andrews and Raymond Crosby, Jim and Bob Montgomery and Harry Donnan all braved the elements in the first week in May – Raymond Crosby on three occasions! James Macdonald, Willie Dempster, Victor Houston and Willie Andrews joined the first group in the second week and it was a full net the following Thursday in preparation for the visit of Pembroke to The Green on the Saturday.

The end of the decade warned of some difficulties ahead, although the 1st XI did well to reach the Senior Challenge Cup final in 1939, albeit soundly defeated by Woodvale. The low league position, seventh, due to only five wins from the 13 games played, highlighted the need for change, even though James Macdonald was again the leading bowler in the NCU.

Perhaps it was inevitable, given that Jack Dearden, TJ Macdonald and Jackie Shields had all retired and illness and age, respectively, were beginning to take their toll on the wonderful cricketing careers of James Macdonald and Willie Andrews.

By 1939 the purchase of the ground had been completed and a circular for funds was sent to members and others interested in the game at North Down.

NCU Senior Challenge Cup 1920, North Down v Cliftonville: Back – Watmore (Pro)*, W Lea*, CE Bebe*, GH Bruce, HE Wood, R McCully. Middle – Bungort (umpire), WH Silk*, DR Wheeler*, WA Miller*, JH Dunn, Campbell (umpire), A Picken. Front – T Maxwell*, FW Willis*, AE Anderson*, DR Taylor*, W Andrews*, SJ Stephenson, GJ Murphy, TA Hargreaves, LM Murphy, WS Haydock. Ground – J Dearden*, S McCully. (*NDCC)

Unfortunately this appeal for financial assistance came shortly before the outbreak of war and the response, looking to raise approximately £1,336, could only muster £294.

But in fairness to everyone around the club, it was impossible to concentrate on cricket as the dark clouds of war had once again descended on Europe and many of the North Down members were already joining the services once again to answer the call of King and Country.

Our little cricket club would never be the same again.

THE SENIOR CHALLENGE CUP BETWEEN THE WARS

The two decades between the wars were probably the greatest playing years at North Down with Willie Andrews's team regularly collecting trophies and our best players regularly representing the province and playing for The Gentlemen of Ireland. Indeed James Macdonald and brother Tom (TJ), wicketkeeper Jack Dearden, William Millar, Albert Anderson, David Taylor, David (DGR) McKibbin and the legendary captain himself were all honoured with international recognition.

On the fringe of international selection were Jackie Shields and Tommy Maxwell who both played with distinction for Ulster and were regular match winners with their fine bowling. Jackie was also a very capable bat who produced many a cameo innings on important occasions.

There is no doubt the North Down players developed a deep affinity with the Senior Challenge Cup, which might explain why it kept coming back to The Green on a regular basis, even when league performances didn't reflect the obvious talent within the team. These were halcyon years at the club as far as the Senior League and Challenge Cup performances were concerned. From 1919 to 1939 the 1st XI won 19 of a possible 42 trophies and contested 16 of the 21 Senior Challenge Cup finals. All this was achieved at a time when Cliftonville, Waringstown, North of Ireland and, later, Woodvale had strong teams.

The senior cup performances during this period are worthy of special recognition as they are up there with the best in the history of this very special NCU competition.

For example, the first round of the cup in 1919 was almost a disaster but, on what was obviously a bowler's wicket, Woodvale's modest total of 58 was passed with only one wicket to spare. Ironically, barely a few weeks later, the cup was won by 69 runs on the back of Tommy Maxwell's bowling against the mighty North of Ireland, Oscar Andrews, Willie Pollock et al.

Such are the fickle fortunes of knock-out competition.

Walter Lea took seven for 55 to beat Armagh in the long drawn-out 1920 semi-final and in a low scoring final added another ten wickets in an easy victory over Cliftonville. Tommy Maxell took nine wickets in that match and, just to show that cricket is a great leveller, both were out for 'ducks'. Ironically the same two teams were drawn against each other in the first round in 1921 when North Down won by only five runs. The bowling of Hiatt, Lea, Maxwell and Hill was the strongest in the NCU at the time and it was the batsmen who failed to fire in the final that year when Waringstown lost eight wickets needing only 51 runs to win. Cliftonville got their revenge in the 1922 semi-

1921 NORTH DOWN 1ST XI: BACK – AE ANDERSON, CAA HIATT, W ANDREWS, J DEARDEN.
FRONT – DC LINDSAY, DR TAYLOR, W LEA, T MAXWELL, J O'PREY, B HILL, JLO ANDREWS.

ONE SHOT MORE...FOR THE HONOUR OF DOWN: A HISTORY OF NORTH DOWN CRICKET CLUB 1857 – 2007

1924 Senior Cup Final, North Down v Waringstown: Back – CE Bebe*, J Macdonald*, J Shields*, R Scott, T McKenzie, T Anderson, C Ferguson. Middle – AE Anderson*, J Dearden*, B Hill*, DR Taylor*, CPR Johnston*, J Gardiner, J Harwood, H McKenzie, R Harwood. Front – WA Miller*, RJE Cadogan*, W Andrews*, J Williamson, W Irwin, J Hampton. (*NDCC)

final shooting out North Down for an all-time low of 26 runs.

A rare first round exit followed against Holywood in 1923, but James Macdonald had entered the scene by 1924 and fortunes were about to turn. Waringstown had a strong team at the time and it was almost inevitable that they would meet in the final but nobody could have predicted such a thrilling and close game at Ormeau, packed full of controversy and excitement. In a rain affected match North Down eventually needed 75 runs to win, six wickets remaining and Willie Andrews and Albert Anderson at the wicket. After only three overs, heavy rain again caused the game to stop for another half hour. On resumption, and without the privilege of covered pitches, wickets fell at regular intervals until James Macdonald, who had been dropped at slip before he had scored, and Teddy Bebe added a vital 13 runs. Tom McKenzie was rampant, but eventually North Down's last pair, Jackie Shields and Bert Hill, found themselves at the wicket with seven runs required to win the cup for the 14th time. Attempting their fourth 'single' both batsmen were completely stranded in the middle of the wicket, but the Waringstown fielder slipped and they scrambled home. The drama and tension increased, but the winning runs came when Hill lofted the ball over mid-off to scenes of wild celebration from the Comber supporters. Such was the tension that a recount was required before North Down was adjudged winners by a single wicket.

Unfortunately, 1925 was an anti-climax in comparison as Cliftonville made it another first round exit, but 1926 produced an epic cup encounter against an up and coming Lisburn side. The finish to this match has remained part of the folklore of both clubs down the years, and centred on the club 'pros' who were standing as umpires. With 266 needed for victory, North Down, the hot favourites, were 178 for nine and looked well beaten, but Jackie Shields had other ideas and proceeded to aggressively attack the Lisburn bowling. Swashbuckling Jackie brought North Down to the brink of victory and then, dramatically, in the dying minutes North Down's 'home' umpire, Mabbott, called a 'no ball' as the Lisburn wicketkeeper took a catch! Unbelievably North Down scraped home and went on to beat cup holders North of Ireland in the final with James Macdonald scoring two half-centuries and taking seven wickets. The inimitable Jackie was not to be denied either, as he scored 51 not out in the second innings.

"There's many a slip twixt the cup and the lip,
And the Lisburn team nearly gave North Down the slip,
But just when we thought that our number was up,
Bert Hill and young Shields put their mark on the cup."

When Lord Justice Andrews two bats did present,
Jack Dearden was there and on good business bent,
He tried to swop Bert a brush for his bat,
For he says you can't paper the kitchen with that.
Tra la la. Tra la lee,
The best team in Ireland is North Down CC."

The 1926 cup win was celebrated in style with a 6.45pm dinner, (Morning Dress), on the 14th October

JACKIE SHIELDS BATTING IN THE 1931 SENIOR CUP FINAL

The Committee Meeting of September 3rd, 1921 was held in Comber Railway Station.

FROM THE CLUB MINUTES

at the Carnival Cabaret in the Andrews Memorial Hall in Comber.

During this time James Macdonald produced some remarkable performances.

In 1927 he took 12 for 45 in the final against Holywood including eight for 18 in the second innings. With either bat or ball he was a match-winner and, without doubt, he was the jewel in the North Down crown. Perhaps in any cricket crown, given his exceptional talents.

The 1928 cup story was notable for the first round centuries against Waringstown from William Andrews (170) and TJ Macdonald (115) and the second round game against Cliftonville, which started on the 30th June with North Down 'posting' 414 for nine wickets and continued on 2nd, 19th and 20th of July. Gerry Spence's 92 was outstanding in the 231 runs victory, and this win was followed by a four wickets semi-final success over Armagh when the Macdonald brothers took nine wickets between them. Old adversaries North of Ireland were waiting in the wings but nine wickets from Jackie Shields were decisive in a seven wickets cup final win. A large crowd followed Comber Amateur Prize Flute Band round the town to the houses of the members of the victorious team, and ended up at Ardara where Mr Willie gave his third winning speech in succession. The proceedings ended with a round of applause and three hearty cheers for Mr Willie, followed by the National Anthem.

But they all came back down to earth in 1929 and ironically it was Lisburn who got their revenge in what has been called "Tommy Martin's final." The young strapping Lisburn pace bowler shot North Down out for 52 in the final and, despite a bit of panic at the end, they got home at 29 for five to secure a famous victory against the hot favourites.

Undeterred, North Down returned for their fifth successive final in 1930 but this time it was Linfield football legend Billy McCleery who did the damage (71 runs and five for 29) as Ulster won by 105 runs. On the way to the final James Macdonald scored a record 197 not out against CPA, 61 against Cliftonville, and 54 against Holywood.

New additions to the side in the early 1930s included George Macdonald, HC Graham, Neville Petts, Reggie Morgan, Percy Clarke and David McKibbin. This was typical of North Down at the time because, despite their success, there were always changes in personnel, a culture that unkindly earned them the dubious title of the 'league of nations' from less complimentary opponents.

Perhaps it was fate that the 1930 finalists should meet again in the 1931 NCU showpiece but this time the gritty McCleery was upstaged by TJ Macdonald (108) and his brother James (13 for 83) as the Challenge Cup went back to Comber. Earlier in the competition 'TJ' Macdonald had scored a brilliant 106 against Strabane and 66 against Armagh, while James had warmed up for the final with eight for 44 against Downpatrick, six for 35 against Strabane and six for 49 against Armagh. George Macdonald joined his brothers in the 1931 cup final team but like most players, friend or foe alike, he always played second fiddle to them when they were on song.

James took 16 wickets in three games as North Down reached their seventh successive cup final in 1932. Armagh's legendary Rev. RJ Barnes excelled with a first innings 40 runs and seven for 49 but, chasing 103 for victory and back-to-back wins, the Macdonald brothers once again saw North Down home with a five-wicket victory.

An unusually poor batting performance in June 1933 saw Woodvale beat North Down at Ballygomartin Road in the first round and go the whole way to become the first junior club to win the Senior Challenge Cup. But North Down responded in style and when the two teams met again in the 1934 final it was the Comber men who triumphed by 131 runs. McCleery was now the guru at Woodvale, with hundreds of Linfield supporters joining the Ballygomartin Road

ALBERT ANDERSON AND TJ MACDONALD GOING OUT TO BAT AT ORMEAU

faithful at cricket matches following their elevation to senior status. However, on this occasion Jackie Shields (six for 13) eclipsed the great Charlie Billingsley (six for 48) in a head-to-head that many people felt should have won Shields an international call-up.

Earlier in the competition, Holywood, Strabane (with Andy McFarlane) and Derry (with Donald Shearer) provided no shocks as Victor Metcalfe followed his 89 at Strabane with an unbeaten 108 against Derry at Cliftonville in the semi-final and FH 'Freddie' Mills (seven for 22) put paid to Derry hopes. Metcalfe and Mills had earned their Senior Challenge Cup final 'spurs' in some style.

The long serving vice-captain Albert Anderson played the last of his eleven senior cup winning appearances in 1934 and when the team returned for the 1935 final popular young local player Harry Donnan was in his place.

*"There's nothing like being a bachelor gay,
At least so I've heard Albert Anderson say,
Though he's fond of the girls, he's not easy to bluff,
With his old 'Yellow Peril' he has trouble enough"
Tra la la. Tra la lee,
The best team in Ireland is North Down CC."*

The season 1935 was the James Macdonald roadshow from start to finish with seven for 30 at Waringstown, 114 runs and six for 31 at Donacloney, seven for 38 against Armagh in the semi-final and a record-breaking 159 not out in the final against North of Ireland. Of course there were other cameos, but nowhere has a player dominated a Senior Challenge Cup campaign to the extent that James Macdonald did in 1935. He was outstanding.

Billy Shields and Gerry Spence made their debuts on the 1936 side that cruised through to the final with wins against Collegians, Donacloney and Waringstown but there was no cruising against a determined Woodvale side at Cliftonville as the narrow four wickets win indicated. Batting number six, Neville Petts scored a crucial 14 not out as North Down struggled to 49 for six to win. However, it was the brilliant bowling of domiciled West Indian Dr. Percy Clarke that took the honours with 13 for 69 runs. Shades of 'league of nations' perhaps!

This was North Down's third win in succession again and their fifth win in six years, but Woodvale was the coming team and about to challenge that supremacy.

Both teams returned for the 1937 final at Cliftonville in August and when North Down took a 105 runs first innings lead, it looked like plain sailing for the Comber men. David McKibbin (80) and TJ Macdonald (45) put on 133 for the first wicket before a middle order collapse was recovered with a 107 runs eighth wicket partnership involving Jackie (67) and Billy Shields (57). The first innings total of 331 looked good, and even better when Freddie Mills and Percy Clarke shared eight wickets in reducing Woodvale to 226. But this Woodvale team was never short of fighting spirit and Harry Armstrong and Charlie Billingsley shot North Down out for 129 second time round.

1926 NORTH DOWN 1ST XI AND 2ND XI, SENIOR CHALLENGE CUP & JUNIOR CUP WINNERS: BACK – R CATHCART, J DEARDEN, B HILL, G SPENCE, TJ MACDONALD, JLO ANDREWS, N BOURKE, J O'PREY, D KIRK, J BROWN, WE BATES. MIDDLE – J MACDONALD, CE BEBE, WA MILLAR, AE ANDERSON, DR TAYLOR, W ANDREWS, FJ BOYD, G MACDONALD, A PATTON, H MEGRATH, WR MORROW. FRONT – J SHIELDS, W WISHART.

1913 Final v Waringstown (North Down 1st innings)

Nevertheless, their batsmen still had a mountain to climb against the formidable bowling of Mills, Macdonald, Shields and Clarke, but McCleery (50) and George Wilson (58) pulled off a miraculous one wicket victory despite another James Macdonald five-wicket haul. Amazingly this match started on the 7th of August and was only finished on the 10th of September. It was also the record aggregate runs in a final with 923 scored.

Although we were not to know it at the time, this was essentially the end of the great North Down era and it was fitting that the emerging Woodvale team should assume that mantle as they were to prove a fine side, unfortunately thwarted by the war years.

Although the semi-final was reached in 1938, the team included WJ Logan, EDR 'Donald' Shearer, W Shanks and DF Bradley, players that would rarely appear again in a North Down team. On this occasion the North Down batting was poor, scoring only 75 runs, and Donacloney won easily to make their one and only Senior Challenge Cup Final appearance. Sadly for this wonderful little factory village club, they lost to North of Ireland by an innings and 17 runs.

In 1939 victories over Cliftonville, Cregagh and Strabane saw North Down reach their last final for 42 years, but poor batting again resulted in an innings defeat against the strong Woodvale side.

The second 'Golden Era' was over.

Five Senior Challenge Cup wins and three Senior League wins in 1932, 1934 and 1936 confirmed North Down domination of Ulster cricket during the Thirties, but war brought it all to an end and it was a long time before the club regained such lofty status.

Between the wars the Challenge Cup became very special to North Down and the Comber community, and even though it would not find its way back to The Green until 1981, the legacy of the 1920s and 1930s teams was the passion they left for future generations. Cup cricket was 'in the blood' and, even if aspirations were constantly thwarted with weaker teams in later years, there was a legacy to build on no matter how long it took. However, nobody expected it to take almost 50 years!

DOWN THE TEAMS

In the early Twenties optimism was also rife within the 2nd XI ranks with the captaincy taken over by SJ Munn, a popular Knock rugby player and Willie Galbraith, of hockey fame, who also acted as secretary for the side.

N Bourke, a capable cricketer from Bangor, joined in 1923 and was part of the team that reached the semi-final of the Junior Cup in 1923 and won through to the final in the following year. The 2nd XI success continued into 1925, the side winning 16 of the 19 matches played, drawing one and losing only two. The young players were coming good. Two of them, Jack Shields and James Macdonald, were already recognised by making the grade at the higher level, but neither was needed in 1926 when the Junior Cup was brought to The Green. They celebrated in style with a November dinner in the Princeton Hotel in Bangor. The squad was made up of the following players:

JLO Andrews (Capt), Joe Boyd, JMB Brown, N Burke, David Kirk, DC Lindsay, George Macdonald, TJ Macdonald Jnr., HN Magrath, DJ Murray, W Milliken, Jackie O'Prey, Andy Patton, Bobby Todd and Willie Wishart.

They had played 23 games with Jack (JLO)

1926 BOYS XI: PROFESSIONAL HL MABBOTT WITH HIS BOYS XI THAT INCLUDED JIM MONTGOMERY, FRED WISHART, BILLY SHIELDS, CHARLES SHUFFLEBOTTOM AND NORMAN MACDONALD.

Andrews averaging 55.4 but it was DGR McKibbin, a player destined for 1st XI and international honours, who shone with 504 runs and 44 wickets.

*"I hear Jackie Andrews is engaged to be wed,
So he can't be as shy as the people all said,
And I think that his uncle will be next on the list,
Now that Jackie has told him all the nice things he's missed!"
Tra la la. Tra la lee,
The best team in Ireland is North Down CC."*

Gerry Spence, Reggie Morgan, Neville Petts, Harry Donnan, George Macdonald, S McAvoy, Billy Shields, A Murphy and Willie Watt made the runs, with McKibbin, Morgan, and Macdonald the main wicket-takers.

The fledgling 3rd XI was created just after the war under the guidance of WT Graham, who acted as an adviser to FJ Boyd, the captain. In 1926, when four games were won, three drawn and seven lost, Victor Houston excelled with both bat and ball, with the other big runs coming from Jim Montgomery, Bobby Rowan and David Shields, with D McNish, Rowan, J Watt and W Allen taking the wickets.

The 2nd XI began the Thirties well, competing for the Junior Cup and the Second Division of the Senior League, under the experienced David Taylor with Jack O'Prey, David Kirk, Willie Cannavan, R Donnan and Neville Petts top run makers and David (DGR) McKibbin, Tommy Maxwell, W McKibbin and especially D McQuade playing major bowling roles.

The 3rd XI played in the Minor Cup under Milton Coulter of New Comber House, and had a lot of Saturday and evening friendlies on their fixture cards. Tom Savage was the top all rounder while Neville Petts and Willie Watt in batting and Joe Watt and Billy Shields were the bowling heroes.

According to William Andrews, young Harry Donnan 'made a most gratifying advance' with the bat. He was later to become a recipient of the unofficial William Andrews-sponsored trip to Lord's for a week's coaching. J Savage was a mainstay in the bowling and Leonard Ward had a promising season as wicket-keeper.

The under 15s, under the guidance of James Macdonald, usually passed the first round of the Graham Cup, but came unstuck against Lurgan and Sydenham in consecutive years. Raymond Crosby, Bob Patton, David Cannavan, John Shields, Bobby Cooke and Drew Hogg all showed great promise. Having won a Graham Cup game by 200 runs in 1932 with Tom Wilson, Raymond Crosby, Hugh McKnight and Frank Andrews outstanding all rounders and Jim Magowan keeping a good wicket, the boys were disqualified through playing an over-age player!

THE PROFESSIONALS

It was the practice for many years to recruit a professional player, with a 'boy' to assist from late in April and this continued between the wars. Basically the position was advertised, contacts used and a detailed application form, that asked for all the necessary background information, issued on request. The lengths to which the club went to ascertain an applicant's suitability for the position, was reflected in the many references asked for, the number of letters written by the much travelled Mr Willie and the advertisements that were placed in 'The Athletic News' and local press.

The 'pro' was able to choose the 'boy', who assisted him in all the menial duties associated with the ground and acted as gatekeeper and vigilante. He informed 'the powers that be' when there was illegal admission to the ground during games or trespass into the pavilion area and for such services received a nominal sum and had free entry into the club dinner and entertainments.

The new spring-locked gate erected in 1922 to assist in 'preventing the destruction of the club's property' required that members provide themselves with a key from Sam Davidson at the refundable price of one shilling and sixpence. Under no circumstances were the professional or his 'boy' to leave their work to open the gate.

The appointment of suitable professionals was not easy, as it was difficult to get reliable information. At North Down it generally worked well, with Arthur Clay from Nottingham, who had been 'pro' from 1884 to 1886 and Charles Lowings (1906-1910), supplying candidates and references during this time. Clay had contacts with 'Gunn & Moore' the sports equipment suppliers and, along with Lowings, also supplied cricket balls to the club. In 1919, Clay referred to the applicant Mr Coates as: 'a good free bat' and 'a most respectable man who is absolutely steady and sober' and quoted averages of 27.29 and 88 wickets at 9.4. He earned his stipend more as a groundsman and coach rather than as a player with his duties carrying a weekly wage of three pounds five shillings and, in this case, a substantial £27 'Benefit' at the end of the season.

In 1920, having secured a dozen county cricket balls from Clay, Mr Willie informed him that Watmore would be pro for the year. Watmore had been 'pro' in 1915 and spent 1919 with Edgeware CC in Middlesex when he showed that his service at the front in the Army had not interfered with his ability as a cricketer. In a letter to Watmore in April, having sorted out his crossing arrangements from London, Mr. Willie wrote:

TOM PEARSON

"As you will have noticed by my last letter, I thought the Sinn Feiners might cause some trouble at Easter, but it was very slight, and no one about here saw any of them, nor is there any chance of them molesting us in any way."

It proved to be an excellent engagement as he subsequently remarked:

"As a groundsman he could not be excelled, having a thorough knowledge of the work in every detail. I have never known our ground to be in better order than he has now left it."

Case, Kingston, Mabbott and Harris had two seasons apiece, Kingston being particularly favoured by Mr. Willie for his all round cricketing ability and was asked back for the 1925 season but declared himself unavailable as a 'pro' but willing to be registered as an amateur. The prospect of Kingston, a former player with Nottinghamshire County 2nd XI, playing as an amateur, underlined the thinking behind the committee's announcement:

'That when the best amateur side was available, the experiment should be tried next season of doing without a professional in league matches'.

In short the 'pro' would coach, act as groundsman, go on tour and play in the 'friendly' games.

In 1925 two boys' teams, the Under-11s and the Under-15s were started under 'pro' Leslie Mabbott. George J Harris coached both age groups at the club and at RBAI and his work on the wickets was excellent. Being 'honest, sober, civil and obliging and good on tour' he fitted in well with the club's perception of the ideal North Down 'Pro'.

After Albert Dodson and Walter Lea, who at that time reputedly held a world record of having taken 14 wickets for no runs, the highly recommended Tom Pearson became 'pro' for the next three years and made an immediate impression by delivering the best bowling figures of any professional since Charles Lowing's first season in 1906. His 77 wickets cost 8.64 and his coaching skills and groundwork convinced the committee that he could be employed for longer than the traditional two years, but the acceptance of a full time post in England brought his association with the club to an end in 1933.

GR Preece, who had been a professional with Liverpool, Birkenhead and County Wicklow cricket clubs was a slow left arm bowler who had taken over 100 wickets in each of the previous three seasons. He excelled as a coach, especially on the fine practice wickets which were top dressed with Daft's famous Nottinghamshire marl. Preece was given notification that he would have 'a boy' at ten shillings a week to help him and it was pointed out that he would have to choose from applicants, some of whom might meet him on the platform at Comber railway station. Mr Willie recommended Willie Wishart or, failing that, Jim Barry.

Later on, evidence of Preece supposedly slacking in his duties did not go down well with the committee. He was reprimanded regarding time spent in Belfast after his duties at Dungannon Royal School when he should have been coaching at The Green.

In 1936, the seasoned North Down player Tommy Maxwell wrote to the committee for the Pro/Groundsman position:

Dear Sir,
Having seen by Ireland's Saturday Night that North Down Cricket Club require Groundsman, able to bowl at nets, play in matches or umpire if required I apply for same. As regards experience any that I have has been with the North Down Club. I have been about the ground all my life & know how to prepare wickets for matches also practice & repair wickets & ground work in general. Hoping sir you & the North Down Committee will consider my application, wages expected 40 shillings per week
Yours Obedient,
T Maxwell

Unfortunately for Tommy, his application was unsuccessful and another local player Robert Patton, was appointed, even though in the words of Mr Willie:

'He is not as well trained, and consequently we are not paying him as high a wage as we usually give our professional.'

Patton accepted £2 per week although the basic wage remained at £3 for the 22 weeks, plus travelling expenses and a benefit, usually raising about £20. Included in his coaching duties for that season was one visit each week to Dungannon Royal School where he earned ten shillings and had his return train fare paid.

Tommy Maxwell was not to be denied and his application in 1943 was successful and he was the key groundsman and coach through the war years, his last season in charge being 1947.

Not all the 'pros' were a great success in dealing with Mr Willie. In 1937 the negotiating was protracted and it wasn't until the 7th May that Riddington was offered the position. He was asked to pay his £1 three shillings for steerage, crossing via Leicester on the Heysham steamer, catch the 8.30am train to Comber, meet with Albert Anderson, see the ground and start work the next morning. It was an ominous start and things obviously got worse in the opinion of Mr. Willie:

"He is the laziest man I have ever known as a professional cricketer, but is undoubtedly a good coach and player."

Riddington was a stylish left-hand batsman and useful spin bowler who made a good impression on the field of play but after a few weeks he had fallen foul of the one person who carried the most influence at The Green. Almost inevitably he resigned, and returned to Leicestershire.

Robert Patton and Albert Dodson finished the 1930s as professionals at The Green, and the workload was much reduced in the six years that followed.

THE GREAT TOURING YEARS

Great eras bring more than trophies, and the camaraderie within the club at this time was epitomised by the regular tours to England and Scotland. A tour to Denmark was also contemplated but numbers were not sufficient to make the trip viable.

Three days before the first tour game in England in 1921, the 1st XI suffered a rare and crushing Senior Challenge Cup defeat at the hands of Cliftonville. The party of 15 included an umpire and a scorer and recorded two early wins against Blackpool and Lytham. In the former game Jack Fleming, a tour 'guest' and Case, the professional, took all the wickets. In the game at Preston their opening bowler produced a meagre two for 16 off 22 overs, 13 of them maidens, but in an exciting finale the Preston last pair added 23 runs for victory.

By Friday the tour excesses were obviously catching up as Shakespeare, who regularly caused hardship for visiting North Down batsmen, held centre stage with seven for 24 to secure another home win for Leyland.

At Poulton-le-Fylde they met some real class when J Winchester hit an amazing 184 not out in a total of 207 for seven. The North Down reply of 61 smacked of yearnings for the Heysham steamer but morale was restored back at The Green the following Tuesday as they 'got back on track' with a victory against the Railway & Steam Packet Company.

Prior to the tour to England the following year, North Down played the Somerset Light Infantry at Palace Barracks and recorded two league wins against Waringstown and Cliftonville. Full of confidence they tackled the English teams 'in their own back yard' with fixtures against the formidable Lancaster, Lytham, Blackpool, Leyland and Preston.

Mr Willie was meticulous in his travel arrangements and costings, with train times and arrival at venues literally timed to the minute, lunch times and menus available to players way in advance of the games, and evening entertainment, especially in Blackpool, arranged to coincide with admission to Blackpool Tower and the circus for which tickets had already been purchased.

As with all of the tours, the 1924 tour was recorded in the compact 'Unrivalled' Pocket Cricket Score Book, which usually had a string attached to hold the scorer's pencil. This tour immediately followed the Challenge Cup final in late July when North Down beat Waringstown in a dramatic finish by a single run, so everyone was in good spirits.

Only three fixtures had been arranged and the party crossed early on Saturday evening so that they could watch the Test match at Old Trafford on the Monday.

By 1925 the tours were becoming very well organised with delegation becoming apparent. The usual North Down equipment was for sale prior to the trip with caps costing four shillings and six pence, and ties, sashes and blazers 'priced on request'.

The tour manager was scorer Bob Cathcart who would look after transport and rail tickets in England, but was caught 'slacking' on more than one occasion:

*"As a scorer Bob Cathcart is very correct,
But I hear that in Blackpool his duties he slacked,
I wonder what that Irish colleen would think,
If he showed her the book in red, white and blue ink"
Tra la la. Tra la lee,
The best team in Ireland is North Down CC."*

Teddy Bebe was in charge of entertainments and amusements, Albert Anderson took responsibility for sweepstakes and auctions and Mr. Bates took charge of photographs. Mabbott the 'Pro' was 'on duty' and for a small fee would carry bags to and from the transport.

*"I hear that in Blackpool the fun it was prime,
And that friend Teddy Bebe had a glorious time,
I'm told that he led all the ladies a dance,
He was perfectly right – for its Teddy's last chance."
Tra la la. Tra la lee,
The best team in Ireland is North Down CC."*

In a season when rain forced the abandonment of games against Armagh, Sion Mills, Lisburn and the

Seaforth Highlanders prior to the English tour, the preparation wasn't ideal, but it didn't deter the tourists from having a great time.

Mr Willie again attempted to resurrect the tour to Denmark but the Danish Steamship Company refused to reduce terms, so the 15-day cost at £19, including a sightseeing trip round Copenhagen and an extra night's accommodation in London, was deemed too expensive.

Liverpool provided a flavour of the forthcoming Lancashire opposition when they played at The Green in July 1927 with North Down winning comfortably by 155 runs. A great win followed against Waringstown in the Challenge Cup semi-final, then it was off to the Heysham boat. As usual Mr. Willie had been meticulous in his arrangements and in a letter to Sidney Catterall didn't pull his punches;

"I regret to say that we had an unsatisfactory match against Fylde on the one occasion on which we played them, so we would prefer not to have a match at all on that date to having another with them"

In Catterall's reply he lamented the difficulties that were facing the cotton trade at that time and since many of his players were heavily involved, it was difficult to arrange midweek matches. Being in the same industry, the difficult economic situation at home was frequently mentioned in this correspondence, but Mr. Willie didn't allow it to interfere with his cricket tour organisation or, indeed, his personal vacations! In January 1928, he returned from a three-week trip to Pontresina in Switzerland after 'a most enjoyable holiday' and immediately started negotiations with 'tried and trusted' Lancashire club secretaries to sort out the tour fixtures.

Headquarters for the 1928 tour was the Grand Hotel in South Shore, Blackpool, a location that became

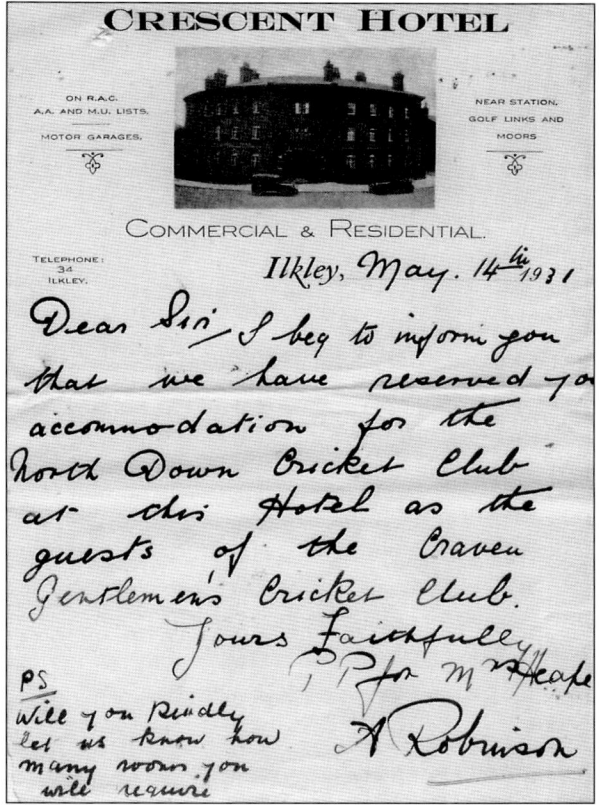

well known to North Down's 1970 tourists who performed with distinction on and off the pitch at South Shore.

In 1931 the touring dates were built around the availability of James and Tom (TJ) Macdonald who played for the Gentlemen of Ireland against the MCC at Lords in early August. On this occasion Tommy Martin of Lisburn CC joined the touring party and was a great success in every way. After a win against the Craven Gentlemen - James Macdonald picking up all 10 wickets – the rain caused the abandonment of the Blackpool game allowing more time for half of the team to enjoy their guinea's worth of fun at the Blackpool Tower.

In his post tour correspondence Willie Andrews wrote to T Wallers Pimley, the Blackpool CC Hon. Sec.:

"After I left you, I heard that your professional was having a benefit at the end of last week. Our players have asked me to send you the enclosed one pound, with our best wishes for its financial success."

In the final game at Lytham the side was Willie Andrews, James Macdonald, TJ Macdonald, George Macdonald, C Watson, Neville Petts, Tom Pearson, Tommy Martin, Teddy Bebe, G McAvoy, M Wild and W North.

It was not unusual in these times for a player to play under an alias and on this occasion Mr. North was actually Jack Dearden, the excellent and long-serving wicketkeeper at the club!

*"I hope that Jack Dearden won't lose of his rag,
If I offer to buy him a new cricket bag,
In Blackpool his old one was in for repairs,
And to get it he waited two hours on the stairs
Tra la la. Tra la lee,
The best team in Ireland is North Down CC."*

There must be many reasons why a player should play under an alias especially on tour.

M. Wild is a typical example and was good enough to bat number four at Ilkley in this strong batting line-up, but was never mentioned again. Ever. Anywhere.

In 1933 the tour changed direction to Scotland with a first match against Ayr. The change of location was largely the result of friendships developed with the Scottish clubs Ayr, Watsonians and Greenock who had been entertained at The Green over the years. This tour produced excellent matches against Ayr, Watsonians, Trojans and a two-day game against Greenock.

As a number of players wished to see the Australians play in England, no tour was undertaken in 1934, another reason being the importance of having strong sides available to play against Phoenix, Greenock and the Gentlemen of Leicestershire at Comber.

West of Scotland was added to the list of Scottish fixtures in 1935 and another excellent tour resulted. The tours continued until 1939 but came to an abrupt end with the outbreak of the Second World War.

JAMES MACDONALD

Every era produces one or two outstanding players and in the period between the wars James Macdonald was arguably the best player in Ulster cricket and one of Ireland's most accomplished. He was a double cricket and hockey international and, at the peak of his cricketing career, he won great praise from the 1938 touring Australians. He captained the Ireland team at Ormeau where he took five for 24 in 16 overs including the wickets of Barnes, White, Fingleton, O'Reilly and Ward.

James was educated at "Inst" and then Queen's University, Belfast, and played for the university side from 1924 to 1928 with his brother Tom. They were the star performers and regular thorns in the flesh of the opposing universities of St Andrews, Glasgow, Durham, Manchester and Trinity College, Dublin. Both went on to play on the same teams many times, at club and international level.

James Macdonald made his debut for North Down as a 15 year-old in 1922 and, over the next four decades,

JAMES MACDONALD (2ND RIGHT) LEADS IRELAND OUT AT ORMEAU TO PLAY THE AUSTRALIANS IN 1938. BROTHER 'TJ' (2ND LEFT).

JAMES MACDONALD AND BROTHER TJ GO OUT TO BAT AT ORMEAU

he became a towering figure in Ulster and Irish sport, both as a player and as an administrator. He was a brilliant all rounder and much of North Down's dominance between the wars was down to James Macdonald's performances.

At international level he marked his debut against Wales in 1926 with a score of 95, ironically ending his career in 1939 with a similar score against Sir Julian Cahn's XI.

He was a stylish left-handed batsman and slow left-arm bowler who varied his flight and pace with great control. He scored a match-winning 108 not out against MCC in 1936 and captained Ireland on 13 occasions, although ironically he never captained North Down for a single season!

Irish cricket historian WP Hone wrote of him in his book "Cricket in Ireland":

"From that year (1926) up to the outbreak of war, he remained one of our most consistent performers with bat and ball. His batting was marked by that easy, graceful style often seen in the best left handers, and his bowling by a high smooth delivery; he depended more on clever variations of flight than on any great spin off the pitch."

James Macdonald was admired by friend and foe alike and played the game with impeccable sportsmanship. His performance against the Australians in 1938 was described by former Australian test spinner Arthur Mailey as "the best piece of left-arm slow bowling he has seen on the tour". Yorkshire's Maurice Leyland went further in this praise when he lamented to a colleague:

"There's now't wrong with James Macdonald except he wasn't born in Yorkshire."

For North Down he was a revelation with both bat and ball. He played in nine Challenge Cup winning teams and six league winning teams. He set high standards in performance and in 1927 he scored 1,072 runs and took 109 wickets. He scored 197 not out against CPA in a 1930 cup game and a record 159 not out in the 1935 final against Cliftonville. In the 1931 final he took 13 for 79 against Ulster. In virtually every game he played James Macdonald made a telling contribution. His record at club level was unparalleled, winning the 1st XI batting award on eleven occasions and the 1st XI bowling award sixteen times. In 1936 he took

JAMES MACDONALD

all ten wickets (10 for 40) against the touring Royal High School FP of Edinburgh in a match North Down lost by two runs.

At the Carnival Cabaret evening the vocal tribute to the team mischievously included a verse on James Macdonald:

*"As one of the best men North Down possess
James Macdonald has been an outstanding success
He has just won two cups, but I hear he'd prefer
A nice game of tennis when ladies are there!
Tra la la. Tra la lee,
The best team in Ireland is North Down CC."*

James played hockey for Ireland 25 times and was a member of the 1933 Triple Crown winning team. He played for the Great Britain XI and was the mainstay in the most successful North Down hockey teams of the Thirties.

When war broke out in 1939 he immediately relinquished his teaching post at Methodist College and joined the Royal Artillery, reaching the rank of Lieut. Colonel. He survived the ravages of Dunkirk and won special recognition for saving the regiment's guns. He was later awarded the OBE (Military Division).

Sadly, ill health and war service limited his appearances for North Down after 1939 and when the war was over, in 1945, there was no James Macdonald to recapture the dizzy heights of success of the Twenties and Thirties.

He was appointed headmaster of Regent House School in 1946 and retained an active interest in the club's affairs through a wide variety of roles. He was, for many years, an Ireland selector and heavily involved within both the ICU and the NCU administration.

1936 Double Winners: Back – W Speers (Scorer), D McKibbin, N Petts, J Dearden, W Shields, R Patton, J Shields.
Front – F Mills, G Macdonald, J Macdonald, W Andrews, V Metcalfe, P Clarke, G Spence.

He was president of the Irish Cricket Union in 1954 and was the first chairman of the NI Youth and Sports Advisory Council.

At Regent House he was a strong disciplinarian but gave sport plenty of support and in particular cricket. Not many of the pupils under his care would have known of the brilliant sporting achievements of their headmaster, except perhaps the 'chosen few' who were taken willingly from lessons to play for Mr Willie's Wednesday XI. James Macdonald and Mr. Willie were lifelong friends and no request of this nature would have been refused.

In 1969 James Macdonald died suddenly, at the age of 63, and one of the finest cricketers in Ireland passed from our midst. Sportsmen and leading dignitaries from all over Ireland attended the special memorial service held at First Newtownards Presbyterian Church.

WILLIAM ANDREWS

"To have a good captain is a very sound plan,
For this Willie Andrews is just the right man,
When over at Blackpool he did the thing right,
By seeing the boys didn't stay out all night.
Tra la la. Tra la lee,
The best team in Ireland is North Down CC"

Willie Andrews was president of the Irish Cricket Union in 1948 and 1952, chairman of the Northern Cricket Union from 1948 to 1966, captain of North Down 1st XI from 1910 to 1949 (excluding 1947) and club chairman and godfather right up to his death in 1966 at the ripe old age of 80. Without doubt he was the greatest character in the history of Irish cricket.

WILLIAM ANDREWS

A tall gaunt man with a squeaky piercing voice, he was an eccentric figure with his yellow and green striped North Down blazer and a club cap perched precariously on his head. He was an authority on most subjects, not least the Laws of Cricket and the Rules of the Northern Cricket Union, and he exploited that knowledge to the full on behalf of club and union, the preference switching according to the occasion. He had the greatest respect for the game, its traditions and its etiquette and he was quick to rebuke those who failed to observe them. At best he was an astute and highly respected cricketing authority, at worst an exacerbating and frustrating adversary.

But he suffered no fools and even in death he was meticulous to the end. Although 80 years old he had carefully planned his bequests to include £50 to go to each of the clubs where he had scored a fifty!

He played in 20 Senior Challenge Cup finals and won on 13 occasions, a record only eclipsed in recent times by the long-serving Waringstown duo of Roy Harrison and Ivan Anderson. Ironically, he scored a century in the 1913 final against Waringstown and in 1928 he also hit his top score of 170 against the same club. That season, at the age of 42 he made his one and only appearance for Ireland, although he captained and selected many Ulster interprovincial teams.

He travelled widely with the MCC and gave talks to local townsfolk about his adventures when he returned home. He was awarded an MBE in 1952 for his services to cricket.

Mr Willie was a director in the family-owned spinning mill in Comber and, at one time, the High Sheriff of County Down. He was the dominant aura at North Down throughout his life and adversaries challenged his authority at their peril. He was an avid collector of autographs, old photos, press cuttings and cricket memorabilia, and if some people found him tiring they usually tolerated his idiosyncrasies because of his fanatical love of the game. He played well into his seventies and, out of respect, he was always allowed a gentle half volley and the accommodation of a 'single'. His big Humber Hawk was as much a part of the North Down scene as his high-pitched voice and in his obituary in Wisden he is referred to as "The Grand Old Man of Irish cricket", a description of which he would have approved.

Willie Andrews was a legend in his time, the like of whom we will never see again. He was frugal but amazingly benevolent in other ways. Ian Shields can certainly pay testimony to the latter when, after being summoned to the Andrews family home at Ardara in 1965, he was informed that he was going to Lord's for a week's coaching in the company of his Regent House headmaster James Macdonald and his son Rory. He can vividly recall that week and its many 'firsts' – flying, Lord's, the plush Clarendon Court Hotel, chauffer-driven cars arriving from Eton, Harrow, and Winchester College and mixing with household names of the rich and privileged. He also recall having to make a full report of the trip to Mr Andrews, a meeting that was held in the billiard room at Ardara, adorned with portraits steeped in Ulster cricket and political history. He was not the first North Down youth to be so treated, as Harry Donnan was an earlier beneficiary of the big man's generosity. Sadly he was the last to report to Ardara because on Christmas Eve the following year Willie Andrews was laid to rest in the family burial place in the grounds of Comber Unitarian Church, adorned with the stained glass window depicting the little boy with the bat and ball, a window that he had previously commissioned in memory of his sister Elizabeth.

Big Willie's legacy to Irish cricket and to the wider community was immense. He had a great sense of responsibility and served with the Royal Army Ordnance Corps and the Royal Navy during World War Two. He had previously served in the First World War as a gunner in the Royal Artillery and then as a Lieutenant in the Ordnance Corps. He bestowed considerable gifts to local causes and was a particularly benevolent patron to his former school "Inst" where he served on the Board of Governors for 26 years.

His character was admirably captured in the following words in Wisden:

THE AGELESS CRICKETER
England had her 'Grand old Man',
The famous Dr Grace,
And many are tales about him told.
But over here in Ireland,
We give the premier place,
'To the Cricketer, who never will grow old.'

His deeds by now are legend,
And opponents to their cost
Found his strategy had left them in the cold.
And when the match was over,
They wondered how they lost,
'To the Cricketer, who never will grow old.'

From Derry down to Dublin,
They know his lengthy stride,
And the way that he watches every ball that's bowled.
And often to a visitor
He's pointed out with pride,
'As the Cricketer, who never will grow old.'

So cricketers salute him,
Who has given to the game,
A devotion, we still marvel to behold.
And with succeeding summers,
May he always stay the same,
'The Cricketer, who never will grow old.'

GOLDEN YEARS FADE INTO THE CLOUDS OF WAR

The 20 years after the Great War were not only the most successful in the club's history, they were full of fun and entertainment off the field, captured so admirably in songs, tours, concerts, fairs and celebrations. North Down had made its mark in club cricket throughout Ireland and beyond, and its top players had won distinction at the highest level. Comber was proud of its cricket club and much of the credit for its drive and good fortune should be given to the inimitable Willie Andrews.

Big Willie was the life and soul of the club, fanatical, eccentric and exasperating to the extreme, but 100% a North Down and a Comber man.

These golden years at The Green were set within a world economic depression but it was difficult to see anything depressing about the club's fortunes in 1939.

But all that was about to change.

RAILWAY STREET, UPPER CRESCENT, MILL STREET AND BRAESIDE TEAMS
THAT PLAYED IN THE STREETS' COMPETITION AT THE GREEN IN 1931

CHAPTER 6
1939 – 1945 : THE WAR YEARS

"THERE'S BIKES AND BIG LORRIES PARKED AT MY DOOR, AND SOLDIERS ARE TRAMPING FROM MORNING TO NIGHT, YOU GET A NICE DOZE AND YOU WAKE UP WITH A FRIGHT, WITH OFFICERS SHOUTING AND SERGEANTS ALL ROAR, AND COMBER, OLD COMBER'S PEACEFUL NO MORE."

FANNIE McROBERTS, RESIDENT OF COMBER SQUARE

COMBER GOES TO WAR

Comber Square in 2007 looks a lot different from what it looked like in 1939 as the dark clouds of war gathered across Europe and the local townsfolk braced themselves for the inevitable. For many families it brought back bitter memories of lost loved ones in the horrors of the Great War, memories that are immortalized in the War Memorial sitting under the shadow of the Gillespie statue. Perhaps ominously, the old First World War field gun strategically pointed to the skies, and travellers from Newtownards going towards Killinchy Street took the shortest route across the angle of the square. The War Memorial was erected in 1923 in memory of the 79 brave Comber men who made the supreme sacrifice, and not long after the outbreak of World War Two the old field gun was dismantled for scrap metal for the war effort and an air-raid shelter had been erected.

It took the rest of the world some time to fully recognize the threat of Adolf Hitler in the Thirties. British Prime Minister Neville Chamberlain and most of America virtually ignored his ruthless anarchy and the ravages caused by the German army as they marched through Poland. Chamberlain's appeasement policy was cruelly exposed as the German tyrant continued his annexation of his neighbours and when war was eventually declared on 3rd September, 1939, Britain was ill prepared for the conflict. Northern Ireland was equally unprepared, but all over the province in towns and villages like Comber, young men and women joined the forces or went to work in factories that were mobilized for the war effort.

Northern Ireland was soon at the forefront of the German Luftwaffe's attacks, a precarious position exacerbated by De Valera's decision to keep Ireland

A note was read from the NCU, stating the Board of Trade had made an allotment of clothing coupons, and these would be allocated to clubs. The secretary was asked to apply for 500 as most members were badly in need of same.

FROM THE MINUTES

neutral. It allowed the German bombers almost free access along the Irish Coast to the Castlereagh Hills and although Comber and Newtownards were hidden by the blackout, the local people could hear the drones of the hundreds of Luftwaffe bombers as they pitched thousands of tons of explosives on Belfast city. Hundreds of people were killed in the Blitz raids on Belfast and De Valera's decision to send supporting fire brigades from Dundalk and Dublin was too little too late for many northerners.

Comber was fortunate to miss the brunt of these attacks although many Belfast people evacuated to the town. One stray shell blew a crater in the road just outside the town and two escaped POW German pilots were recaptured at 'Eusemere', the home of Lord Justice Andrews.

In truth the war didn't come to Comber, but Comber went to war.

CRICKET IN THE WAR YEARS

Many members of the club enlisted in the services during the Second World War while others made huge contributions, working in the factories that made munitions, building planes and ships, making clothing and hosting overseas troops. Some served in the Home Guard but, all in all, the townsfolk of Comber, rallied to serve their country in its hour of need.

But times were tough and cricket, like many sports, had to take a back seat as the war effort was mobilized. There was great uncertainty throughout Britain, but once Winston Churchill became Prime Minister there was a clear focus on the enemy and what each man and woman was expected to do in the service of their country. Churchill was arguably the greatest war leader of all time and in Field-Marshall Montgomery he found a military commander of similar stature. Both had lived through the Great War and learned from its harsh experiences, not least the importance of the war effort at home as much as on the front. Although there were many critics of their strategy, both encouraged sport to be played at home to maintain and boost morale, and after initially banning the congregation of people, the ban was gradually lifted and many sports became important fund-raising mediums that greatly benefited the war effort. Cricket was at the fore of these efforts, although the visiting West Indian tourists didn't hang around too long in August 1939. As soon as it became clear that war was going to be declared they caught the first available ship and were off home to the Caribbean. It mattered little to the English county season, as within a few weeks of the formal

Mr Willie

declaration of war, all games were suspended and many clubs saw their membership join the forces, virtually en bloc.

In 1940 the German army overran Belgium, Holland and France. It was a bleak picture for the beleaguered British troops that were forced back to Dunkirk within days of being obliterated but, miraculously, in the face of adversity, hundreds of boats of every shape and size sailed across the English Channel to rescue them. It was a turning point in the war and, within weeks, many cricketers, including those who had returned from Dunkirk, were on their way back to France as the British war machine started to regain lost ground. The same could be said for the gallant RAF pilots that fought so heroically to preserve British supremacy in the skies, and cricketers throughout Ulster could hear and see their fellow countrymen and women win the historic "Battle of Britain" during the summer of 1940.

Both the Northern Cricket Union and the North West Cricket Union took immediate steps to accommodate the war effort as they prepared for the 1940 season. Many NCU cricket officials had enlisted and were already on active service, while some clubs had folded because their membership was so severely depleted. Committee meetings were held during the winter to determine what cricket, if any, could be played, but the NCU decided to keep the game alive. Inevitably this meant restrictions, especially as clubs couldn't travel too far due to the petrol shortage, so war-time rules and regulations were implemented. There were no official registrations, teams were allowed to scratch without penalty if the reason was connected to the war effort, union fees were reduced by 25%, no rulebook was printed, interprovincial matches were postponed, committee meetings were reduced, and the union trophies were put into storage. The Senior Challenge Cup final was reduced to one innings and a set of stumps was awarded to the winners, if requested. Otherwise the competition was played much as it is still played today, albeit some teams were often below strength on match days.

For their part the clubs recognized the difficult circumstances and some recruited new players from clubs that had struggled to keep playing during the war. Clubs were also encouraged to play matches against the services and to accommodate any forces personnel who wished to play at a club. There were no challenges to the NCU during the war years and this made administration much easier. Lisburn, Muckamore and Holywood enlisted some outstanding military men in their ranks and North Down benefited in the same way.

Cricket had answered the call and while many players went off to war, there were many others playing their part at home in the war effort against tyranny and oppression.

SERVICE TO THE CAUSE

The war years marked a major decline in the fortunes of North Down, a decline that was to last virtually another 36 years. For a club steeped in success since 1887, this was a total transformation, and although there was never any alternative to the 100% commitment to the war effort, it was always expected that the good times would return when the conflict was over. Sadly it was not to be and the golden years between the wars became distant memories for the old hands during the barren 1950s and 1960s.

Two of the club's most distinguished players led the way when it became apparent war was inevitable. It was reputed Mr. Willie recruited over 70 people to the services and this is not hard to believe given his strong sense of loyalty. Willie also held a captain's commission in the Royal Army Ordinance Corps (RAOC) until 1943 before joining the Royal Navy, while James Macdonald joined the Territorial Army

Jim Montgomery

WILLIE WATT
DFC

in 1938 and was called up in 1939. He rose to the rank of Lieutenant Colonel and his regiment in the Royal Artillery was said to be the only one that returned from Dunkirk with all its guns. He was later awarded the OBE (Military Division).

Twenty North Down members were on active service during the war and this decimated the playing ranks to such an extent that the club faced the possibility of folding on numerous occasions. But to their credit the members kept the flag flying in the face of adversity and serving soldiers home from war duty were always welcomed with open arms. The spirit of the club was resilient at a desperate time, and despite enduring the worst cricketing seasons in their history, North Down Cricket Club survived the war years and played its part at home and away from the conflict in Europe.

Jim Montgomery was an excellent hockey player and useful cricketer who made many valuable contributions to the North Down club before the war. He played in the 1939 cricket Senior Challenge Cup final before joining the RAF. Early in 1941, while serving as an air gunner, he received a serious foot injury but after a fourteen month break he resumed his operational career and on the 15th May 1943 he repelled a sustained attack from German fighters over Bochum (Ruhr Valley). His citation informs us that he completed 36 operations successfully and showed great courage and devotion to duty. In early 1944 he was awarded the Distinguished Flying Cross (DFC) by His Majesty the King and later was feted with a great party held in the Andrews Memorial Hall.

Harry Morgan played at North Down in 1932 before moving to Ormeau. He lost a leg during the D-Day drop into France where his brother Reggie was killed and young Tom McLeod who played for the 3rd XI was killed in an air crash while serving with the RAF.

William Thompson Hamilton Watt (Bill) was born in Comber in 1911, educated at Comber National School and the Belfast College of Technology and joined the Air Force in August 1940. He took part in a large number of sorties, including numerous attacks against many of the major and most heavily defended industrial targets in Germany. The success of an attack

WILLIE WATT'S
DFC

against railway sidings at Cham in Czechoslovakia was mainly due to Flight Lieutenant Watt's skilful navigation, and his citation reads:

"This officer has proved to be an excellent leader who by his skill and courage has inspired confidence in all the crews with whom he has flown."

Bill, like so many of his colleagues at the time, was adept in most sports and he was a keen golfer who helped design the clubhouse at Mahee Island and later became club captain in 1969.

These members, and many more, made their contribution and sacrifice to enable us to live with the freedom that we enjoy today.

TOUGH TIMES AT THE GREEN

Finance to keep North Down going was a major challenge with limited gate money, but stalwarts like Jim Baxter rallied to the cause and played a significant role in maintaining the ground and the pavilion. The Ministry of Home Affairs needed a hut for shooting practice and the Nissen hut was erected at the top of the ground on a ten-year lease at a fiver a year. The club treasurer was also pleased to receive £70 when the top field was used for assault course training.

Not surprisingly, Willie Andrews lost no opportunity to secure military assistance and in 1942 he received help from the commanding officer of the Ordnance Corps, who were stationed in Comber, to assist with work on the ground.

Most surviving Ulster cricket clubs adapted to the challenge of war-time cricket, and there was the added bonus of seeing top class players like England test cricketers Hedley Verity and Norman Yardley in action either at Strabane, playing in representative matches or for the Green Howards, the regiment that was stationed in Omagh in 1940. American troops were also billeted in the province but while they didn't take to cricket some Canadian soldiers got into the spirit of the game playing in their pyjamas due to the shortage of cricket gear. Perhaps the earliest Twenty/20 exponents?

Charity games were played against the Services teams to raise funds for the war effort and cricket played a big part in these events both in England and in Ulster. The Governor's Red Cross Fund was one of the most popular Appeals and at times North Down players like James Macdonald and Willie Dempster played their part, while North Down's international umpires Neil Petts and Jim Baxter stood in many of these games without asking for their match fee.

Several of the members also served on NCU committees with Willie Andrews, Raymond Crosby and Gerry Spence being mentioned in the NCU minutes of the time. As expected, the Andrews family took a prominent role in many aspects of everyday life and James Andrews was awarded a Baronet in 1942 for his services to the legal fraternity and became Sir James Andrews, while his brother John Miller took over the demanding role of Northern Ireland Prime Minister from 1940 to 1943.

On the field of play club results could not have been much worse, as the club languished at the bottom of the 'Friendly League' table in four of the six war seasons with creditable mid-table placings in 1943 and 1944. First round exits in the Senior Challenge Cup became the norm, and for a club with such a distinguished cup record these were ignominious occasions. But it was a fight for survival at The Green rather than the pursuit of cricket honours.

Wartime North Down teams were barely recognizable from the pre-war teams as was evident when

DGR McKibbin

the club lost to Waringstown by seven wickets in 1941. The ten-man team read: Willie Andrews (Capt.), Gerry Spence, Willie Dempster, JH Abernethy, Sergt. Footitt, Young, Colour-Sergt. Prince, Pte. Williams, Pte. Faulkner, and Sergt. Gascoyne.

Low totals were a feature of wartime cricket and, unfortunately, North Down was on the receiving end of many of them. League wins were a rarity and cup wins non-existent. Muckamore (by five wickets) knocked us out in the first round in 1940 after only 68 runs were posted, while Woodvale gave us a cricket blitz in 1941 skittling us out for a paltry 26 runs in 35 minutes! It was said 1941 was the worst season on record for North Down but 1942 wasn't much better and in the cup competition Waringstown's 187 total, including a sparkling 106 by the Reverend Bobby Barnes was 105 runs too many for North Down.

The Villagers were the best team around during the latter war years and they showed no mercy on North Down the following year when they dismissed them for only 44 in the cup again, and then scored the required runs in just under 30 minutes. Waringstown played their part in the war effort, just as much as any other club in the Province, but in contrast to their rivals, when it came to important cricket matches they always seemed to field a strong team.

Downpatrick knocked us out of the cup in 1944, a tough season with barely a win to record and serious difficulties in fielding a team of any description on several occasions. In 1945 Cregagh had the dubious honour of adding to our cup demise, a sad occasion because James Macdonald was in attendance, just days after it had been announced that he had been forced to retire from the game on medical grounds. In more ways than one it was the end of an era because victory in Europe and the Far East was imminent.

Throughout the period DGR McKibbin was in a class of his own and a useful bowler when needed. He was ably supported by JH Abernethy, Gerry Spence, JA Hunter, Tom Magowan and Raymond Crosby. Willie Dempster was the leading bowler supported by Norman Murphy and G Cargo. There was also mention of a promising young wicketkeeper EA 'Eddie' Marks who would later play for Ireland, and of the good work achieved at boys level by some of the older members.

The seconds suffered badly and struggled to put out full teams let alone competitive teams. Their key batsmen were AD May, WJ Baxter Jnr., T Patton and JV McDowell, while Roy Maxwell and F McCullough were promising young players. Marks and Baxter were the bowling stars but when AD May left for military

WJ Baxter

duties in the Far East the team was further decimated. Some of the 2nd XI teams during the war years were almost military teams but, slowly, more young local players emerged after 1943. In 1945 there was some semblance of order and hope for the future, when five members of the Maxwell family featured in a junior league game, a match that also saw a young Walter Wishart emerge. Shades of better things to follow?

The war did finally end in the spring of 1945 and acting NCU secretary Jimmy Picken later recorded the season as "successful and enjoyable wartime cricket." There was certainly a great feeling of jubilation and relief all round, as barely 11 days after the Germans surrendered on 7th May 1945, Warrant Officer Lindsay Hassett led the Australian Services team out at Lords to face Wally Hammond's England in the first of the Victory tests.

Slowly but surely cricket returned to normality but for North Down Cricket Club it was to be a long time before the club got back to its pre-war position at the top of NCU cricket. The war years were tough times at The Green and more of the same was to follow for the next three decades.

JOHN MILLER ANDREWS

The second son of Thomas Andrews, John Miller was born at Ardara in 1871 into one of the most prominent and influential families in Ulster society. Like the rest of his family he grew up with a keen interest in sport and cricket in particular, but his destiny in life was to be politics. He was particularly close to his brother Thomas and took his untimely death in 1912 particularly badly. He had grown up playing cricket with Thomas and James at Ardara and at The Green, and he was a guiding influence with young Willie,

JOHN MILLAR ANDREWS

who was 15 years his junior but arguably the most fanatical cricketer in the family. He enjoyed the fellowship of sport and family, and was particularly fond of the annual Andrews family challenge match against his fellow members at North Down where he spent so many happy days at cricket.

John Miller never rose to the cricketing heights of his talented brothers largely because he was so committed to working at the spinning mill and later because of his heavy commitment to politics. He was essentially a 2nd XI player, making only sporadic appearances for the 1st XI in friendly and tour games. He played in the inaugural Junior Cup final in 1891, which North Down lost, but he later captained the seconds to Junior Cup wins in 1897, 1902 and 1904.

He was MP for County Down and Mid-Down from 1921 to 1953 and was a key member of the first government of Northern Ireland following partition in 1921. He was Minister of Labour from 1921 to 1939, Minister of Finance from 1937 to 1940 and then Prime Minister from 1940 to 1943 in the difficult war years. He was also chairman of the family firm John Andrews and Son, a director in the Belfast and County Down Railway Company (1916 to 1921), Belfast Ropeworks Co Limited (1919 to 1941) and was President of the Chamber of Commerce in 1936. Like most of his family he was a staunch Unionist and held senior positions within the Ulster Unionist Council and the Orange Order.

John Miller's son JLO 'Jack' Andrews inherited both his father's passion for sport and politics. He was also primarily a 2nd XI player although he played in the losing Challenge Cup final team of 1921 against Waringstown. He succeeded his father as managing director of the Spinning Mill and was also an MP and a prominent Ulster Unionist. He rose to the lofty status of Deputy Prime Minister and Leader of the Senate.

John Miller Andrews was almost 70 when he became Prime Minister and the heavy responsibility and stress of the job took its toll on his health. Although he continued as an MP until 1953 he reduced his commitment considerably as each year passed. He died in 1956, aged 85.

GERRY SPENCE

The war years brought out the best in the members who had to keep the club alive during the toughest of times on and off the field of play. North Down had a small core of willing workhorses, some of whom had enjoyed the good years before 1939, but who stayed loyal to North Down in its hour of need. One of these loyal club stalwarts was the effervescent Gerry Spence.

Gerald Spence was a Comber man who lived most of his life in Railway Street, a location that produced as many critics as cricketers. He was 14 when he made his senior team debut, rubbing shoulders with seasoned club legends and scoring 20 runs. From this modest start he went from strength to strength and played for

35 years, winning many admirers, as much for his charm and charisma off the field as his excellent batting on it. He helped the club to many Senior Challenge Cup and Senior League successes and played inter-provincial cricket for Ulster at senior and junior level. He was a great traveller to away games and did more for team spirit than any other member of the team. He was a warm friendly character and while he played to win, he enjoyed sport and the camaraderie it brought to those who participated.

In an era when there were many talented players vying for 1st XI places, Gerry Spence held a middle-order batting position in the strongest of North Down teams and played in seven senior cup finals from 1926 to 1939. He played on four winning sides including the hat-trick of wins from 1926 to 1928 and in the 1936 senior league and cup double 'dream team'. Unlike many senior cricketers, Gerry continued to play on after 1939. He topped the batting averages in 1941 and captained a much-changed side for two years in the early Fifties, dealing with relegation into the Qualifying League. When times were difficult Gerry was always there to assist during the war years, especially when Willie Andrews was stationed away from home.

GERRY SPENCE

Almost every time it was Gerry who dealt with the demanding off-field captaincy issues.

He was a great tourist and played against some useful cricketers like Blackpool's Cecil Parkin, stealing more than a few runs in tandem with James Macdonald and the rest of his fellow travellers. Off the field on tour he was full of fun and music and hosting club members loved his company.

So did all of his colleagues, both at cricket and at hockey. He played in the great North Down hockey teams of the 1930s and won two interprovincial caps and many accolades. He won Senior League and Kirk Cup medals and featured in Anderson and Irish Cup finals. He also had the distinction of playing for the Ulidians, an Ulster touring side renowned for playing with success in the Irish hockey tournaments.

Whether it was a sign of 'misspent youth' or a matter of convenience to his place of work we don't know, but top-class billiards players need time at the table or exceptional talent and Gerry was one of the best billiards players to come from the town! He played in a talented 1931 Andrews Memorial Hall team that won the Belfast and District Senior League and Senior Charity Cup and he also won the Individual Championship one year and was runner up the following year.

At golf Gerry was a useful eight-handicapper who played most of his golf at Mahee Island, where he won a beautiful and much treasured clock as the Captain's Prize in 1937 and where he became club captain in 1968.

Throughout his life Gerry played his sport like a true sportsman and won many friends and admirers, none more so than his daughter Barbara and son John, the former a hockey player at Regent House and the latter a promising fast bowler who, like his father, had diverse sporting talents.

WILLIE DEMPSTER

All his life Gerry worked as a bookkeeper in Comber Spinning Mill, an institution renowned for its association with Willie Andrews and the cricket club and what a loyal, devoted and talented servant to North Down he proved to be.

WILLIE DEMPSTER

Willie Dempster emerged into the North Down senior team at the start of the war and was to leave an indelible imprint on the club for many years. He assumed a wide variety of roles in his time, not least as an excellent spin bowler in an era in Ulster cricket when many of the best spin bowlers were at their peak.

Willie had a great ability to set a field to his own bowling and then put the ball on a nagging length so that his well-placed fielders would snare the errant shot. He was an astute captain in the post-war era and a tough opponent who gave no quarter. His round-arm slinging action was hardly textbook orthodox bowling, but it was very effective and won him the nickname of 'Spin King' with the younger members. Unfortunately, Willie never played in the great North Down teams so representative honours were hard-earned, although he did represent Ulster on several

> *The Club horse was sold for £12 and it was reported that horses and dogs had been running over the square, especially Willie Wishart's greyhounds that were being exercised. A letter was written to same.*
>
> FROM THE MINUTES

occasions. He also lived and played in an era when there was a plethora of top class spin bowlers in NCU cricket and most of them were playing in Senior One while North Down struggled down the leagues.

Willie donned many hats at North Down over 50 years and his name is deservedly up there with the all time greats who served the club with distinction. He captained the 1st XI from 1954 to 1961, and in 1964 and 1965. He was a staunch supporter of 'Mr. Willie' and James Macdonald, and followed in their footsteps as a dedicated and stalwart committee member. He was later appointed as a trustee of the club and for many years he was the groundsman, the one-man grounds committee and the man who got things done. Many of the improvements around the clubhouse and on the ground were almost single-handedly undertaken, including the transformation of the top field into an excellent cricket ground. Willie severed his day-to-day connections with the club in the late Eighties and will always be remembered as a colossus at a time when fortunes on and off the field had dropped to an all-time low.

During the war years the young Willie Dempster became North Down's most successful bowler and from as early as 1941 his name was engraved on the 1st XI Bowling Cup, an occurrence that was to become all too familiar in the years that followed. He was a regular wicket-taker in every match and a useful bat in his early years, renowned for always batting without gloves. He gave plenty of encouragement to the younger players and was never short of an opinion on every subject.

He had a deep interest in the ground and, after several unsuccessful appointments, he took on the role himself and in time became judge and jury on whether the ground was fit for play or not. He virtually lived at The Green during the day and every evening returned to the club via the stepping-stones across the river Enler from his Dunsy Way home, some ten minutes walk across the meadow. Willie's arrival from the Scrabo Road end was invariably preceded by Rusty and Ranger, his faithful patrol dogs for many years.

Willie's part-time employment as groundsman brought controversy in 1963 when the NCU Senior Committee deemed him a professional and threw North Down out of the Challenge Cup, a decision that was later rescinded when it was accepted that the role was only part-time.

He was a tireless fundraiser and his general handy-man skills played a major part in the successful extension of the clubhouse in 1957. He was also responsible for bringing the 'Guiney Stones' to the Green and everyone sees them immediately they walk through the gate. These stones have a long history as a meeting place for locals at the top of Castle Lane and when the road was being widened they risked being lost, but Willie saw their historical importance and quickly had them 'resettled' at The Green.

As they say in Ulster, 'he wasn't everybody's cup of tea,' but for commitment and service to North Down over the years there weren't many members who gave more to the cause. Willie also produced two cricketers in sons Geoffrey and Ivan, who played many fine innings for North Down before leaving to join Woodvale.

Their departure was another twist to the Willie Dempster story, a story that should be remembered for all the positive things he brought to the club.

THE END OF AN ERA

In stark contrast to the halcyon years between the wars, the period 1939 to 1945 was the worst in the club's history. Gone was the playing supremacy that had produced so many wonderful victories in the 1930s, gone were so many of the old stars of yester-year and gone was the status that had made visits to The Green such a wonderful cricketing experience for opposing teams and supporters. Times had been tough in the war years with so many members on active service and a heavy responsibility was placed on the chosen few left to keep the club afloat. But in their own way they succeeded, and North Down Cricket Club came through the doldrums, albeit severely scarred by ill fortune. There was no immediate return to the successful golden years and in the wake of World War Two the club had to start afresh and rebuild without so many of its best players. This was an awesome challenge and while a hardened band of willing stalwarts set about the task with great optimism, the sad fact was that is was going to be a long time before North Down got back to its lofty position at the top of Ulster club cricket.

CHAPTER 7
1946 – 1968 : 'HOW ARE THE MIGHTY FALLEN'

"THIS HAS BEEN COMING FOR SOME TIME IN COMBER, AND NO DOUBT THEY WILL ACCEPT IT AS PART OF THE BARGAIN. OUTSIDE COMBER TOO, THERE ARE SOME WHO SAY THAT NORTH DOWN ARE NO DIFFERENT FROM ANY OTHER CLUB AND THAT HAVING BEEN SUCH STICKLERS FOR RULES, THEY ARE NOW GETTING THEIR JUST DESSERTS. HOW ARE THE MIGHTY FALLEN."

IRELAND SATURDAY NIGHT 1947 WHEN NORTH DOWN WAS RELEGATED

POST WAR COMBER

The headlines said it all: 'Japan Surrenders Unconditionally', 'Germany's Surrender'; and the celebrations began throughout the British Empire, Russia, the USA and all the countries liberated from German and Japanese oppression.

Comber celebrated too with a united thanksgiving service conducted by the local clergy in the Andrews Memorial Hall. Following the service, the bands paraded through the town accompanied by their enthusiastic supporters and when darkness set in a huge bonfire was lit on Maryborough Hill. The bands played into the night and the dancing and rejoicing continued in floodlit Comber Square.

On the following morning after a parade of the local services, a drumhead service was held at The Green when all the local clergy officiated and where the afternoon was given over to sports for the children. In the evening at the Andrews Memorial Hall a big crowd patronised a victory dance well into the early hours.

A concert in aid of the 'Welcome Home Fund' was also organised in the Andrews Memorial Hall and the crowd was entertained to three hours of variety including the stars of the show, the 'Faulat Minstrels', a group of coloured dancing and singing ladies.

It was relief and rejoicing at the same time and who could blame them? But after the euphoria had died away, reality quickly set in and the problems of social decay became very apparent.

Difficulties with provision of adequate housing, suitable water and sanitary conditions had been put on the back burner during the war years, but they now became major priorities. At that time many houses in Comber had dry toilets, although the new Public Convenience had been opened in 1955, but it wasn't until 1957 that piped water replaced pumps and street fountains in the older houses. The town was expanded with the building of council housing estates in the early 1950s and two of the streets were named after war heroes and former North Down members, De Wind Drive and Bruce Avenue.

The Coronation of Queen Elizabeth II in 1953 provided much excitement in the town and plans were drawn up for a Coronation Eve competition for the best

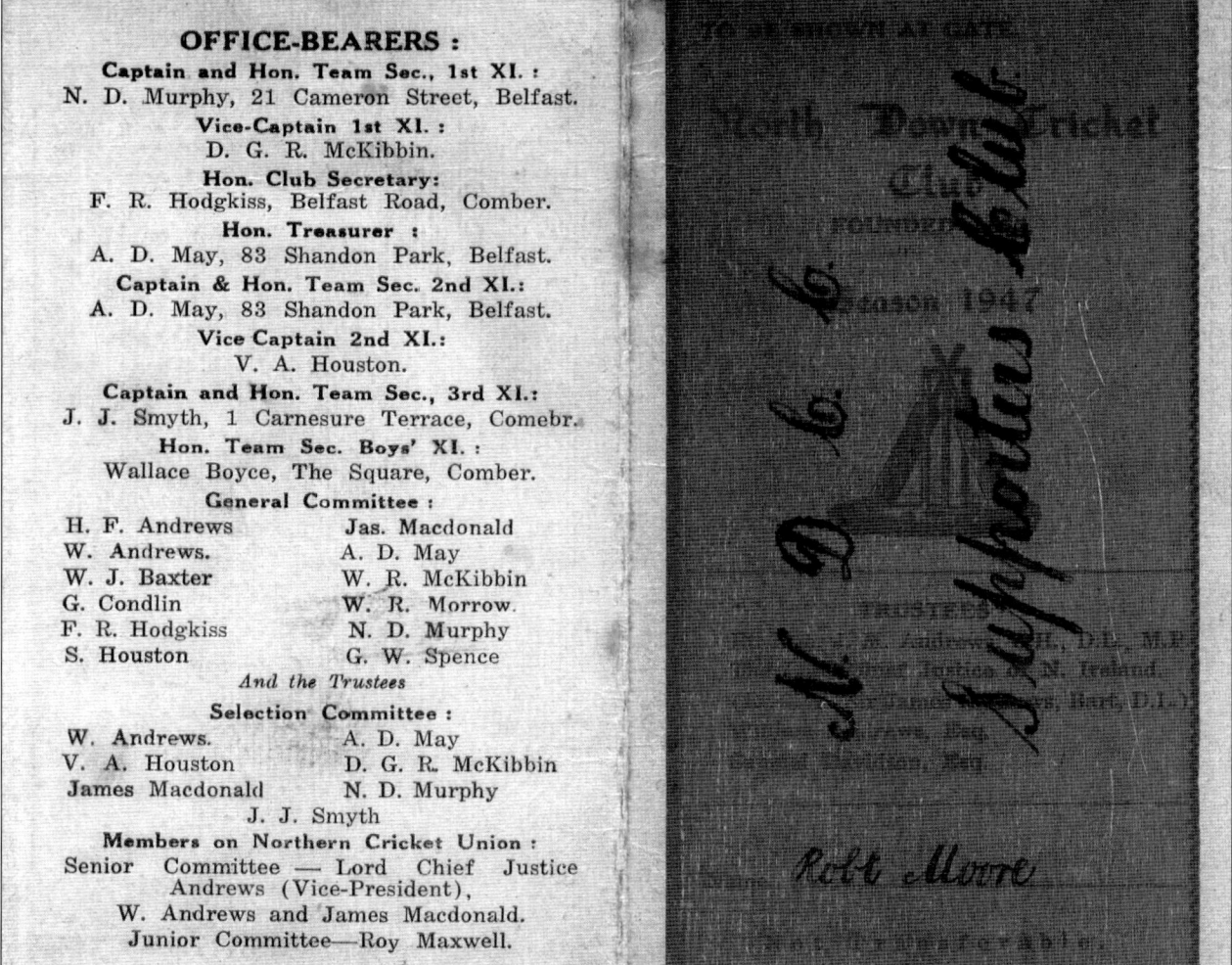

'dressed' street, house and business premise. A Coronation Wagon toured the town and all the children assembled in the Square and paraded, to the accompaniment of bands, to The Green where a 'monster' sports day was held. Each child received sweets and a souvenir and in the evening a fireworks display and bonfire was followed by a late night dance in the Andrews Memorial Hall.

Life returned to normal when the Chronicle reported on the new films available in Comber cinema, detailing the Wills of the dead, naming pools winners, and scrutinising the 450 entrants for the Comber Cage Bird Show!

CRICKET IN ULSTER

The administration of the NCU from 1929 until 1947 had been expertly marshalled through the chairmanship of Sydney Jackson, a former North of Ireland and Ulster player, and a popular man of many talents and expertise. Other fine administrators who loyally guided the NCU during and immediately after the war included Cliftonville men JC 'Jimmy' Picken, who received an MBE for services to the game, and WL McClay, secretary from 1946 to 1958. The chairman of the senior committee was in effect the chairman of the union and in 1948 the reins of office passed to our own William Andrews at the mature age of 62.

In a way his elevation to this position was almost inevitable but when it finally came it was ironic that his years of leadership coincided with a period of struggle within his own club that was sinking fast into the obscurity of the Senior Qualifying League.

The war had taken its toll on many clubs but not all had suffered the same fate as North Down. The Belfast clubs seemed to get their act together in post-war NCU cricket much quicker and Lisburn emerged as the best of the country clubs. Cregagh won the Senior League twice and North of Ireland, Woodvale and Waringstown each won the accolade before Lisburn took over in the early Fifties with a hat trick of wins.

In the Senior Challenge Cup, Lisburn's win in 1946 was followed by the only outright win from a North-West side when Sion Mills beat Armagh by one wicket, after winning both the North West Senior Cup and their Senior League. Then Woodvale took over with a tremendous hat trick of Challenge Cup wins, a feat they had threatened to accomplish after their 1939 victory over North Down.

There were also signs of growing strength in Mid Down with the Intermediate Cup and Lindsay Minor Cup heading to Downpatrick and the latter to Crossgar in the late 1940s.

James Macdonald may have retired as a player but the North Down man was an influential member of the senior committee, alongside the great EDR 'Donald' Shearer who had briefly been a member of the club in the pre-war years, but who played post-war at North of Ireland with some distinction.

TOUGH TIMES AT THE GREEN

Despite the demands on his time at work, within the NCU and as 1st XI captain, Willie Andrews continued as chairman of the club until his death in 1966. He was ably assisted by James Macdonald who acted as secretary from 1949 to 1951 with assistance from Walter Fawcett and John Smyth, the latter taking over until 1959.

Willie Morrow had the financial responsibilities of the club through the war years until 1946, but AD May, who was secretary of the NCU until his posting to the Far East, took over in 1947. Gerry Spence was much to the fore as well, but the administrative input of Andrews and Macdonald at the time was arguably as important as their pre-war contributions on the field.

Mr Willie had captained North Down 1st XI since 1910 and throughout that time he rarely missed a committee meeting or a match. But after 36 years, Norman Murphy, who had joined the club in 1940, was able to rally enough support to win the captaincy vote at the Annual General Meeting for the 1947 season. It didn't affect Mr Willie's cricket as he went on to top the run makers and turn in more than useful bowling figures for the season, but the rare 'misjudgement' was rectified the following year when Willie Andrews won back the captaincy going into his 62nd year.

Mr. Willie had an inherent belief in his own leadership qualities and was certainly not going to bow to old age without a fight!

The war years had raised many questions relating to the club's future and such was the concern that an audit on the state of cricket in Comber was commissioned by the chairman and penned by Terence G Andrews, who had assisted with treasurer's duties before the war. The object of the report was to set down certain facts about the club and to outline proposals for broadening the scope of the club with a view to setting it on a sound financial footing and, at the same time, enabling it to cater effectively to the sporting and recreational requirements of the community as a whole. So wide were the implications contained in the report that the members of the committee were given the opportunity to consider and discuss the whole matter before it was raised officially. For this reason the report was circulated privately among the committee members with their comments to be written confidentially in the report book.

The financial position of the club was at the heart of the report, both the current position and the prospects. At the time of the issue of the report in May 1946, the club was in debt to the tune of £126, though it owned the 16 acres of land that had been bought for £428, and various other fixed assets.

At a seemingly inappropriate time, a 'Special Appeal Fund' was launched in 1939 for rebuilding the pavilion and improving the ground. But by 1946 this fund had reached only £300.

The average annual income for the five years prior to the war was £177; the average expenditure over the same period was £170 but the bank overdraft had risen from £63 in 1927 to £125 by 1938. It was judged that the existing borderline situation in 1946 was going to become much more serious when lack of success on the field was augmented by the increase in wages and cost of equipment.

The report was detailed to the point of costing the 'pro' and his 'boy' at £8 in 1946 against £3 ten shillings pre-war. The cost of cricket gear, which the club paid, had spiralled post-war, as had repairs and even postage, and the audit reckoned that an annual additional £100 was needed to run the club.

Adding to the foreseen financial problems was the decline in membership, which fell from 107 members in 1929 to 76 in 1938 and 53 members in 1946 with no optimism about an upturn. This 'ever decreasing measure of public support' caused great dismay. The report stated:

"If the Club continues on its present basis I doubt very much whether it can survive for the simple reason that there is not adequate popular support for it among local people or even real enthusiasm among the majority of the members."

There was another concern added to finance and membership as the audit notes.

"More and more people are giving up cricket in favour of other sports. Why is this happening? It is happening because in recent years there has been a great extension of facilities for other sports. Moreover, many of the newly popularised sports are those in which women as well as men can take part. As time goes on an ever increasing number of young women are turning to sport for their recreation. They don't want to watch — they want to take part. It is this fact which explains the rapid growth and increasing popularity of tennis, golf, badminton, cycling and sailing clubs throughout the province. As might be expected husbands and boy friends have been 'encouraged' to take up those sports in which their ladies could join. In the event cricket has suffered more than any other old established game — firstly because it is played in summer in the best weather and, secondly, because it occupies so much time. Most wives would not grudge an hour or two of their men's leisure time but they definitely do grudge the loss of the whole of every Saturday and of several mid week evenings throughout the summer. Therefore however much they may wish to play cricket, many men give it up simply because they are not prepared to be entirely selfish about their recreation at their wives' expense."

Nothing changes. Not even the proposals as to what would have to be done to change the situation. The following and final section of the audit asks what can be done? It makes for interesting reading, as some of the comments are as relevant today as they were 61 years ago:

"The cricket club is ideally situated in the very centre of the town but, at present, it caters for a very small proportion of the local people. That must change. We have a splendid opportunity now to broaden the scope of the Club and thus essentially to increase its value and its

1960 v Kilmarnock: Back – Umpire, D Lapsley, W Dalzell, P Craig, W Artt, J Dalzell, visitor, Scorer, D Nesbitt, W Andrews, J Boucher, D Shields, G Menagh, Dai Jones.
Front – Kilmarnock team with NDCC Captain Willie Dempster 6th from left.

appeal to the community as a whole. We can do this by cooperating with other interested parties and transforming the cricket club to a Sports Club that will provide facilities for a really wide variety of healthy outdoor and indoor sports.

The location is ideal and we already own the ground. There is plenty of room in the field at the north end of the ground to make a first class football pitch and with modern equipment the necessary levelling could be done very quickly. Cricket and hockey are already catered for. Tennis courts can be built.

The Club must cater for men and women of all ages. It must have a really comfortable clubhouse with central heating, electric light and ample bathing and dressing room accommodation. It must have nicely furnished lounges, a snack bar serving light refreshments and rooms set aside for table tennis, darts, billiards etc. It must have a hall large enough to be used for entertainment, club dances, badminton, boxing etc. It must be a home from home where people can go and read, write letters, listen to the wireless. In brief, it must be a real recreation centre for the whole town.

In the reorganisation and running of the Club all sections and interests in the town must be fully represented. One of the first steps must be to put the ideas over to people at a big public meeting. If this is done I believe that at least 400 members can be enrolled. With such a large membership the Club would be in a position financially to provide really first class facilities for all types of sport and a high standard of comfort in the clubhouse itself."

Was this report woefully out of touch with reality as a later report in the 1980s was deemed to be? This may have been the case as no action was taken on the audit and the club continued to scramble through the post-war era towards the celebration of the centenary in 1957.

> *"We must look after the potential England batsmen," said Mr J.O.H. Long, RM., when seven boys appeared before Comber Petty Sessions on Monday, charged with playing cricket in the street on May 6th. Accordingly he gave them all an absolute discharge.*
>
> NEWTOWNARDS CHRONICLE 1953

Sadly James Macdonald's illness prevented him from playing much after the war, while his brothers, George and Tom, moved to England. Jackie Shields had gone to live in Ballymena, in those days a long way from Comber, and Neville Petts had carved out a successful career in England. William Miller, Albert Anderson, David Taylor and DC Lindsay had passed to a greater calling. Cadogan, who became a Colonel, was captured by the Japanese Army and spent two years in a Prisoner of War camp. Jack Dearden, Bert Hill and Willie Morrow had all given up the game while Teddy Bebe became a Major in the Army and remained in the service after the war.

Jim Montgomery received the DFC from His Majesty the King in 1943 but struggled to recover from his combat injuries and didn't play after the war. Jim, now in his Nineties, lives in Cranbrook, Kent and remembers, with great clarity, the 1939 cup final against Woodvale and the pre-war cricket and hockey successes.

Gerry Spence and Tommy Maxwell were still playing, the former doing a good job on the 1st XI but Tommy's best days were gone and he struggled to regain former glories under captains David Kirk, Gerry Condlin and AD May on the 2nd XI.

Although the club fielded three elevens the falling membership was a concern and it was recommended that a positive effort be made to attract young players.

Of the nine teams in the Senior League in 1946, North Down had probably suffered more than any other with regard to loss of key personnel, but the 1947 fixtures were as substantial as ever with military games against the Headquarters of the Northern Ireland Command, RAF Aldergrove and the 28th Training Battalion based at Palace Barracks. The tours to the mainland were replaced by a tour to the North West and matches were scheduled against Eglinton, Sion Mills and Brigade, but before that the side made yet another early exit from the Senior Challenge Cup when beaten by City of Derry at Duncreggan. In an effort to continue to attract teams to The Green, Thornlebank and Kilmarnock were entertained at home.

These were tough times but reality finally sank in when a defeat by CPA in 1947 relegated the club, for the first time in its illustrious history, from the Senior League. The view was taken that since North Down had been unequivocal in their attitude in applying the rules of the union to other clubs they had no way out. The press took the view that the rules of the union were abysmally out of date with regard to the percentage system. Friendly matches were still filling clubs' fixture cards and taking precedence over rearranged league games and with the weather intervening North Down were caught out on all counts and paid the price, even though there was a belief that pressure might be brought to give North Down an escape route.

However, despite the rumour mongering, this didn't happen.

The harsh reality was that the players that had replaced the old guard weren't of the same calibre and had to find their level, but it didn't help when the excellent young wicketkeeper Eddie Marks joined an ever-strengthening North of Ireland.

Was it a coincidence that the first year of the club being relegated out of senior cricket was the only year that Mr Willie wasn't captain in a 39-year span!

The advent of the Senior Qualifying League in 1948 brought better results in a lower standard of cricket.

It wasn't all doom and gloom as the club won the Senior Qualifying League in 1949 and began the new decade back in senior cricket. Strength in depth would be critical in trying to maintain this status and there were encouraging signs when the 3rd XI gained success against a strong Woodvale team. North Down scored 217 for nine with H Farran scoring 38 and Wallace Boyce 35. The team was; D Maxwell, B Scott, J Heaney, Wallace Boyce, H Farran, Jack Maxwell, Miller O'Prey, J Mills, J Oliver and one other.

The Senior Challenge Cup matches immediately after the war were few, with first round exits in 1945

RAYMOND CROSBY

against Cregagh, 1947 against Derry and 1949 against Armagh. Second round exits in 1946 against Cliftonville and North of Ireland in 1948 reflected the difficulties in batting; the firsts averaged 100 runs in all cup games between 1945 and 1950 yet Basil Irwin, Walter Wishart and Willie Dempster showed that they were capable of matching senior opposition in the bowling department.

The 1950 season was seriously interrupted by bad weather to the extent that North Down played only seven of their scheduled 18 games.

Armagh, CPA, Cliftonville, Cregagh, Downpatrick, Lisburn and Waringstown provided the opposition and North Down had Basil Irwin as their new captain. He had a fair side with Walter Wishart and John Copeland providing back-up to his own pace bowling and Bobby Todd and Willie Dempster two of the best slow bowlers in the league. There was also the aggressive stroke play of Wallace Boyce and the excellent wicket-keeping of Walter Fawcett, later to be capped by Ireland. The batting was centred on David McKibbin, Willie Watt, Dennis Murray and Gerry Spence. LC Head was a useful all rounder that Mr Willie brought in from time to time to avert a crisis. In the wings was Raymond Crosby, who epitomised everything that was good about the club, on and off the field. He had a distinguished career as an all round sportsman, starting with the Boys' XI and eventually winning a place in the 1st XI in the late 1930s at the age of 16. He was of great value to the club during and after the Second World War when he was a mainstay of the team. Capped by Scotland at hockey he also played a number of times for the Ulster team and won a Steel and Sons Cup medal at football. Raymond was not only a fine all round sportsman, he was a lovely person and in later life extremely popular with the members.

Willie Dempster took 42 wickets in 1951 and won the relegation match against Cliftonville despite a dismal North Down batting display. Young Bobby Todd played his first senior season and took 37 wickets for the 1st XI and 27 for the 2nd XI. They played in Section B of their Division and, like the previous season, finished third with Tom Magowan and Raymond Crosby the main run makers and Bobby Todd and Leslie Thompson taking the wickets.

Gerry Spence succeeded Basil Irwin as 1st XI captain, but the team finished bottom of the league and into Qualifying league cricket in 1952 where they finished runners up. Occasionally glimpses of ability shone through as when Lisburn, who were the strongest NCU team in 1952, were the cup opposition at Wallace Park in June and Raymond Crosby scored

> *It was reported that the flagpole had been blown down and broken and the Chairman mentioned that he had a tree growing which, when felled and seasoned, would be most suitable. This offer was unanimously accepted.*
>
> FROM THE MINUTES

61, with Walter Wishart taking three for 37 in a creditable five-wicket defeat.

Willie Watt inherited the general apathy and lacklustre performances of the firsts when his side were 68 all out against CPA in the league in the first match the following year. The opposition was St Mary's, Holywood, Muckamore, Drumaness, CPA, Hilden, and Queen's University. He wasn't helped by the loss to Waringstown of Walter Fawcett and the non-availability of Walter Wishart who had gone to work in Kenya. On the plus side, the arrival of the Lapsley brothers, the Reverend David and Josh along with M Ford, was some compensation.

Willie Dempster took over as captain in 1954 and a year later the Senior Qualifying League was won. Two crucial games at the end of the season would determine their fate but they lost the first one to Instonians. Willie Watt, Wallace Boyce and Walter Coey all hit thirties in the 145 for eight total, but Instonians passed the score with four wickets remaining. The final match against Drumaness had to be won and with Watt and Dempster scoring twenties, it was left to a young Alex Gregg, with an unbeaten 77, to be the hero of the day. It won the league, but with the complex percentages taken over a number of years it didn't win promotion. The following year Instonians won the promotion race in another nail-biting finish and it wasn't until 1957 that promotion was attained by North Down.

Back in the senior league, Jackie McBurney and Willie Dempster each took over 50 wickets, supported by 32 from Bobby Todd and 28 from the rising star Jimmy Boucher. It was the custom at the time to leave the wickets uncovered and open to the elements that greatly favoured the bowlers, and the new groundsman, Jimmy Cairnduff, wasn't going to apply new fangled ideas about covering the wickets.

HOW THE TIMES HAVE CHANGED!

The McBurney family, Sam, Jackie and Ronnie had spells of success at the club, with Ronnie showing a lot of promise as a quick bowler at youth level and Sam playing good 2nd XI cricket. But Jackie was the best of the McBurney boys and played cricket at Regent House and Ulster Schools before turning in many good performances as an all rounder for North Down. He was one of the few players at the time who would have made an impression at the higher level, but he was a Comber man and stayed loyal to the cause.

1955 QUALIFYING LEAGUE A WINNERS: BACK – W ANDREWS, W WATT, A GREGG, B FOWLES, B IRWIN, J MACDONALD. MIDDLE – B TODD, W COEY, W DEMPSTER, T BOYD, R CROSBY. FRONT – W BOYCE, J JORDAN. INSET – L BRYSON, J MCBURNEY.

1951 NORTH DOWN XI: BACK – W ANDREWS, T KILLICK, S GLOVER, C RICHARDSON, J MCBURNEY B ROWAN, J O'PREY. MIDDLE – J MAXWELL, D O'PREY, M O'PREY, S MCBURNEY, M CAIRNDUFF. FRONT – M O'PREY JNR., H MCGREEGHAN.

The Senior Challenge Cup matches in the 1950s followed the pattern of the previous decade with first or second round exits every year apart from 1955, when victories against CPA and Cregagh produced an unexpected semi-final tie against the very strong Lisburn side. Almost inevitably North Down lost by 145 runs.

Willie Watt captained the 1st XI in 1953 and usually opened the batting with the forerunner to the 'pinch hitter', Alex Gregg. Left-hander Jack Maxwell, Dr. Denis Murray, Miller O'Prey, swashbuckling Stanley Glover and David O'Prey occupied the middle order. There was a strong and varied opening attack with Leslie Thompson, Jimmy 'Slinger' Boucher and John Craig. John bowled sharply off two paces and could unsettle any opposition, while the O'Prey brothers provided guile with the slower variety.

The 2nd XI performed well in the 1950s in a variety of sections within Division 2 and played in the Intermediate and Junior Qualifying Cups, being defeated in the latter in 1951 by Ards, when 65 year-old Mr Willie opened the batting and was run out for one run.

The O'Prey brothers, Miller and David, were the principal run makers and towards the end of the period a young Malcolm Campbell began to show a lot of batting promise.

By 1957 Alan Simpson was captain and wins over Sirocco Works and Short & Harlands in the Junior Qualifying Cup set up a difficult third round tie away to Hollerith. The batsmen could not have been confident chasing a victory target of 233 runs after tea, but it was Malcolm Campbell's day, as he proceeded to score a century, receiving great support from the up and coming Billy Artt and Dennis Murray. A semi-final place was booked but it was as far as the team went, despite another sound batting performance from Campbell. At Woodvale they crumpled to 94 all out and a six wickets defeat.

Bobby Rowan, Miller O'Prey, Alan Simpson and Jim Barry each took their turn to captain the side during this period, with mixed fortunes.

THE SWINGING SIXTIES

The 1960s started poorly for the 1st XI, with a seventh position out of eight in the 1960 Senior League. They played 27 games winning only five and marginally improved on the situation the following year, with 10 wins from 25 starts. The 12 sides in the league in 1961 were reduced to eight in 1962 and although the team finished fifth in 1961, on the basis of percentage wins over the previous two seasons, they were relegated again to Senior Qualifying cricket.

The 2nd XI, in contrast, won their Second Division Section B title in 1960 on a wet day play-off against Downpatrick II. Under the captaincy of Raymond Crosby, veteran of many games at the higher level, the experienced side also contained two young players, Malcolm Campbell and Don Shields, who would become regulars at the top.

There were a lot of cry-offs on the 2nd XI in 1962, and the selected side on a Monday evening rarely appeared on the Saturday. The situation became acute when as many as six cry-offs became habitual and the lack of team spirit that ensued became the main factor in the fight to stave off relegation. The 3rd XI suffered to the point where an abandonment of the side in 1962 looked imminent as they 'scratched' four games and the club was penalised by the union for the first time in its history.

Wallace Boyce left for New York in 1965, but there was some compensation in having Stanley Glover back in the ranks after a two years absence. Times had changed dramatically in 20 years and the senior team was, in effect, playing third division cricket against Dungannon, Portadown, Milford, Collegians, Donacloney, Bangor and Civil Service. Worse still, they were having little success.

The first match of the 1965 season with Donacloney was a two-innings affair, as only 44 overs were used to dismiss both sides in the 100 overs match. The bowlers' paradise saw Walter Wishart take six for 14 for North Down before Carson (eight for 40) and Poots (eight for 51) gave Donacloney an easy win.

Defeats against Portadown and Civil Service indicated that it was going to be a struggle, but wins against Dungannon, Bangor, Milford and Collegians was enough to stop the slide to an even lower standard.

It was difficult to find a batsman who hit a 'fifty' during the season and when he did, bowler Jack Dalzell's 67 against Civil Service wasn't good enough to avoid a seven wickets defeat.

But throughout these tough times the bowlers could not be faulted and turned in fine performances week in week out, with Willie Dempster, Walter

1960 SECOND DIVISION SECTION B LEAGUE WINNERS: BACK – A GREGG, M O'PREY, D O'PREY, S GLOVER, J CRAIG, J MAXWELL, D KIRK. MIDDLE – L THOMPSON, W WATT, R CROSBY, D MURRAY, J BOUCHER. FRONT – D SHIELDS, M CAMPBELL.

1958 NORTH DOWN BOYS XI: BACK – G PORTER,
W MCKIBBIN, R MCBURNEY, T SAVAGE, J BOUCHER.
MIDDLE – R WARNOCK, J MYERS, D ARTT,
A THOMPSON, A HENRY.
FRONT – D SHIELDS, J MORELAND.

Wishart and paceman Dalzell all regular wicket-takers.

One of the more significant 'signings' of the period was that of Queen's University graduate Sydney Elliott in 1967, a year that saw Billy Artt return to the game after a lay-off. Sydney was one of the most promising batsmen of the day and he was to serve the club with great distinction on and off the field for almost 40 years.

Another positive development was the ability to turn out three elevens with every prospect of a fourth. The 3rd XI under Jimmy Boucher won their league in 1967, a rare success for the club at this time.

The inability to score runs at the club was painful and had been for twenty years, so the introduction of the Rothmans Cup was warmly welcomed. It was a midweek 20 overs thrash and designed to bring out the aggression in the batsmen. As noted cricket journalist Carl Anderson said at the time:

'The game should appeal to the players' brighter cricketing instincts.'

Holywood, Donaghadee, North Down, Ards, Bangor and Berkshire contested the inaugural tournament, which was won by Holywood.

The Boys XI held the potential for the future, although they lost to Bangor in the Graham Cup in 1965. Norman Beck hit 68 runs in a side that included Miller O'Prey, Geoffrey Dempster, David McVeigh and Derek McCracken, all promising young players who would later experience senior cricket. The following year, under coach Jimmy Boucher and captain Norman Beck, they defeated Drumaness in the semi-final thanks to a brilliant 76 from Miller O'Prey and

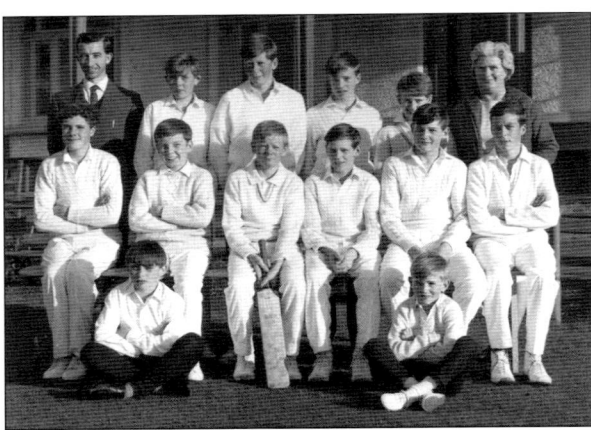

1966 BOYS' XI: BACK – J BOUCHER (COACH),
T MCMILLAN, G CROSBY, W MCCONVILLE,
G DEMPSTER, MRS CAMPBELL. FRONT – D MCVEIGH,
D MCCRACKEN, N BECK, W CAMPBELL, J CAMPBELL,
M O'PREY. GROUND – A MCKENZIE, K CAMPBELL

1966 GRAHAM CUP PARTY

a supporting 27 from Wesley Campbell. David McVeigh's six for 21 ensured a final place. But was the Graham Cup, a trophy that had not been won by North Down since its inauguration, coming to The Green at last?

The final against Donacloney was bitterly disappointing, as the side crumbled to 54 all out against the pace of mighty Michael Lumb, an aggressive bowler who would cause plenty of problems for many senior cricketers in later years. His seven for 22 destroyed our batting, despite some spirited resistance from Wesley Campbell and Derek McCracken. It would take another 29 years for the club to achieve that unique Graham Cup victory.

As the 1960s drew to a close the 1st XI was denied a league title in a decider at home to Collegians. The Collegians total of 129 looked vulnerable, Des Sterritt scoring 84 of the runs, but Ernie Rea's seven for 37 ruined the party. Nevertheless, 1968 had been a good season, runners-up in the league and Challenge Cup semi-finalists, but the real bonus was that, in the reshuffle of the leagues, North Down was placed in a new 12-team Senior League 2.

The 'Sixties' Challenge Cup runs were limited to 1963 and 1968, both admirable in that North Down was playing Qualifying League cricket. In the preliminary round in 1963 St Mary's fell victim to the spin and accuracy of Willie Dempster and Walter Wishart, Warwick Dalzell having posted 61, but North Down were sensationally disqualified as Dempster was deemed a 'professional' for his full time work on the ground. With North Down subsequently reinstated to the first round proper, Jackie McBurney's century in a 234 total against Cregagh still needed eight wickets from Dempster and Wishart to ensure a 27 runs victory. Harry Blair, who tragically lost his life during the 'Troubles' of the Seventies, batted down the order for the visitors but his brilliant 87 wasn't good enough on the day. Sparkling cricket was not on show at Shane Park in June when North Down scored 156 off 97 overs in the second round. Patience was not evident in the reply as Dempster's six for 37 showed. So, despite losing league games every week, North Down surprisingly had a

1967 AWARD WINNERS: BACK – I SHIELDS (1ST XI BATTING CUP), S WILSON (3RD XI BATTING CUP). FRONT – W DEMPSTER (1ST XI BOWLING CUP), MRS J BARRY, J BOUCHER (3RD & 4TH XI BOWLING CUP).

semi-final place against Muckamore at Wallace Park. Wishart's four for 16 and Jack Dalzell's four for 23 reduced the opposition to a meagre 83 all out and a shock was on the cards. But hopes of a first final in 24 years were dashed by Jimmy Reid's five for 15 in 20 overs and the dream disappeared in a dramatic eight runs defeat.

The batting order in that semi final was: - Malcolm Campbell, Billy Artt, Jackie McBurney, Warwick Dalzell, Walter Wishart, Rev. Hamilton Leckey, Willie Dempster, Artie Coey, Rev. Paddy Craig, Jack Dalzell and wicketkeeper Bert Jordan.

Only five of the 1963 team remained for the 1968 semi final. New and younger players had made their mark and wins against YMCA, Instonians and Muckamore set up a semi-final with Waringstown, the giants of Ulster cricket, at The Green.

On this occasion North Down had an ace up their sleeve in a confident Regent House schoolboy, George Norris, who hailed from the Ballystockart area. George threatened to lower the Waringstown 'colours' with his confidence and self-belief, in much the same way as his fiery left-arm bowling and big hitting had already accounted for some Qualifying League sides but, although he scored a defiant 34, it was clear that George and North Down weren't ready for the big stage yet. Adrian Thompson and Ian Shields made valuable contributions in the cup run, and the 'Sixties' ended with a lot more promise than they had begun with signs that, perhaps, better days lay ahead.

THE DUNDONALD LEAGUE

In the days when the highs of the 1930s had long gone and the struggle to keep afloat was real, with falling membership and few trophies in the cabinet, a new adventure for the enthusiasts was born. Great fun was had in the late 1950s when teams like Ballydrain, Ballystockart, Cherryhill and Millmount played in the summer evenings for sheer enjoyment. These teams featured players who had played at the highest level, those who had never been affiliated to any club and much younger ones who later went on to greater things under the NCU umbrella, when they left the precarious cowpat dappled fields to play at Ards, Shorts or The Green. They mostly featured enthusiastic players who did not aspire to any dizzy heights, or elder statesmen who had played their part in the good times, but all brought a great charisma to the game. Charlie Wilson, Orr Morrow, James Caughey, Ray Gibson and David Shannon epitomised these keen cricketers, from all walks of life, willing to devote their evenings to clearing a field and organising a game. The league was not short of 'characters' like the eccentric Francie McLaughlin who, with Caribbean demeanour and running commentary, bowled his flighted leg-spin. His 'trial' at North Down didn't run the full term!

When Ballydrain won the league the team was feted in the British Legion Hall in Dundonald where they were presented with commemorative ties. James B Caughey, an enthusiast and headmaster of Ballydrain Primary School, led the side, with Billy Shields, Raymond Crosby, Gerry Spence, Willie Watt, John Shields, and Miller O'Prey as the experienced cricketers in the ranks. Raymond McIlveen and wicketkeeper Bert Jordan were joined by youngsters Wilmer McKibbin, Don Shields, Sammy Alexander, Ronnie McBurney and Ian Shields who learned the game playing beside their illustrious seniors.

North Down's scorer for many years, John Patton, had close connections with the Ballystockart team and had many tales to tell of the intriguing personalities who did battle in the fields around the countryside in the summer evenings.

After the construction of Moat Park, all games were switched to Dundonald, although facing quickies like North Down's erratic Ronnie McBurney or Jack Dalzell at this venue was a frightening experience.

THE HOCKEY CONNECTION

The close relationship between the cricket and hockey clubs continued during the war and after it, with many members playing both codes. The hockey club celebrated its 50th birthday with barely a whimper in 1946. Its fortunes had obviously taken a knock during the war years, as there was no return to the halcyon years of the 1930s. But they were still in good shape and when Raymond Crosby returned from Scotland in 1947 both clubs benefited. Raymond was the star hockey player of the era and cricketers Walter Fawcett, Willie Dempster, Walter Wishart, Neville Petts, and Bobby Rowan joined him in the hockey 1st XI. Down the teams were Roy Maxwell, Davy O'Prey, Wally Boyce, William Shields, Jack Maxwell and many others, as these were years when players from both clubs mixed their sports comfortably. In the 1950s Wallace Boyce played for Ulster and JLO 'Jack' Andrews became president, a role he also held with the cricket club for many years.

In 1957 the hockey club celebrated its Jubilee as the cricket club celebrated its Centenary, and guest of honour was Mr. Willie in his guise of NCU chairman, cricket club chairman, and strong supporter of the hockey club.

In truth, both clubs were celebrating 60 years of sporting friendship and camaraderie.

WALTER WISHART

The name of Walter Wishart first appeared in North Down scorebooks as long ago as the mid-Forties and was still around in the mid-Eighties. Rarely was it seen outside the 1st XI until he stepped down voluntarily in 1979 to captain the 2nd XI. It speaks volumes for both the ability and the loyalty of a player who has given a lifetime to our club and won the respect of visiting teams for almost 40 years.

In the Forties, Fifties and early Sixties the fortunes of North Down were at a low ebb. Playing strengths were far removed from the halcyon pre-war days and the facilities were far removed from those of today. Players like Raymond Crosby, Willie Dempster, Bobby Todd and Walter Wishart emerged to carry the club through this difficult period, and much is owed to them. It was one of Walter's hallmarks that he was up for any challenge, fortified by a seemingly endless stamina. He was one of those athletes who was naturally fit and he became a mainstay in both hockey and cricket post-war teams at The Green. Walter performed long and arduous bowling heroics that became characteristic of his playing career. He was the most economic of bowlers both in terms of runs conceded and the energy he exerted. Like a true thoroughbred he was tailor-made to stay the distance, so it was a bitter blow in 1953 when he departed to Kenya and later to Uganda to work at the construction of diesel powered stations at the massive Owen Falls Dam. Thankfully, he returned in 1956.

In his early career Walter was an opening batsman, but he later developed into a bowler of even greater ability. He always made the best use of a helpful wicket but perhaps his biggest asset was his ability to set a field that he could bowl to. He had few equals when it came

WALTER WISHART

to the placement of his fielders, as the Milford batsmen could testify on one very special occasion when Walter took seven wickets for only nine runs.

Although quiet and unassuming, Walter was far from casual. He was a fierce competitor on the field, and he gave no quarter nor expected any. He hid his feelings well but when the situation demanded he wasn't afraid to air his views. He did a good job when captain of the 2nd XI and skilfully managed the capabilities of a young side. He was over 50 when he made his last appearance against Waringstown II and the North Down victory was a fitting tribute from his fellow players. His 'retirement' at the end of the 1980 season was recognized at the Club's Annual Dinner when Ian Shields delivered a glowing tribute and Jack Newel, the president of the NCU, made a presentation on behalf of the Club. It should have marked a well-earned finale to a long playing career, but Walter was always a sucker for another game and over the next few years he was occasionally throwing over the arm for the 1st XI. On 9th September, 1984 against Lisburn he took his last senior wicket, a catch from Graham Benson sending the great Dermott Monteith back to the pavilion. It was a treasured wicket to remove the Ireland captain and a poignant moment for Dermott who was injured in an accident that winter and never played senior cricket again. Walter had finally gone out on a high after an amazing 40 years playing senior cricket.

But, as so often happens when one door closes another door opens, and while Walter Wishart could have been excused for stepping into the background this was not the case.

Walter then launched himself into a second North Down 'career' and over the next 20 years he donned many roles including groundsman, bar convener, and club president.

In 2007, by his own admission, the legs have all but seized, but given the passage of time they have carried this doughty little fighter through adversity and we expect to see him around The Green for many years to come.

JIM BARRY

Born before the Great War, Jim Barry's life spanned over 90 years during which he served North Down manfully for over 70 of them. He donned many roles not least as club chairman from 1966 to 1979 during the challenging transition years. He followed in the footsteps of Willie Andrews and James MacDonald as a committed administrator with both club and union, although at times he could be brusque and abrasive. But behind his stoic exterior was a heart of gold and, like a good wine, Jim mellowed in later years and became a much loved and highly respected member. He played at every level for the club from boys to 1st XI, but his best years as a cricketer were as the 2nd XI wicketkeeper where he was never afraid to sound off when returns from the outfield failed to match his expectations. The younger members affectionately nicknamed him "Wasim Bari" after the legendary Pakistan test star, but typically Jim took it all in his stride. He was a tireless worker within the club during the tough post-war era and also joined his life-long friend George Orr of YMCA to serve on the NCU Junior Committee. He was chairman of that committee in 1975 when it was amalgamated with the senior committee and then served for almost 20 years as a divisional chairman. He was also an Ulster Town selector for many years.

Like his mentor, Mr Willie, he was a staunch North Down man within the union and never afraid to wear both hats if the situation demanded. He turned down the presidency of the NCU several times but was later deservedly awarded an Honorary Life Membership in recognition of his long service.

Jim's official positions within the club included the presidency and, in later years, patron, but he never forgot his roots and was just as happy marking the wicket or serving tea from the huge teapot with his white apron around his waist. His wife Sally was totally supportive within the Ladies Committee and a willing chauffeur picking him up when "meetings" in the clubhouse lasted longer than expected!

He umpired for some time and was a popular

JIM BARRY

President of the Northern Ireland Association of Cricket Umpires and Scorers (NIACUS), for over 20 years. He always ensured every umpire was well treated at The Green and loved nothing better than to enjoy a few drams with them after the match. In a similar vein he was a member of the North Down "Thursday Club" of Eddie Doherty, Sammy Haire and himself, who, after working diligently on the ground, appeared to sort out all the problems in the North Down world over a few tots in the bar!

If Jim was a modest cricketer then the same could not be said for his hockey prowess. He played in the best ever North Down hockey teams of the Thirties,

> *The Committee agreed that as Mr Andrews had always been accustomed to having his own dressing room the store room in the new pavilion be set aside for his use.*
>
> FROM THE MINUTES

teams that won the Ulster Senior League, Kirk Cup and contested the Irish Senior Cup final. He was also a hockey umpire and in 1978 became president of the Ulster Branch.

In the twilight of life, Jim and George Orr travelled together to many North Down games home and away, and they were engaging conversationalists to anyone walking the boundary. He revelled in North Down's success in the modern era and as club President took immense pride in the club's achievements at every level. One of our last photographs of him was in the middle of the 1st XI champagne celebrations after the 2003 Challenge Cup final victory over Waringstown. He loved every minute of it.

We didn't know at the time but it was to be his last North Down celebration, as he declined in health during the winter and, although he put up a brave fight, he passed away.

Jim "Wasim Bari" was a gentleman at heart and gave trojan service to North Down.

A WHOLE NEW WORLD

At the end of the 1969 season it was 30 years since North Down had contested a Challenge Cup final and the fortunes of the club during that period were far removed from the golden years of the 1930s. The war years decimated the club in so many ways, and while many of the 'old hands' did their best to keep the club afloat, the mantle was handed down to a different generation in the 1950s and 1960s.

The Swinging Sixties were a whole new world and for North Down it marked the end of another era when, on 22nd December, 1966, Mr. Willie Andrews passed to a greater calling. His life was a magnificent innings full of so many cameos and riddled with so many eccentricities. North Down would never be the same again and, as Jim Barry took over the challenging role of chairman, he knew that change was already in the air.

North Down hadn't got their act totally together at the end of 1969 but there were many positive things happening at The Green and a new generation was coming into the club that would eventually lay the foundations of better things to come.

The club was on the way up again.

CHAPTER 8
1969 – 1979 : THE ROLLER COASTER YEARS

"WHEN I THOUGHT OF ALL THE LEGENDS CENTRED AROUND THE OLD NORTH DOWN OF WILLIE ANDREWS' DAY, THE FAMOUS CHARACTERS IN THE SIDE, ITS VIRTUAL MONOPOLY OF LEAGUE AND CUP, I WONDERED WHAT THE MODERN NORTH DOWN HAD TO PUT ON THE SCALES. I SENSED SOME SORT OF AWAKENING AFTER A LONG FRETFUL SLEEP AND OLD TIMERS LIKE JIM BARRY WERE DETERMINED THAT THE REJUVENATION WOULD CONTINUE."

ERNIE McCLEARY, SUNDAY NEWS 1974

COMBER IN 1969

Would you believe that the North Down Rural District Council recommended NO WAITING on either side of Castle Street and High Street and more than a generation later we're still waiting?

The constant improvements to our roads and housing conditions kept the planners busy and the introduction of the new Strangford Ferry was a welcome boost to the tourism industry and to the locals who had to make regular crossings from Portaferry.

Major JD Chichester Clarke visited Newtownards at a time when 110 'B' Specials resigned and Private Robert Smyth, an 18 year-old member of the 3rd Battalion of the UDR, received a military funeral after he had been murdered near Castlewellan.

Noel Orr took over as headmaster at Regent House with 'cricket coach' part of his CV but, like his predecessor James Macdonald, the chances of finding time to actually coach cricket were very limited.

The 2nd Comber Girls 'Brigade celebrated with a 21st birthday party and celebrations extended to the sporting community, as the Rifle Club undertook a major building programme and, with continued success, took six first places in the Ulster Rifle Association's Open Full Bore Rifle meeting at Ballykinler.

Ards Football Club held the might of Roma to a scoreless draw at the Oval and then beat Distillery in the Irish Cup final, with all four goals coming from Greyabbey's Billy McAvoy, a Cliftonville Cricket Club supporter in later years.

Ards Rugby Club won the Towns' Cup and was soon to celebrate the opening of Hamilton Park with a new clubhouse and three new pitches, while North Down Hockey Club climbed back into senior hockey after topping the Qualifying League.

The Annual Sportsman's Service was held in St Mary's Parish Church with Michael Crooks, one of North of Ireland's finest cricketers, a special guest and at which the Rector Hamilton Leckey spoke of the sad loss of James Macdonald.

Comber played its part in the 'Ulster 71' Festival; the hockey club played a President's XI, a junior table tennis championship took place and Comber Rec. played Glentoran in one of a number of football features. There was also a round the houses pram race and an Army Cadet display. The culmination to a busy week was a youth parade and service in the Andrews Memorial Hall.

The Spinning Mill continued to be the town's

1970 1st XI: Back – W Dempster, G Dempster, G Norris, W Wilson, W Wishart, R Thompson.
Front – P Gilliland, W Artt, M Campbell, I Shields.

major employer, but it was a tough industry and many people commuted to Belfast and Newtownards for work. Comber was a busy little town but it had retained much of its village character. However, all that was about to change in the 1970s when the Troubles were at their worst and more and more people fled the city for a quieter environment.

ULSTER IN THE SEVENTIES

The carefree Sixties gave way to a more sinister movement in Ulster when republican supporters infiltrated peaceful Civil Rights marches and within a few years Belfast, Londonderry, Newry and Dungannon were known worldwide for some of the more barbarous acts of inhumanity imaginable. Normal everyday life was changed for the next 30 years and when the army came in to support the beleaguered police force, the civil atrocities got worse not better.

The Ulster economy suffered badly and the social life of the province was almost brought to a standstill, as no one travelled after dark unless with good cause.

In the midst of this unparalleled violence, some sporting moments united a divided community and when Mary Peters won the pentathlon gold medal in the 1972 Munich Olympics everyone celebrated a true sporting hero. But it was a rare glimpse of hope and, just as quickly, it was back to violence the day after.

Direct rule from Westminster was inevitable but the cricket spin-off was a series of cricketing Secretaries of State at Stormont in Willie Whitelaw, Tom King and Nicholas Scott.

The decent people of Ulster got on with their lives despite the conflict and sport set a shining example in its resilience and never-say-die attitude to the terrorists. Every sport suffered, and sadly many sportsmen and women lost their lives in senseless killings and bombings, but life went on because everyone believed it would end.

Unfortunately, nobody knew it would take another three decades and more than 4,000 people would lose their lives on the way.

CRICKET IN THE TROUBLES

Cricket suffered badly during the Troubles. Visiting teams from 'across the water' stopped coming and games were called off when travelling to potentially hazardous areas. The whole culture of cricket changed and the much-enjoyed after-match analysis in the bar, so much a part of the enjoyment of the game, no longer happened, as teams wanted to make the homeward journey in daylight.

Club pavilions and grounds were regularly vandalised, bombed or burnt out and innocent individuals assaulted or, in the case of several of our cricketers, killed while in the course of their daily work.

The administrators of Irish cricket, and particularly those in the NCU and North West, dealt with many sensitive issues and did it with understanding and compassion. Despite the security issues the interprovincial Guinness Cup fixtures were fulfilled and the Combined Services played Ireland at Beechgrove in 1970, the last of the big matches in Londonderry during the Seventies.

Scotland played at Ormeau in 1970 but it would be eight more years before Ireland would play in Belfast.

The administrators switched the NCU and North West cup finals to more country venues at Downpatrick and Eglinton after arson and bombing attacks at Ormeau and Beechgrove.

1973 Winning Captains with Chairman Jim Barry: A Maginnis (Midweek XI), I Shields (1st XI), J Galway (2nd XI), D Steen (3rd XI).

During this time Queen's University, Post Office, Lurgan, Portadown, Sion Mills, City of Derry, Brigade, Cliftonville and Instonians suffered greatly when the Troubles escalated and the Belfast Cricket League, a long-standing institution catering for many small and enthusiastic Belfast clubs, folded in 1972 after 70 years in existence.

Unique amongst clubs was the Royal Ulster Constabulary, the RUC, which amazingly survived through the dark days of the Seventies.

Many cricketers and their families were caught up in the Troubles but, thankfully, North Down, due principally to its rural location, remained free from the worst of the civil unrest.

In the midst of this civil mayhem the NCU settled a 50 year-old dispute between the seniors and the juniors and amalgamated both committees in 1975. Our own Jim Barry was the last chairman of the Junior Committee and then became a divisional chairman for many years after the restructure.

Waringstown was the club of the period winning eight of the 11 Senior Challenge Cup finals and the same number of Senior League titles, sharing the league twice in 1970 and 1971.

UPS AND DOWNS AT THE GREEN

The Sixties ended on a sad note with the deaths of James Macdonald and Gerry Spence, but there was hope on the horizon as many younger members joined the club during the Seventies and North Down started to come alive.

Jim Barry was a 'no frills' straightforward chairman who led a vibrant committee with plenty of experience. It included Raymond Crosby, Willie Dempster, Robert Rowan and JLO Andrews as club trustees, Willie Watt, a former 1st XI captain, Robert Foley and James Burgess represented the supporters and business interests, while Billy Artt, Jimmy Boucher, Adrian Thompson, Sydney Elliott, Roy Thompson, Wesley Graham and Alan Reid were experienced cricketers sprinkled throughout the teams. Youth had its representation through Hammie Mills and Ian Shields, while the Reverend Hamilton Leckey was the quiet, counselling voice of reason when required!

Roy Thompson's crucial period as secretary, from the mid-sixties to 1973, saw the club begin to blossom. He was actively involved in promoting the club at every level and played for both the first and second elevens as a batsman and wicketkeeper. He was a natural motivator and brought enthusiasm and energy to his various roles, encouraging and supporting the hard work being carried out with the boys' teams and bringing teams like the Pedagogues to Comber for midweek cricket.

The treasurer in the early roller coaster years was the versatile Adrian Thompson, a high order 1st XI batsman, a useful medium pace bowler and a capable stand-in wicketkeeper, before Raymond Crosby took over the treasurer duties in 1972.

North Down 1st XI had done enough in 1968 by finishing second to return to senior cricket, albeit Senior League Two the following year and for the first time in a decade there was real optimism at The Green.

Despite a preliminary round exit from the Challenge Cup in 1969, to Cliftonville by 61 runs, morale was good with the enthusiastic and capable Billy Artt as captain. Billy had the experienced Walter Wishart and Willie Dempster to call on plus the youth of George Norris and Adrian Thompson in the bowling department. A fine all round sportsman in his own right he was a dashing motivating skipper who led by example, scoring plenty of runs. His opening partner

1ST XI LEAGUE CHAMPIONS 1973: BACK — R CROSBY (TRUSTEE), G DEMPSTER, A THOMPSON, L HUNTER, M O'PREY, D ARTT, J MCDONOUGH, J PATTON (SCORER). FRONT — M CAMPBELL, D SHIELDS, I SHIELDS (CAPT), J BARRY (CHAIRMAN), W WISHART, W ARTT, W MONTGOMERY.

was the dependable Malcolm Campbell and the promise of Paul Gilliland and Ian Shields gave grounds for great optimism.

Paul, cousin of John Gilliland, was a fine player with pure natural ability whose short stay at the club in the early Seventies produced some spectacular innings, including a polished 71 against Donacloney and a great century against Muckamore.

Unbeknown at the time, a decade of triumphs and disasters lay ahead, but the club officials handled challenging situations on and off the field with tact and surety that only experience brings.

The club had three elevens and a midweek side and had a growing membership that raised hopes of a 4th XI. But the burning desire throughout the membership was to return to the premier senior league and, as the years passed, there was a growing realisation that something or someone, was missing to enable the club to complete that transition.

Section Two was competitive and to get back into the top tier it had to be successfully negotiated. Teams like Ballymena, Bangor and Donacloney had quality players and it was a dogfight to determine who would lift the trophy at the end of each season.

1970 was a good example of how tight Senior Two was, as North Down and local rivals Bangor finished joint top, leading to a play-off at Stormont to decide the outcome. North Down considered itself unlucky to be in this situation, as in August they played Bangor at The Green, dismissed them for 55 and were thwarted in their attempt to finish the game by a teatime drizzle. The doughty Conn McCall and his team refused to leave the dressing room until the drizzle ceased. It didn't.

Unfortunately skipper Billy Artt missed the play off, holidaying in Majorca, and the team could not

1ST XI LEAGUE CHAMPIONS 1979: BACK – J PATTON (SCORER), B PATTON, K CAMPBELL, B JOHNSTON, L HUNTER, D ARTT, E DOHERTY (CHAIRMAN). FRONT – I SHIELDS, R HAIRE, J GALWAY, S ELLIOTT (CAPT), J BARRY (PRESIDENT), G DEMPSTER, J McMILLAN, G MOWAT.

reach the 132 Bangor total, losing by 29 runs with Brian King taking six for 31. Walter Montgomery, who had joined from Ards, was a bright light in an otherwise ordinary team effort, but his four for 36 was not enough to stave off defeat.

The talented Lawrence Hunter, who had played his cricket at Dunmurry and Lisburn, was a great acquisition in 1971. He missed the early games that season but from then until the end of the decade he was our best bowler by a long way.

Otherwise it was a determined and relatively unchanged North Down 1st XI that stuttered into the 1971 season against the unfancied YMCA at The Green. Batting first the top scorer, in a poor total of 52, was Walter Montgomery with ten! But this was to be Walter's day as he then took six for 16 in 17 overs, overshadowing his great slow bowling team mate Willie Dempster, who took three for seven.

2ND XI LEAGUE CHAMPIONS 1973: BACK – R McVeigh, J McMillan, W McKibbin, W Wilson, D McVeigh, J Boucher, S Elliott, D Kirk. FRONT – D McCracken, P Artt, J Galway (Capt), J Barry (Chairman), J Armstrong, W Montgomery.

CHAPTER 8 : 1969 – 1979 : THE ROLLER COASTER YEARS

3RD XI LEAGUE CHAMPIONS 1973: BACK – D KIRK, P ALLEN, W GRAHAM, J CAMPBELL, W CAMPBELL, A MAGINNIS, J BOUCHER, R MCVEIGH. FRONT – J MCKITTRICK, H KYLE, D STEEN (CAPT), E DEARDEN, W BARKER, T RITCHIE.

YMCA were all out for 43 and this unlikely victory began a run of wins that culminated in a 100% record with the defeat of Armagh in September.

Promotion and time for another celebration!

But the 1972 season saw the team struggle in the big league, and it was a big league in every way consisting of 16 teams. Wins against Downpatrick, Donacloney, RUC and Laurelvale gave the team 13th place.

In another NCU reshuffle in 1973 the league was split into three sections, with North Down in Section 2 and our team was amongst the pacemakers for most of the season. The crucial tie was against nearest rivals Donacloney at The Green on 25th August and what a thriller it turned out to be. Batting first, the home side were decimated by an outstanding bowling performance from Michael Lumb who took eight wickets for 32 runs to leave North Down 77 all out with only Geoffrey Dempster and Lawrence Hunter scoring in the twenties.

Donacloney had scored 33 before they lost their first wicket and then Hunter and Wishart took control with four for 23 and four for 19 respectively. The figures tell only part of the story, as the game was interspersed with good and dropped catches, run outs and near misses, and panic batting aplenty. The unsung hero was Walter Montgomery who, although taking no wickets, bowled five overs for three runs at the crucial stage, enabling a dramatic one run win that guaranteed promotion.

The 1st XI was a well-balanced side. Lawrence Hunter, Walter Wishart, Miller O'Prey, Adrian Thompson, Ronnie Elliott and Don Shields were augmented in the bowling by Walter Montgomery with his left-arm spinners. Denis Artt had moved from Collegians to The Green and was arguably the best wicketkeeper in the country at this time. His brilliance behind the stumps enhanced all the bowlers' performances and he was a useful contributor with the bat although the bulk of the runs came from Malcolm Campbell, Billy Artt, Ian Shields and Geoffrey Dempster.

From the relative obscurity of Loopvale in the Belfast Cricket League, Billy Dale had gone to Civil Service but in 1974 he came to The Green thus beginning a long and distinguished cricketing career that saw him play through the not so good times, to later win senior league and cup honours.

It was still a struggle in the premier league although a sixth position retained premier status. However, that was to change in the most dramatic of fashions in 1975 when Woodvale's Ken Kirkpatrick pulled Lawrence Hunter's last ball past a well-patrolled boundary, to send North Down back into Section Two. It was a bitter pill to swallow and highlighted our plight of being too good for Section Two but not good enough to stay in Section One. We all knew something was missing but didn't know what!

Nomination for Club Bore of the Year award: Prolific previous winner wee Ivan picked up his usual bag of votes for his unlimited ramblings of nonsense, intrigue, mystery and balls, but this year's recipient surpassed him by far in terms of the quality of his boredom, drunk or sober!
FROM 'THE BOWLER', 1979

Another change of captaincy saw Hunter faced with the same highs and lows that Billy Artt and Ian Shields had had to deal with in previous years. A disappointing third place behind Ballymena and Instonians in 1976 was followed by another title in 1977, losing only two of the 14 fixtures.

At Laurelvale in June, a young left arm bowler took two for 21 in his four overs and began a career that would be difficult to match in the annals of the club. Robin Haire's emergence was certainly one of the reasons why Hunter felt that the side was ready to compete and remain in the top league.

The first three games in 1978 set the tone. Walter Wishart's six for 42 was matched by Simon Corlett's six for 49 at Ormeau and North Down lost by 16 runs. At the Lawn, Waringstown were 68 for six chasing 109 when the rain intervened and in another nail-biter at Comber the following Saturday, Woodvale won off the penultimate ball. With only one victory against RUC to show for a lot of effort, another bitter relegation pill was swallowed at the end of the season.

At that time the club was experiencing a great surge in popularity, mostly built around a strong social scene centred on the clubhouse. The committee had new faces and new ideas and these were starting to bring success down the club. In a short time they were to have a profound influence on the 1st XI.

The astute Sydney Elliott accepted the leadership in 1979 in another bid to win promotion, but diplomatic activities behind the scenes were already taking place amongst some of the club's administrators who realised that some new initiative was needed to give the team a competitive edge and end the up and down culture that had plagued the club for most of the Seventies.

Elliott's team won the league with another 100% performance, but on the negative side was Ken Campbell's departure to golf and fast bowler Brian Johnston's departure to new pastures. Both served the club well and deserved their winners' medals.

It was a new era and new names were becoming established. They included John Gilliland, Clarence Hiles, Jimmy Galway, Garson Mowat, Stephen Barry, Peter Orr, Jack McMillan and Sammy Wilson.

Shades of things to come and maybe better days ahead?

MORE AGONY THAN ECSTASY IN THE SENIOR CUP

There were more Challenge cup games in the Seventies than any other decade since the war, but the RUC gave us a first round exit in 1970, Comber man Richard Barker causing the damage with five for 18.

Bangor did the same the following year with six wickets to spare and Donacloney successfully chased 184 at the Factory Ground in 1972 to compound the agony.

The team travelled to draughty Mossley in 1973 to play nomads Cliftonville, the outcome being another last ball boundary defeat and further despondency.

It wasn't until 1974 that some progress was finally made in the Challenge Cup and the old bogey was put to bed.

A total of 160 was good enough against Bangor, Walter Wishart and Derek McCracken the key men, but Lurgan's Alan Johnston put paid to any hopes of further progress when he took eight for 21 in a comfortable second round win.

A lengthy cup run seemed years away but in 1975 the team set aside poor league form and played some really good cup cricket. A great eight wickets win at Lurgan Park, chasing 152 courtesy of Billy Dale's four for 25 and Malcolm Campbell's unbeaten 88, was followed by a Ken Campbell-inspired 32 runs win against the strong Downpatrick side at the Meadow. A semi-final tie at home to Civil Service was the reward and high hopes of a possible cup final place in early August.

On a glorious day at The Green, North Down's first six batsmen contributed to a 245 total and Brian Johnston, Ken Campbell and Walter Montgomery shared the wickets to secure a 100 runs semi-final victory.

It was a monumental milestone for a club that had lived in the shadow of its great past and finally there was an opportunity for the 1st XI to savour the unique cup final atmosphere and perhaps acquire a taste for more. For the first time in 34 years North Down would contest a Challenge Cup final but, sadly, it turned out to be a huge disappointment. Unlike North Down,

Waringstown had won senior league titles and Challenge cups regularly since 1970 and were hot favourites to win again.

On a blistering hot Friday at Ormeau, Waringstown scored 192 for four including a measured century from Jim Harrison and North Down replied with a paltry 56, Bertie McGill taking four for 28.

As a contest the game was over, but Lawrence Hunter's four for 40 and Jimmy Galway's three for 21 were fine bowling performances in Waringstown's 130 for nine in the second innings, which was matched by North Down's 135 for 6 when Denis Artt hit a defiant 66 runs.

Perhaps the cup final appearance rekindled the old competitive cup spirit, because there was another good cup run in 1976 with away victories against RUC, Woodvale and Cregagh setting up a semi-final clash with Waringstown at Comber.

North Down's batting let the team down on their big day and the 110 total was never going to be good enough to test the best batting line-up in Irish club cricket and we deservedly lost by four wickets.

A year later the visit to Lurgan Park saw defeat defending 213 runs, an impressive total courtesy of a Don Shields' 76 and Geoffrey Dempster with 56.

Wins over RUC and Muckamore in 1978 set up another semi-final opportunity against Waringstown at The Green but, after so many cup defeats at the hands of the Villagers, there was a severe psychological barrier to overcome. Defending only 143 runs a defeat was almost inevitable, and 'Snow' Harrison survived a caught behind and went on to score 78 not out to win the game, much to the chagrin of the locals.

The decade finished with another cup defeat at Waringstown but it was the first round win against Saintfield at the Demesne that produced one of the most exciting games of the season.

David Napier, later to captain North of Ireland to Challenge Cup success, and later still to play at The Green, hit a typical swashbuckling unbeaten 83 in the Saintfield total of 153 with Lawrence Hunter and Clarence Hiles taking four wickets apiece. Was it enough?

The Saintfield 'critics' on the bank certainly thought so when North Down slumped to 64 for six and one of our batsmen had packed his bag and headed home. The game looked lost, but Hiles, who had been caught off a 'no ball' in his vital 37 runs innings, won support from Robin Haire, Stephen Barry and Hunter. But Jimmy Galway and Hunter still had to scramble 15 runs from 16 balls to pull off an unlikely victory.

Two hours later, in Comber, our bemused opening batsman Adrian Thompson learned that the team had won in his 'absence'.

It was all part of a new spirit emerging at the club and although we didn't know it at the time, the decade ended with a scent of a Challenge Cup success that was carried into the Eighties by Sydney Elliott's team.

DOWN THE CLUB

The top field was turned into a cricket ground almost exclusively by Willie Dempster over a long period as groundsman. It was perfect for junior cricket and from 1971 it provided a wonderful asset to the club. It wasn't long after it was opened that a 4th XI was formed and used it along with the thirds and the midweek teams.

The pinnacle of success down the club occurred in 1973 when, along with the 1st XI winning Section Two, the seconds, thirds and midweek teams each won their respective leagues. Remarkably, of the 52 league

CELEBRATION AT THE NORTH DOWN ANNUAL DINNER

FRANCES MCVEIGH, MAVIS CROSBY, RAYMOND CROSBY, SAMMY HAIRE AND MARGARET HAIRE ENJOY THE EVENING

games played, only four were lost throughout the club.

In 1969 the 2nd XI lost to Ards in the Junior Cup with the rugby score of 47 to 28 and had mixed fortunes in their league programme, winning four of the 12 games played.

Sam Wilson and Jack Bennett were the principal run makers, but the strong-room of the team lay with Wesley Graham, Hammie Mills and popular captain, off-spinner Willie Wilson. Indeed has there ever been a more popular captain at the club?

The following year they were edged out of the Junior Cup by Downpatrick after Roy Thompson and Wesley Campbell had scored thirties in a 137 total. Walter Montgomery and Sydney Elliott between them took seven wickets for 26 runs but the side lost by one wicket. The 2nd XI team that day, in batting order was: James Campbell, Geoffrey Dempster, David McVeigh, Sydney Elliott, Roy Thompson, Wesley Campbell, Walter Montgomery, Rodney Kerr, Wesley Graham, Tudor Hopkins and Willie Wilson.

The 2nd XI had no fewer than eight captains during the seventies and compounded their misery in 1979 with relegation.

John Craig, Wesley Graham, Norman McLeod and Derek Steen captained the 3rd XI throughout the Seventies with varying fortunes, ably supported by Robert McVeigh and David Kirk who loyally scored and umpired. These two great club stalwarts gave sterling service down the club and many aspiring young members found Davy and Robert their first mentors at The Green. Their names are deservedly perpetuated on trophies awarded at the annual dinner.

The thirds beat North of Ireland in the Minor Cup when John Craig and Peter Artt bowled out the opposition for 108 and Derek Steen replied with 31 opening the batting. Peter Artt, Charlie Richardson and Derek McCracken all contributed, but Robin Mitchell, noted more for his hockey exploits and making a rare appearance at the crease, made a crucial 15 not out and with Roy Beck saw the team home to a memorable win.

In 1974 the thirds won the Section 3B league with the following formidable squad: Derek Steen, Jack McMillan, David McVeigh, Trevor McMillan, Ivan Dempster, Jimmy McKittrick, Clarence Hiles, Jimmy Boucher, Wesley Graham, Alvin Maginnis, Billy Allen, Colin Campbell, Paul McIlfatrick, Eric Dearden, Peter Allen and James Campbell.

The club had worked hard at establishing a strong 3rd XI and, as the decade ended, they could boast a well-established middle of the league placing, although their one run defeat in the Minor Cup against North of Ireland was very disappointing. Much of the credit should go to Derek Steen and Alvin Maginnis who did much to foster a strong social aspect, and in the process cajole players into the ranks who may otherwise have drifted away from the club. David McVeigh, James Campbell, Wesley Campbell and Hammie Mills scored most of the runs while the bowling honours usually lay with John Craig, James Boucher and Wesley Campbell.

Harry Morrow, Harry Kyle and Jimmy McKittrick captained the 4th XI during the seventies. There were many unsung heroes at this level and plenty of exciting

CHAPTER 8 : 1969 – 1979 : THE ROLLER COASTER YEARS

performances to record, with runs coming in great numbers from the bats of Raymond 'Jumadeen' McIlveen, Ivan Dempster and Jack McMillan. At Musgrave Park, against Holywood III, the inimitable Billy Allen senior scored an unbeaten 76 and then watched his son David take nine for 44 to secure a memorable 'family' win. David was a prolific wicket-taker at this level, ably supported by two great characters in Peter Allen and Jimmy McKittrick. The team on that memorable family outing was: Jimmy McKittrick, Raymond McIlveen, Billy Allen Snr., David Allen, Ivan Dempster, Hammie Coulter, J Graham, A McMorran, Stephen Gibson, Chris Thompsett and Stephen Potter. Against Collegians III the effervescent Will Barker took a hat trick and reversed a losing situation to win by three runs.

In 1971 North Down entered a team into the NCU Belfast and District Midweek League. The format was 20 overs a side with batsmen retiring on reaching 30 runs. This form of cricket was not only to prove successful for the club but was enjoyable to play and created a wonderful social aspect to the working week. Midweek captains like Derek Steen and Alvin Maginnis built the backbone of the club in the Seventies and laid the foundations for its strong social base in the years that followed. For many years selection was by 'invitation' and the midweek teams provided platforms for some players to go as high as the 1st XI.

The first year saw a team captained by Derek Steen beat a strong Academy XI in a league play-off final. The next four years saw the Midweek XI win this league again under captains Alvin Maginess, David McVeigh and the McMillan brothers, Trevor and Jack.

Stories of after-match hospitality are part of midweek cricket folklore and some great nights were had at Shane Park or the I.C.I. Social Club. These were the darkest years of the Troubles with little night entertainment in Belfast and it is a sobering thought to remember that one night the North Down team arrived to play Instonians only to see the Shane Park clubhouse had been demolished by an IRA bomb an hour earlier. Relations between the two clubs have remained strong from those years and occasional social evenings between North Down and Instonians players from that midweek era are still held.

Every era has its characters but there was something special about the characters down the club in those years. Derek Steen, a former Leinster schools' opening bowler, was a fiery captain of the 3rd XI, but an endearing socialite in the clubhouse. He was an inspirational leader and a fine chairman who did much to get North Down back to the top of Ulster cricket.

Alvin Maginnis was an excellent motivator who knew his players better than they knew themselves; at least that's what he kept telling them. Affectionately nicknamed 'Shockinbowler' by his colleagues, he was a deep thinker of the game, well informed and a very capable medium pace bowler at 2nd XI standard. As arguably one of the worst number eleven batsmen the club has produced, he nevertheless knew what the

AWARDS EVENING: WALTER WISHART, SYDNEY ELLIOTT, IAN SHIELDS, JIMMY GALWAY, JIMMY BOUCHER, EDDIE DOHERTY, JIM BARRY AND GUEST DERMOTT MONTEITH.

requirements were with the bat and when the unfortunate Harry Kyle was struggling to hit the ball off the 'square', Alvin 'invited' him to retire and give someone else a chance! After his playing days were over, Alvin continued as a valued member within the NCU umpires' panel.

Midweek cricket was competitive and great fun and all 10 matches were won in 1973 and the final play-off for the trophy against BRAFP was won in great style when Jimmy Boucher, Clarence Hiles and captain Maginnis took the wickets and the 81 runs total was chased down with David McVeigh, Peter Artt, Derek Steen all contributing and big Wes Campbell finishing it off in some style.

There were major contributions during the season from North Down's dual sportsmen, the Ards rugby stalwarts Wesley and James Campbell, and Will Barker while Jack McMillan and David McVeigh were a prolific opening partnership and Derek Steen, Clarence Hiles and big Wes scored the bulk of the runs. Maginness, Barker, Peter Allen and Jimmy McKittrick took the wickets with the reliable Norman McLeod as wicketkeeper.

All these personalities were suited to the cavalier approach of the shortened game and there is no doubt that the comradeship generated by these games spread through the club and made it a much stronger social scene.

THE 'SIXES'

This was the era when North Down played a lot of six-a-side cricket and regularly entered winning teams for the prestigious Ballymena and RUC competitions. Cricket attributes weren't always the main criteria for selection, as availability over two evenings and an insatiable appetite for socialising post-event were prime requirements. The ability to hit the ball a long way, bowl straight and field keenly was a bonus.

Denis Artt captained Derek McCracken, Billy Dale, Clarence Hiles, Jimmy Galway and Miller O'Prey to victory in the RUC Jack Newell Shield in 1975. The following year, having reached the semi-finals at Ballymena, Miller O'Prey captained the side that won at Newforge again, with Adrian Thompson, Ian Shields and Wesley Graham joining the retained Hiles and Galway. Adrian Thompson scored 82 runs in his three innings, rated the best effort since its inauguration in 1969.

In 1978 Clarence Hiles captained the side to yet another RUC title but missed out at Ballymena, going down by one run to the RUC in the semi-final.

North Down won the Ballymena title the following year, Clarence Hiles, as captain, picking up a cheque for £150 and Miller O'Prey winning the bat provided by the sponsors for the outstanding performance of the tournament. Denis Artt, Lawrence Hunter, Robin Haire and Ian Shields made up the side that celebrated at Eaton Park into the 'wee small hours'…and then made off to Scotland on tour with the proceeds, much to the disgust of 'Wasim Bari!'

Success in the national Sixes competitions generated a lot of interest at the club so it was inevitable that a similar competition should be introduced at The Green. Harp Lager provided the sponsorship and

ANNUAL NORTH DOWN 'SIXES': R McIlveen, S Barry, W Wilson, M O'Prey, R Thompson, J Galway, H Kyle, I Shields, J Boomer, W Artt, L Hunter, J Armstrong

RUC 1975 'SIXES' WINNERS: BACK – D MCCRACKEN, W DALE, C HILES, R CROSBY. FRONT – M O'PREY, D ARTT, J GALWAY.

Sydney Elliott's team won the inaugural North Down Sixes final in 1974, an event organised to coincide with the opening of the new club bar and annually thereafter the 'Sixes' provided great fun for the eight sides involved.

Walter Montgomery's team won the following year courtesy of two boundaries by Hammie Coulter off the last two balls of the match and, after the early exit by the 'hockey' team in 1977, 'Hunter's Hoods' won in the dark. These twilight finals became part of the culture of the early competitions and ensured a packed clubhouse for the presentation of the trophies and the ensuing bragging rights over a few pints.

'Artt's Antiques', 'Syd's Sextet', 'Donald's Ducks', and 'The Whizz Kids' were half of the 1978 line-up, a competition sponsored by local entrepreneur Ivan Adair and the Ards Borough Council, and providing another success for captain Syd Elliott.

By the end of the era David McVeigh, Wesley Graham and Syd had established reputations as 'Sixes' winners.

This tremendously successful competition was synonymous with the name of our regular sponsors, Harp Lager, and for that association we thanked Derek Stanbridge, the local executive, who took a keen interest in the event and made himself available each year to present the awards at the end of the tournament.

THE HOCKEY CLUB

The Seventies saw a significant change in the culture of the cricket club and, in particular, a decline in the number of dual members.

The hockey 1st XI had returned to senior hockey in 1968 after winning Qualifying League 'B' with Raymond McIlveen, George Harper and Stanley Glover the only cricketers of note. A few years later it was a distinguished international cricketer that kept the side in the senior league with his goal against Bangor in the last league game of the season. Unfortunately Simon Corlett played his cricket at North of Ireland!

Floodlighting was established at The Green to enable the hockey players to train, but it proved damaging to the ground and the sessions came to an end. The drive to unite the two clubs socially continued and the refurbishment of the pavilion and the licence to sell alcohol meant that the hockey players could use the premises for after-match relaxation and refreshment to the benefit of the cricket coffers.

To comply with legislation all senior members of the hockey club became associate members of the cricket club and, in so doing, the two sports returned to the original set-up of 1896 when the cricketers established the hockey club.

But the new structure didn't improve relations between the two clubs and with so many 'outsiders' in the hockey ranks, there was no tradition or loyalty to fall back on when the problems got worse. Members of both clubs worked voluntarily behind the bar and

HARP LAGER REPRESENTATIVE DEREK STANBRIDGE AND NORTH DOWN CHAIRMAN DEREK STEEN

the cricket club, in exchange for the help, covered certain hockey expenses, but it was a strained agreement that was full of cracks.

On the playing front Ian Shields and Jimmy Galway scored vital goals at Newry for the 2nd XI as they came back three times to win 4-3 and John Craig, a long time bowler, captained the hockey 3rd XI.

One of North Down's best post-war cricketers was left-arm slow bowler RM 'Bobby' Todd, and while he denied himself the chance to play regular senior cricket, this was not so with his hockey career. Bobby played for several years with Cliftonville at the highest level and when he returned to Comber, captained the 2nd XI to the league win that took the side into Junior League 1 for the first time.

Long time hockey club member and barman at the club Robert Johnston, captained his 3rd XI to a Mulholland Shield win. The side included Jimmy Galway, Denis Artt, Stanley Glover, John Craig, Jack McMillan and David McVeigh and had as travelling umpire Robert McVeigh, as enthusiastic and helpful about hockey as he was about cricket.

Towards the end of the Seventies, improvements in the pavilion and on the grass pitch indicated that co-operation could be mutually beneficial between both sporting interests and an uneasy peace was carried into the Eighties.

CLUB TOURS

The great touring years had long disappeared, so it wasn't customary for the club to tour regularly during the Seventies. The tours that actually took place amounted to no more than a pre-season trip to play in Dublin. However, in 1974 that all changed and, reminiscent of the annual tours of the Twenties, a touring party of 13 members flew from Aldergrove for a three-match tour to Lancashire. Ian Shields captained the squad made up of an almost full compliment of 1st XI players.

The first match against Kirkham Prison was rained off, but on Sunday the game against Springfield resulted in an emphatic 78 runs win for the visitors. Ian Shields, Lawrence Hunter and Geoffrey Dempster scored the bulk of the runs with Don Shields, Billy Dale and Lawrence Hunter taking three wickets each.

A confident South Shore side put North Down in to bat in Blackpool the following day and an equally confident Miller O'Prey made them suffer with a belligerent 82, supported by Don Shields with 64.

Billy Dale, Don Shields, Miller O'Prey, Jimmy Galway, Wes Campbell and Peter Allen took the wickets in the 51 runs win.

The lack of Ulster-style hospitality from the hosts meant for nothing, as North Down's off the field activities more than compensated.

Scotland was the destination for another tour in 1979 with three fixtures planned by tour organiser Denis Artt. Club chairman Eddie Doherty chaperoned the group captained by Ian Shields and the first fixture was played in Glasgow against Kelvin Academicals. It was a strange game, as thereafter most of the party suffered from serious hangovers and didn't give of their best. This condition was largely due to Denis Artt's maiden century and, in particular, the celebration that he orchestrated in the clubhouse on an evening most will never forget, certainly not Denis!

At 17 for four the visitors were in danger of total embarrassment but Artt, in partnership with Ian Shields took the score to 236 and a 107 runs victory ensued.

Denis set the tone for the celebrations by removing the huge rack of cigars from behind the bar as his initial gesture of merrymaking but the copious glasses of the potent 'Black-outs' buried our star wicketkeeper for three days!

Amongst some interesting items returned to The Green were a pick and shovel and a stump to commemorate the 'ton'.

At the Dunlop CC village ground, outside Kilmarnock, the home side succumbed to five wickets from Clarence Hiles while Jimmy Galway played a star role as an opening bat with a memorable 74 against Glasgow Academicals in a seven run victory. Noted in that win was a running catch at deep midwicket by Davy Donaldson, who picked up his nickname 'Goffer' for services rendered in the Railway Hotel in Ayr. Davy was a great tourist and travelled on many occasions with the firsts and was called into the field on several occasions, sometimes to the bowler's cost!

Played three, won three, and plenty of stories still untold!

Not everyone was happy with the tour, clashing as it did with an important league game against Cregagh and when a telephone call was made to The Green to enquire about the result, the unfortunate caller found a belligerent Jim Barry at the other end of the line. He told the caller that North Down had won easily, that they didn't need to come home, and hung up!

LAWRENCE HUNTER

After his marriage to Maureen in 1971, Lawrence Hunter moved to live in Comber and joined North Down from Lisburn. He was to make a huge impact at the club during the Seventies. At the time, the big strapping pace bowler had already established a

LAWRENCE HUNTER

reputation as one of the best bowlers in the country and was also a rugby international. In many ways he followed in the footsteps of his older brother Raymond who had made the same short journey from Dunmurry to Wallace Park and became an instant hit. Big Ray went on to win both cricket and rugby international honours and Lawrence came painfully close. Many cricket followers deemed him very unlucky not to have won a place in the Ireland cricket team, having been the bowling reserve on several occasions. It would have been a fitting reward as Lawrence was an exceptional sportsman and if rugby was his first love then cricket came a very close second. He was the mainstay of the Ulster Country and Ulster Town interprovincial teams for almost a decade and a prolific wicket-taker who conceded few runs. He was tailor-made for the limited overs game and in tandem with the aggressive wicket-keeping of Denis Artt, they were a fearsome combination.

Lawrence played in four Challenge Cup and one Junior Cup final, but lost on each occasion! However, his eight for 76 in the 1966 final against Downpatrick is one of the all-time great cup bowling records and if senior cup success eluded him, then he had the satisfaction of being a senior league winner on several occasions in Lisburn's fine team of the Sixties. His last cup final appearance was against Waringstown for North Down in the 1975 final and although by that time some of the speed had disappeared from his game, he tactfully sacrificed it for accuracy. There were few better bowlers around for line and length, and when swing bowling and Artt were added to his armoury then big Lawrence was a formidable bowler against any opposition. In the days when there were no limitations on the number of overs a bowler could bowl, he could effectively tie up one end, and in 1980 when North Down recruited Michael Reith from Waringstown, it appeared that they had the 'dream' attack for limited overs cricket. Alas it was not to be, and although Lawrence took a full part in the secret negotiations with Reith, he was struck down with illness at the start of the season and they never had the opportunity to bowl together at North Down. Unfortunately Lawrence never played again and it was a travesty for such a fine athlete to end his sporting career on such a negative.

Lawrence Hunter was the epitome of sportsmanship in both his favourite sporting codes. He was an inspirational captain, 100% committed to the cause and as gracious in defeat as in victory. He played a full part in North Down's development on and off the field during the Seventies and served the club well as both captain and committee member. He was a role model to the younger players and if his North Down career was short on quantity it was blessed with quality. That's the legacy he left at The Green.

IAN SHIELDS

Sons of Billy and nephews of Jackie, Ian and Don Shields were born with a North Down cricket and hockey pedigree second to none. It was a mantle they bore with great pride and a credit to them that in 2007 they continued to serve the club with such distinction. Ian's son Peter has followed in father's footsteps and it seems likely the Shields dynasty will be preserved for many years to come.

Although he successfully played tennis in his teens, Ian Shields had a natural ability at cricket that was nurtured at Regent House School under the watchful eye of the legendary James Macdonald and at The Green under the even more watchful eye of Willie Andrews. Both played significant roles in the development of Ian's cricket career and his evolvement into the 1st XI in the mid-Sixties was almost seamless and predictable, given the reputation he had built as a solid if cautious opening batsman.

Ian's greatest cricket attribute was his ability to build an innings, an ability built around a solid technique and total focus. He had great powers of

IAN SHIELDS

concentration, perhaps better suited to the longer game, but those that felt his game was often pedestrian usually overlooked the free-flowing broad bat that was much in evidence when he switched to fast mode later in the innings. In truth, Ian's cautious approach to opening was more a reflection of the times in which he played, and his team's requirements, as there were fewer better strikers of the ball when he was on a run chase. Not surprisingly this was highlighted in his performances in Sixes competitions.

Ian played in the North Down teams of the challenging Sixties and Seventies but like all great club players his career had longevity that brought much more satisfaction and success in the twilight of his career.

He was an ideal 1st XI captain because of his dedication and commitment to the team and he carried the club through some tough years. He was a prolific runs accumulator, his name a standing order on the 1st XI batting rose bowl, an award that he has won more than any other batsman since 1857. He played for both Ulster Country and Ulster Town interprovincial teams and in another era, when batting was not as strong at the highest level, he would surely have won full international honours. He was the prize wicket for opponents but rarely gave his wicket cheaply, and if he practised religiously it was just another facet of his dedication and focus. Off the field he was a 100% committed club member and in just under five decades he has served the club in a wide variety of roles that embraced President, team captain, fund-raiser, PRO, team manager, coach, groundsman, archivist, historian, and, in more recent times, the tireless webmaster of the North Down website. He has meticulously preserved club records and memorabilia, and when it came to writing this history there was none better equipped to do the job. His passion and commitment to the task are strikingly similar to the way he opens an innings!

By his own admission Ian's most rewarding cricket experiences were playing with the great Raman Lamba. In many ways he was the perfect foil, the team player that fully understood his part and played the supporting role to its fullest for the overall benefit of the team. At the height of their prowess they were probably the best opening partnership in local cricket.

Ian's status as a player and as a sportsman stretches far beyond The Green and there are few more popular cricket personalities in the Province. He was elected vice-president of the Northern Cricket Union in 2005, but other commitments prevented him from accepting the presidency, an accolade that surely sits in waiting. If and when that happens, it will be a fitting honour and one richly deserved.

No appreciation of Ian Shields would be complete without mention of his family, all of whom made huge contributions to his development as a cricketer and a sportsman. The legacy left by his dad and uncle Jackie, the support and encouragement from a proud mum, the endless 'back yard' matches with sister Christine and brother Don, the fulfilment provided from seeing Kevin and Peter evolve, and finally the long-suffering Brenda who has given him the love and support to follow his passion.

In any North Down Roll of Honour Ian Shields would be one of the first names on the list. *(JCH)*

A PHOENIX RISES

The 1970s was a great era for the club because our teams started winning again and there was a great buzz in the clubhouse built around a strong social culture that had developed from the junior teams. Ironically, the Troubles was the catalyst that made the club bar such a social focal point, as teams stopped staying behind on away games and retuned immediately to The Green. This built a wonderful club spirit that was enhanced by a visionary committee that encouraged the organization of a wide variety of social events.

The playing success down the club fired the ambition further up the club and the determination to regain full senior status on a more permanent and competitive basis gathered momentum during the winter of 1979 when several of North Down's senior administrators hatched a plot that would change the face of Ulster cricket forever.

The Seventies at North Down were characterised by relegation and promotion peaks and troughs for the 1st XI, but entering the Eighties in the premier section the club was not only determined to stay at the top, it was about to guarantee that status in a way nobody could have envisaged. The good times were just around the corner.

Roll in the eighties.

CHAPTER 9
1980 – 1997 : BACK IN THE BIG TIME

"WE ARE DELIGHTED TO BE ABLE TO ANNOUNCE CONTINUED SPONSORSHIP OF THE NORTH DOWN CRICKET CLUB. WE RECOGNISE THE PROMINENT POSITION IN THE GAME THAT THE CLUB HABITUALLY OCCUPIES BOTH ON AND OFF THE FIELD OF PLAY. WE ARE ALSO VERY HAPPY THAT NORTH DOWN WILL AGAIN WIDEN THE SPHERE OF CRICKET BY ORGANISING THE EVER-POPULAR 'SIXES' COMPETITION AND WISH THEM ALL THE BEST IN THEIR EFFORTS. WE ALSO WISH ALL THE TEAMS IN THE CLUB SUCCESS IN THEIR RESPECTIVE LEAGUE AND CUP COMPETITIONS IN THE SEASON AHEAD."

MICHAEL COOKE, HARP LAGER MARKETING DIRECTOR 1985

COMBER IN 1980

In 1980 Comber was a growing town and the population had risen to 6,500 boosted by the migration of people from the city seeking a better life away from the main centres of civil disturbance. New housing to accommodate the rising population had stretched the town boundaries and lands that had been earmarked for development within the Ards Area Plan had largely been used up restricting further growth.

Two popular Comber landmarks had disappeared, both deemed to be as a result of acts of vandalism. The first was officially sanctioned by local government but many local people were disgusted when the old Irish Oak tree that had stood for hundreds of years in front of the Andrews 'Old House' in Castle Street was cut down to, supposedly, facilitate progress.

Much less organised but just as devastating was the destruction of the famous old 'Piggery' just behind The Green. Built at the grand cost of £1,750 in 1863 as a grain store, it was later used in the manufacture of rice starch and during the Second World War as billeting quarters for American troops. After the war it was taken over by two Indian Army colonels and used as a piggery. When that enterprise ended it was used to store a variety of goods. The vast six-storey building was an impressive example of Industrial Revolution architecture and for over 115 years it had been an integral part of the club's heritage and just as important as a landmark as Scrabo Tower in the distance. Vandals callously burned it down and in the midst of the heavy black smoke that clouded the town for several hours, went a bevy of cricketers' stories, mostly relating to tales or otherwise of the gable wall having been hit by powerful shots. It would certainly have taken a powerful strike but, true or false, the stories were all part of North Down cricket folklore, sadly gone forever.

Ulster struggled economically in the Eighties as over a decade of violence and civil unrest took its toll. Unemployment rose as factories closed all over the province.

Comber's culture had also changed and while most of the old stock remained, many new families were being absorbed into the community and gone were the days when everybody knew everybody in the town. The village culture had gone and Comber was now a dormitory town servicing Belfast and Newtownards.

CRICKET IN THE NCU

Sport was a breath of fresh air throughout the Troubles and both the NCU and the ICU ensured cricket was well administered and had a vision for the future. North/South relations were improving and they were significantly strengthened by the introduction of the Irish Senior Cup, a new competition embracing clubs from all the provinces. Some northern clubs were initially tentative, as indeed were some southern clubs when drawn away to the Londonderry or Belfast 'hot-spots', but the competition survived and in time it became the main goal of all senior clubs to win it.

The new competition was in keeping with the development of the one-day game, one of the much debated issues of the times, but not as controversial as the influx of professional cricketers into the Ulster scene.

Club professionals were nothing new as Lisburn, North of Ireland, North Down and others had employed overseas cricketers, usually English, from very early times, and indeed North Down's first recorded 'pro' was Arthur Clay in 1884. The 'pros' were not allowed to play in some competitions over the years and there was also a stigma attached to their status, almost a class issue with some people. North Down could relate to the issue as late as 1963 when they were thrown out of the Senior Challenge Cup for allegedly playing Willie Dempster who was a part-time groundsman at the time receiving token remuneration for his services. As reported by Peter McMullan, the excellent cricket correspondent of the Belfast Telegraph:

"The sensational announcement was made last night by the senior emergency committee that North Down has been disqualified from the Senior Cup."

The decision was later reversed but the undercurrent remained and Ulster cricket was polarised between those who supported and those who opposed professionals. This contentious debate was coloured by other issues, not least the emergence of a new generation of more affluent cricket clubs blossoming on the back of lucrative clubhouse bar takings, and with committee members who had little time for traditions and the status quo of Ulster cricket. They were ambitious, visionary and had clear goals, and at the top of their priority list was a craving for success. In their path stood Waringstown, the kings of local cricket whose domination had reduced everyone else to also-ran status for virtually 15 years.

But was all that about to change?

THE MICHAEL REITH AFFAIR

The shock news in 1980 that North Down had signed Michael Reith, the Waringstown and Ireland international all rounder, was greeted with amazement in local cricketing circles. Michael was Waringstown born and bred, the team's opening batsman and

CHAPTER 9 : 1980 – 1997 : BACK IN THE BIG TIME

CLARENCE HILES AND MICHAEL REITH

bowler in an era when the Villagers dominated club cricket and had the strongest team in Ireland. He was also a highly respected player with a proven pedigree and extremely popular at the Lawn. He was the complete cricketer. A deep-thinking strategist and highly motivated leader, he was an attacking batsman of great talent and a medium-pace swing bowler who conceded few runs and could bowl long spells. He had vast experience and in cricketing terms he had done it all; numerous Challenge Cup and league wins, interprovincial honours with both Ulster Country and Ulster Town and 44 caps for Ireland since his debut at Sion Mills against the West Indies in that famous victory in 1969.

He was no stranger to the professional debate as the Lawn was the strongest bastion of the amateur code in Ulster cricket and, of course, he had first-hand experience of it when Lisburn's new professional John Solanky and then Woodvale's mercurial Indian spinner Uday Joshi challenged Waringstown's supremacy.

It was therefore unthinkable that he would move, let alone join the professional ranks.

During the winter of 1979 some members of the North Down committee hatched a plan to hire a local professional and for many reasons Michael Reith topped the list. In due course an approach was made and when he responded positively a series of secret meetings took place to complete the details.

The announcement of Reith's appointment as club coach sent shockwaves throughout local cricket but it was a classic coup made for the right reasons and in the best interests of North Down Cricket Club. It was also another huge stepping stone in getting the club back to the top of NCU cricket and if critics could only see short-term 'damage' to the amateur code, the visionaries at The Green were miles ahead in their enterprise and ambition.

In his three years with the club Michael Reith was the model professional and made a huge impact with both the playing members and the supporters. He rarely missed a practice and he not only coached the younger members, he took time to work with established players to improve their skills and their focus. He was a great motivator and he instilled a Waringstown will-to-win that brought the club its first Challenge Cup success in 45 years. He mixed well socially and became a great favourite with the members, but above all he delivered, both as a coach and as a player, and history has shown that he was the catalyst that sparked North Down's return to the big time. He led by example, and when it was time to return to Waringstown he handed over the captaincy to Robin Haire, a player he had tutored with great care and commitment.

Michael Reith showed a lot of courage and resolve to make the move to Comber and he will always have a special place in our history, not just as a cricketer but also as a person. He was a true sportsman and a gentleman in every way.

NCU CENTENARY CELEBRATIONS

The Northern Cricket Union (1986) and the North West Cricket Union (1988) celebrated their centenaries in the Eighties, as did Donemana, Woodvale, Drummond and CIYMS, while Lisburn, the second oldest club in Ireland, celebrated its sesquicentenary in style in 1986. Their Patron's XI in their special celebratory match included the great Ian Botham, Graham Roope and North Down's Asjit Jayaprakasham, each giving a memorable batting display and enthralling one of the largest crowds ever seen at Wallace Park.

The NCU administrators did a tremendous job in their centenary year celebration organizing a number of special games across the province and inviting many leading cricketing personalities to participate.

Ireland played a star-studded Indian side captained by Ravi Shastri and the North Down 'pro' Raman Lamba opened the batting for India with Kris Srikkanth at Ormeau.

North Down welcomed Bermuda to the Green to play an NCU President's XI that featured Robin Haire, while Ian Shields played at the Mall for an Armagh Invitation XI that included Desmond Haynes, Mudassar Nazar and Rahul Mankad. In the President's XI was Asjit Jayaprakasham.

The NCU also produced a special Centenary Brochure with North Down's Sam Turner on the front page and there was plenty of coverage of the club in the text plus two feature articles on Willie Andrews and James Macdonald. Clarence Hiles and Jim Barry were heavily involved in the organizing committees within the union throughout the year.

The culmination of the season's celebrations off the field included a special centenary church service

SAMMY HAIRE, JIM BARRY & EDDIE DOHERTY

at St Anne's Cathedral where the preacher was former North Down all-rounder Canon Hamilton Leckey, and in October 1986 a Grand Centenary Dinner at the Europa Hotel.

CRICKET AT THE GREEN

Throughout this period there were no less than four chairmen, Eddie Doherty until 1981, Derek Steen up to 1987, Sydney Elliott through to 1992 and then Billy Crawford.

The secretary throughout most of this time was Terry Ritchie from 1982 until 1993, preceded by Sydney Elliott and followed by Gordon Scott up to 1997. Terry mixed his secretarial duties with useful cricketing contributions on virtually every North Down team and, after a long lay off, resumed playing in our sesquicentenary year with great benefit to the 3rd XI.

Wilmer McKibbin was treasurer from the mid-Seventies except for one season when Trevor McMillan balanced the books. 'Kibbie', who had done an excellent job, finally passed the accounts to Tom Mills in 1994.

For a time during this era Eddie Doherty, Jim Barry and Sammy Haire met in the pavilion every Thursday to discuss the internal affairs of the club and enjoy their favourite 'tipple' and they became affectionately known as the Thursday Club. Each with his own skill and experience did tremendous work for North Down. Sammy, a non cricketer himself, knew everything there was to know about groundsmanship and even today is consulted from time to time on the best approach to preparing wickets. Our Club Patron, he has held the office of president and was wise counsel in the committee for many years.

Towards the end of the era, in January 1995, an initial application was made to the Lottery Sports Fund and with a lot of dedicated work from chairman Billy Crawford and secretary Gordon Scott, the plans were drawn up for a pavilion extension. On the 15th August, 1996 a North Down Select XI played The Free Forresters to mark the official opening performed by Don Allen, chairman of the Sports Council for Northern Ireland and attended by Robert Gibson, the Mayor of Ards, councillor Tom Benson, Michael Rea, the president of the ICU, and Comber resident John Law, the NCU president. The new addition to the clubhouse made North Down's facilities amongst the best of any club in Ireland.

On the playing side, the 1st XI under Sydney Elliott's captaincy finished mid-table in 1980 with Ian Shields finishing fourth in the NCU batting averages and Clarence Hiles sixth in the bowling averages with

IRISH SENIOR CUP WINNERS 1989: BACK – E DOHERTY (PRES), S HAIRE, JD GAMBLE, W ADAMS, J GILLILAND, G BENSON, J PATTON, S ELLIOTT (CHAIR). FRONT: G MOWAT, R HAIRE, R LAMBA, M QUINN, I CARSER (CAPT), I SHIELDS, W DOHERTY, I CONNOLLY.

IAN CARSER WITH IRISH SENIOR CUP 1989

42 wickets. Clarence had taken on the difficult role of replacing the unavailable Lawrence Hunter.

Under Michael Reith's captaincy in 1981 and 1982 the side retained its senior status, but only just, finishing eighth and tenth. However, this was still progress compared to the Seventies. Robin Haire's XI fared no better with ninth and seventh league placings in 1983 and 1984, but after Raman Lamba arrived at Comber to replace Javed Mohammed as the professional, all the anxieties regarding relegation disappeared overnight. The brilliant Indian inspired youngsters and veterans alike, and became an integral part of the North Down scene for more than a decade.

On his first visit to the Lawn, Lamba hit a sparkling century in an exciting seven runs win, and according to Michael Reith it was one of the best centuries ever seen there.

Despite his huge contribution, the senior league title was never won during Raman's time although the team was 'knocking on the door' most seasons and attained the runners-up spot in 1987, 1991 and 1994. Captains Robin Haire and Ian Carser may not have registered any league championships, but they had great success with Irish Senior Cup wins in 1989, 1993 and 1995.

The Irish Senior Cup had become the premier club competition in Irish cricket, a barometer to measure the club's progress and return to the big time. North Down has one of the best records in this competition and from 1982 until 1997 they played 49 games, winning 36 and losing only 13.

There were cup final wins in 1989 against Donemana, in 1993 against Brigade and in 1995 against Bready and losing final appearances in 1985 to Downpatrick, and in 1988 to Lurgan.

There were many exciting games, none more dramatic than the one-run win at The Green against Bready. Chasing 228 runs for victory, Alan Rutherford, Bready's aggressive international wicketkeeper, needed two runs to win off the last ball when Charlie McCrum bowled him. It was a dramatic finish but there were many other moments in that match to savour. Gavin Rodgers, with an accurate boundary throw, ran out Sam McConnell at a crucial stage and Ian Carser, David Moreland, Robin Haire and Michael Quinn all held vital catches as the Bready batsmen attempted to hit the ball out of the ground. Paul McCrum was awarded the Man-of-the-Match from Sir Everton Weekes for a fine century and two wickets.

There was no less excitement in North Down's first Schweppes-sponsored Irish Senior Cup game played at the Holm in 1982. At 22 for three, Donemana rallied to 112 without losing a further wicket but when the rain poured down there was no other option but to have a 'bowl out'.

With the scores level at two strikes each, Michael Reith missed and Roy McBrine sent the local supporters home happy with a last ball win. It was a miserable feeling that, fortunately, North Down suffered only once more, in 1991, when Lisburn won a second round tie 4–3. But in the meantime we won a few on the way.

The North Down tour to Barbados clashed with the Irish Cup semi-final match against Lurgan in 1984 although there was an opportunity for Lurgan to play on another date. However, no rearrangement was offered and the remnants of a North Down 1st XI were soundly thrashed at Pollock Park.

TENSE FINISH TO IRISH CUP FINAL: GRAHAM BENSON AND ROBIN HAIRE RUSH TO CONGRATULATE MICHAEL QUINN, SUPPORTED BY LEONARD COEY AS VICTORY IS SECURED.

Barbados Touring Squad 1984: Back – I Connolly, M O'Prey, R Nield, P Artt, W Campbell, M Rodgers, R Moreland, J Galway, T Ritchie, J McCall, N Beck.
Front – D Artt, J Gilliland, J Barry (President), R Haire (Captain), D Steen (Chairman), C Hiles, S Haire.

Senior & Junior Cup Winners 1981: Back – D Shields, G Dempster, I Dempster, W Dale, J Armstrong, G Mowat, S Barry, J McCall. Middle – W Dempster, R Crosby, J Gilliland, S Elliott, R Glover, J Hiles, A Donaldson, J Wilson, T Ritchie, E Doherty (Chair), J Patton. Front – J Galway, D Artt, T McMillan, M Reith, J Barry (Pres), J McMillan, I Shields, R Haire, C Hiles.

The 'bowl out' against Fox Lodge was welcomed in the first round at Ballymagorry in 1986 and when big fast bowler Kevin Copeland scattered the stumps off a splashing full run up, the visitors came away with a 4-3 win courtesy of Garson Mowat, Ken Boucher and the ever reliable John Gilliland.

Two years later on a wet day that wiped out six Irish Senior Cup second round games, North Down returned from Castle Avenue with a 2-0 win over Clontarf and proceeded to the final.

Old Belvedere looked beaten at The Green in the 1986 second round game, when chasing 117 they found themselves 89 for nine. However, Asjit Jayaprakasham's Man-of-the-Match award for 29 runs and four for 11, was scant compensation as the tied match resulted in a countback of wickets lost and a North Down defeat.

The preliminary round tie against Waterford in 1987 was exceptional. The visitors arrived with seven players and were supplemented by four volunteers from North Down. For the record, Dessie Savage, Raymond Moreland, Colin McCaughey and Colin Montgomery played for Waterford.

Their excellence in the field, especially Savage, the wicketkeeper, resulted in a mediocre North Down total of 129 runs. It was then game on. However, at 51 for seven and with only the 'North Down Four' to bat, Waterford sportingly conceded the tie.

Reith's arrival in 1980 allowed North Down to take advantage of a kind Challenge Cup draw and victories over Laurelvale, Dunmurry and Holywood took the side to Downpatrick and a final against high-flying North of Ireland.

For the first time in a cup final Reith failed with the bat and shades of the disastrous 1975 final returned,

Robin Haire

Irish Senior Cup Winners 1995: Back – G Rodgers, J Gilliland, J Montgomery, W Crawford (Chair), D Moreland, A Semple, I Carser, A Macrory. Front – S Haire (Pres), P Moore, M Quinn, R Haire (Capt), C McCrum, P McCrum, J Patton (Scorer).

when Gilliland and Corlett reduced the side to 35 for four, but Robin Haire and Geoffrey Dempster repaired the damage to give North Down, the underdogs, a first innings total of 107.

Reith, Haire and Hiles didn't make things easy for the Ormeau Road team and they totalled only 158, a good lead but certainly not 'out of sight.'

Despite another unusual Reith failure with the bat, North Down's second innings score of 172 was much better, Geoffrey Dempster hitting 48, Denis Artt 41 not out and Don Shields 37, but it was not enough as North's South African 'pro' Kevin Skjoldhammer's 74 not out was the difference between the sides.

A year later the team faced a difficult second round tie with Lisburn, resulting in a thrilling and surprising win, defending a modest 153. Michael Reith's five for 35 more than made up for his 'duck' and such was Denis Artt's enthusiasm behind the wicket that square leg umpire Murray Power, controversially 'no balled' him five times for encroaching in front of the stumps. With tension mounting Artt stumped Lisburn's key player Dermott Monteith off Clarence Hiles' bowling, only to be 'no balled' yet again, and the pendulum swung in favour of the home side and all looked lost. Amazingly, Artt then legitimately stumped Monteith off a well-flighted Robin Haire delivery and Lisburn never recovered. North Down booked a quarter-final place against Lurgan at Pollock Park where Robin Haire's fine six for 12 and Don Shields' equally fine 57 not out were good enough to secure a semi-final place against old adversaries Donacloney.

The game was played in front of a good crowd basking in the sun at the picturesque Factory Ground and while the 'dress rehearsal' two weeks earlier had been a close encounter, it was not half as exciting as the semi-final turned out to be. In a brave attempt to reach their first senior cup final, Donacloney dismissed North Down for a modest 153 and were 88 for 1 before they started to drop wickets at regular intervals. It all came down to six runs needed with their last pair at the wicket, and when Robin Haire dropped a simple catch he still had the presence of mind to quickly react when he saw both Donacloney batsmen, John Quigley and George Martin, panic-stricken in the middle. Robin returned the ball over the stumps for a run out and North Down was back into the cup final. What a match!

The jubilation in the North Down dressing room was enhanced further when the players learned that the 2nd XI had beaten North of Ireland in the Junior Cup semi-final at The Green.

The 1981 Senior Challenge Cup final against Ballymena needed three days before it was resolved and Ballymena required 148 runs to win with all their wickets intact and 49 overs at their disposal on day three. Yajurvindra Singh and Wilfie Ridge took the score to 83 without too much trouble and Ballymena looked set for victory. They had been slow, and when the first wickets fell the panic set in, and after three run outs and brilliant bowling from the North Down captain, Michael Reith, Ballymena collapsed and finished 38 runs short of their target.

The victory saw Reith at his best, the master

He listened in awe to countless stories and tales some true, most not, about North Down's greatest piece of folklore, the infamous Dodger (Willie Andrews). After sitting in on numerous sessions the frustrated starlet of the modern generation unleashed this astonishing statement at Bangor — "Who is this bloody Dodger anyway?"

THE 'FLY ON THE WALL', ACE REPORTER FOR 'THE BOWLER', QUOTING ROBIN HAIRE

tactician who tightened the screw at the right time and piled the pressure on the batsmen, and the ace bowler that conceded few runs. He was ably supported by Robin Haire and Billy Dale, but his dominance was highlighted by the fact that he bowled a marathon 58.4 overs and took 12 wickets for 103 runs. Winning the coveted Man-of-the-Match award was a formality.

The tension built as the, so far, unique end to the first innings saw both teams on the same 149 total. The poor weather didn't ease the nerves, as the game was continued into the following Monday. The North Down second innings score of 165 featured another John Gilliland '50,' but this match was won in the field on the last day when Reith reigned supreme.

The Senior Challenge Cup returned to The Green after a 45-year absence and the icing on the cake was provided by Jack McMillan's 2nd XI winning the Junior Cup and a rare double, only the fourth time since 1887.

But the historic Senior cup win didn't ignite further successes in the Eighties and, sadly, from 1981 to 1991 cup performances were poor with only two semi-final appearances in 1984 and 1990.

However, 1991 produced something very special. Victories over Instonians, Cregagh and Ballymena, with a big contribution from the New Zealander Michael Clarke, led to a semi-final against North of Ireland at Comber, and when the home side slumped to 165 for 7 chasing 241, it looked a lost cause. Big hitting Michael Quinn had other ideas and he delivered a blistering 39 before he was bowled. Twenty runs were required from 11 deliveries and Miller O'Prey and Robin Haire scrambled 14 from eight balls. With six required Haire didn't score off the fourth and fifth balls and needed to hit a six of the last ball to win the game. It required 'One shot more for the honour of Down' and what a shot it was! A flat bat straight six that split mid-on and mid-off and sent the crowd into a state of wild celebration.

BILLY ADAMS

CHARLIE MCCRUM

The dramatic win set up one of the greatest finals of the modern era, a match that was dubbed the 'professionals final' by the anti-pro lobby because of the performances of professionals Michael Clarke and Woodvale's Akram Raza.

The Meadow at Downpatrick was bathed in sunshine for both days of this historic final. Raza hit 146, the highest individual score in a limited overs final, more than matching New Zealander Clarke's 111. Charlie McCrum scored 60s in both innings and John

SENIOR CHALLENGE CUP WINNERS 1991: BACK — E DOHERTY, J BARRY, I CARSER, M O'PREY, P MOORE, W ADAMS, I SHIELDS, J GILLILAND, S HAIRE, J PATTON. FRONT — M QUINN, M CLARKE, C MCCRUM, R HAIRE (CAPT), L SEMPLE, RJ MONTGOMERY.

Gilliland made two valuable batting contributions, but the game was swinging Woodvale's way until Billy Adams caught Akram in the deep, in front of the pavilion. At the end of the first day only seven runs separated the sides and when the final ball was bowled, North Down had won the game by the same narrow margin.

Despite what the anti-professional critics claimed, it was a classic game of cricket and not only the 'pros' had impressed.

Paul Moore had taken over the wicket-keeping duties from Ivan Connolly in 1991 and immediately made an impact. He was good enough to earn international recognition in 1992 against Scotland and two years later against the MCC and won back-to-back NCU Dai Jones awards in 1993 and 1994 for the top performance behind the stumps.

The McCrums' move to The Green in 1990 had sparked widespread condemnation and much media focus, but although Paul moved on in 1991 after taking 42 wickets, Charlie stayed until 1996 and in those years scored 4,635 runs and took 287 wickets — a remarkable set of statistics. He won the in-house batting rose bowl four times and the bowling rose bowl three times and won the praise of all at The Green for his ability and attitude. It was no surprise that he was acclaimed as the top all rounder in the NCU when he won the Bowden Cup in 1993 and 1994. His made his international debut at Coleraine in 1990 and, in all, played 22 times for Ireland including one against Barbados at The Green when he scored 49. His final game was against Canada at the Premier Club in Nairobi in the 1994 ICC Trophy.

Lionel Semple made a brief appearance for the club in 1991, but brother Adrian became part of the 1st XI scene for the next three years and took almost 100 wickets and he also won a cup final Man of the Match award in 1994.

After the euphoria of cup success in 1991 the side crashed out after a disappointing batting performance in the semi-final against North of Ireland in 1992, but convincingly reached the 1993 final with victories over Ballymena, Bangor and Downpatrick. After a first innings stalemate, North Down was 'put to the sword' by Garfield Harrison's five for 13 and were well beaten by seven wickets.

GAVIN RODGERS

This was one of the rare occasions when Charlie McCrum missed out in his seven seasons at The Green and it was at the expense of brother Paul who captured his wicket in each innings.

Another good cup run in 1994 with wins against Laurelvale, Waringstown, Downpatrick and Woodvale, set up a clash with Lisburn, a repeat of the 1929 final!

Lisburn had a very talented team with internationals Derek Heasley, Uel Graham and Neil Doak, Bruce Topping a fine wicketkeeper and Davy McDowell, Stephen Hutchinson and Henry McAuley possessing a wealth of experience.

The North Down side, under Ian Carser, had had a good league run and were strong and experienced with Charlie McCrum, Robin Haire, Paul Moore and Adrian Semple in the ranks, so it was always going to be a close run affair.

But nobody could have guessed how close, as for the first time in 107 years, the final ended in a tie. It didn't look likely when Lisburn were 61 for five, 144 runs adrift, but Michael Blair and skipper Trevor McKeown added 97 for the sixth wicket. Two runs were required off the last ball to Henry McAuley and one was scrambled for the tie. An historic occasion.

This era ended with a semi-final defeat by North of Ireland and the much more serious situation of relegation to Section Two.

Rumblings of discontent at the importation of players from outside the club led to major changes both at committee level and on the field.

A conflict of opinion as to the best way forward, whether strengthening the 1st XI with imports or persevering, probably at a lower standard, with the home grown youngsters, led to Robin Haire leaving for Downpatrick after 24 years at The Green and with him went opening bowler Billy Adams.

The days of Paul and Charlie McCrum, the Semple brothers Adrian and Lionel and Paul Moore were over, quality players who had been instrumental in bringing the Senior Challenge Cup and Irish Senior Cup to Comber during their stay. The charismatic Raman Lamba had also played his last game at The Green.

Back came Gavin Rodgers and South African professional Greg Smith, and it was left to the experienced Michael Quinn to try to weld a new generation into a strong cricketing unit.

He had the proven talents of John Gilliland, Billy Dale and Ian Carser to assist and the promise of talented young players Ryan Haire, Peter Shields, Alan O'Prey, Martin Moreland and Jonathan Montgomery, as yet unproven in senior cricket.

The 1997 season got off to the perfect start with a win over Muckamore, thanks mainly to an unbeaten 62 from Rodgers who had left Moylena the previous year. But Rodgers, with 647 runs and 'pro' Smith with 40 wickets still couldn't stave off relegation, and with only four wins, the side went down into Section Two for the first time in 18 years.

It was the end of an era within the club, but while outsiders in the anti-professional lobby basked in our demise, they didn't see the bigger picture, and when North Down bounced back, it was to begin a new era of cricket dominance that would match any that had gone before.

DOWN THE CLUB

While the 1st XI settled into the top league in the Eighties, the 2nd XI went through an abundance of captains during the period, with Walter Wishart,

SYD ELLIOTT WITH THE JUNIOR CUP

Jimmy Galway, Adrian Thompson, Alvin Maginnis, Miller O'Prey, Don Shields, Sydney Elliott, Dessie Savage and David Wishart each taking a turn.

Although they crashed out of the Junior Cup early and finished in the bottom half of the league in 1980, the seconds called on 34 players, most of them young and some, like John Gilliland, Trevor McMillan and Stephen Barry, the team's award winners that year, would go on to play 1st XI cricket.

In 1981, the 2nd XI defeated North of Ireland by 13 runs in the Junior Cup semi-final and went on to recover a first innings deficit to win the final against Civil Service. Willie Wilson's three for 32 restricted the opposition to 145, but it took a John Hiles 40 and

JUNIOR CUP WINNERS 1986: BACK – D ELLIOTT (SCORER), J GALWAY, J HILES, M O'PREY, B PATTON, D ORR, J WILSON, D WISHART. FRONT – F HILES, S ELLIOTT (CAPT), C HILES, G HASLETT.

tail-ender Jim Wilson with 26 to keep in touch. Stephen Barry's four for 27 and another fine bowling performance from 'Bimbo' Wilson with three for 31, left North Down needing 130 to win. Adrian Thompson's 34 and Ivan Dempster's 26 were invaluable, but it was Andrew Donaldson's unbeaten 53 that proved the winning innings.

More 2nd XI success was to follow in 1986 when the 'double' was achieved with the side winning Division Two Section Two and the Junior Cup against Lisburn in a sporting game at Comber. This team had a wealth of experience and was not short of characters either. The experienced all rounder Sydney Elliott captained the cup final side that included three Hiles brothers, Clarence, Frank and John. Brian Patton and Graham Haslett opened the batting and the run-making middle order of all rounders, David Orr and Miller O'Prey, rarely failed. David Wishart was a strong hit or miss batsman who, on his day, could change the course of a game. Jimmy Galway provided the left arm pace and Jim Wilson bowled good left arm spin. The seven runs lead in the first innings featured a half-century from Sydney, and was followed that evening by a long drinking session between two teams who were determined to enjoy the occasion. Next day the second innings belonged to the North Down bowling trio, of Clarence Hiles, Orr and O'Prey who each took three wickets for few runs, leaving North Down 111 to win. Another sound start from the openers and a batting reshuffle, promoting Frank Hiles up the order, worked well, and while Elliott picked up the singles, Hiles powered boundaries and North Down won the Junior Cup for the seventh time since 1891.

It was fitting that Cecil Walker, president of the NCU, presented the medals and paid a glowing tribute to the North Down players for their sportsmanship and to the club for their facilities and hospitality. Another celebratory session ensued for what must have been the most congenial junior cup final in the history of the competition.

However, it was to be the last Junior Cup win for 20 years.

Jimmy Boucher, Norman McLeod, John Hiles, Roy Thompson, Norman Beck, Miller O'Prey, Jimmy Galway, Mike Dallas, David Patton and Raymond Moreland shared the leadership duties for the 3rd XI, and it was Jimmy Boucher's team that, in 1980, brought home the silverware with victory in the Intermediate Cup against Woodvale and a third position in the league. The main contributors were Andrew Donaldson with the bat and Richard Glover with the ball.

The Lindsay Minor Cup came to Comber in 1988 when the 3rd XI defeated Lurgan at Ballymena, but it wasn't all plain sailing and it took an eighth wicket stand of 69 between Stephen Gregg and Keith Graham to lift the side from 67 for five. Gregg finished on 50 not out in a 151 for 8 total. Lurgan didn't reach three figures as Trevor Burney took three for 20, Keith Graham and Miller O'Prey each took two for 15 and Colin Montgomery two for 17.

The decade came to a close with the 3rd XI again winners, lifting the Division Three Section Two title with big Raymond Moreland scoring over 400 runs and Jim Wilson taking 44 wickets.

Not to be outdone, the 4th XI won their league in 1983 under Peter Artt and completed another 'double' in 1987 winning their league unbeaten and beating Armagh in the Minor Qualifying Cup final. Raymond Moreland galvanised a competitive and talented squad that included the Campbell brothers, Wesley, James and Ken, Raymond McIlveen who brought a vast experience to the side, Derek Steen, a former Ireland schoolboy international in his last year as club chairman, George Harper, Brian Patton, Tony McBride, Peter Wishart, Colin Montgomery, Geoff Johnston, Terry Ritchie, the club secretary, and wicketkeeper Dessie Savage.

David McKibbin, Peter Artt, David Patton, Raymond Moreland, Geoff Johnston, Colin McCaughey, Don Barry and Aiden Williams each took a turn at leading the 4th XI until the late Nineties.

With the firsts and thirds finishing runners-up in their respective leagues, the disappointment was that the 2nd XI, double winners in 1986, were relegated back into Section Two.

The North Down Annual Sixes Competition was still in full swing in the Eighties and our success in the RUC tournament at Newforge and the Ballymena Sixes at Eaton Park continued as well. Clarence Hiles led the team to victory in the Ballymena event in 1983, with John Gilliland the tournament's top run maker. Ken Boucher was the successful captain at Ballymena in 1985 with Michael Quinn, Kevin Copeland, Raman Lamba, David Orr and John Gilliland in the side when Jimmy Boyce, manager of Sun Life Assurance Society, handed over the cheque for £175.

In 1980, new coach Michael Reith won the North Down Sixes in his first year with his 'Pros & Cons' and again with 'Sachs' in 1982. Billy Dale's 'Comber's Boys' won in 1983 and Raman Lamba won it in his first year with 'New Delhi' in 1984. Clarence Hiles' 'Kaliber Kids' won in 1985 in the failing light, having been mysteriously put in to bat first, and 'Sangster' Moreland sang about it for most of the night! Robin Haire led his 'Haire Raisers' to another dark and rain-swept win in 1987 as the Sixes tradition at The Green continued, providing the opportunity for the lesser mortals to mix it with the stars causing major upsets and a lot of fun.

It was during this period that some of our better youngsters caught the eye of 'the critics' who predicted a bright future. The 'Test' matches that began in O'Prey's garden were often finished at The Green and the exploits of their 1st XI hero, Raman Lamba, were re-enacted many times over. The talents of this very special little group of up and coming players were to blossom with rich rewards and bring youth trophies to Comber in the Nineties, including the prestigious and elusive Graham Cup.

In 1993, the under 13 side lost to Bangor by three runs at Eaton Park in the Ballymena CC-sponsored league cup final, after Marty Moreland had scored 45, but dropped catches cost them the game. Two years later, in the Graham Cup Final, the result was a comprehensive, record-making win against the same opposition at Holywood, with captain Alan O'Prey hitting a fine 77 out of 206 for eight. Marty Moreland then took three for 21 in a memorable 106 runs win.

The famous old Graham Cup had never been won before, so this was a notable achievement, although from time to time, the club had reached the latter stages.

In 1929 the semi-final team that was defeated by Cliftonville at Ballynafeigh included Jim Montgomery, Billy Shields and Harry Donnan, who were to play 1st XI cricket in the Thirties. Another great chance to reach the final came in 1958 when visitors Downpatrick were dismissed for only 64 due to the bowling of Alan Henry, Don Shields, Jim Moreland and Ronnie McBurney. Wilmer McKibbin gave North Down a great start with 29 runs, but from 38 without loss they slumped to 62 for six and the home side failed to get another run!

Eleven years later, Ken Campbell captained the side at the age of 13 and hit a tremendous 105 against Holywood in the second round but the side lost in the next round. This failure to progress in the competition must have been frustrating for the players and coaches alike and particularly Jimmy Boucher, who gave over 20 years service to youth cricket at The Green.

Alan O'Prey was a confident and mature 15 year-old all rounder who led a talented side that included

Graham Cup Winners 1995: Back – Raman Lamba (Coach), B Ireland, D Miskelly, P Law, N Russell, R Haire, Robin Haire (Coach). Front – A Norman, P Shields, A O'Prey (Capt), M Moreland, P Coey. Ground – A Haire.

Peter Law, David Miskelly, Neil Russell, Ryan Haire, Peter Shields and Martin Moreland. Just how talented they were can be measured by the contributions of Russell, Haire, Shields and Moreland in their later domination of the NCU Colts Cup, and their impact in the Senior League and Senior Challenge Cup from 1999 to the present day.

This talented Graham Cup team ominously progressed to the Colts Cup stage and won their matches in style. The nucleus of the side had strong cricket family roots and their enthusiasm knew no bounds. Their invincibility was further enhanced when Andrew White joined the ranks from Ards. Jonathan Montgomery led the side to a six-wicket win over Lurgan in 1996, with Ryan Haire taking three for 18 and Marty Moreland two for 12 and Peter Shields scoring an unbeaten 39.

In 1998, under Martin Moreland's captaincy, they demonstrated their superiority with White taking five for 11 in the eight wickets victory over Ballymena at Armagh.

Regent House School, for so many years the nursery and provider of North Down players, struck gold in the late Nineties, winning the Junior Schools' Cup and Jubilee Trophy in 1995 with North Down players David Miskelly, Ryan Haire, Peter Law, Paul McLaughlin and captain Peter Shields playing their part.

Another former North Down player, Andrew Laird, captained the school 1st XI in 1996 and the Colts side that year included Ryan Haire, Peter Law, Christopher Fry, Barry Ireland and Michael Dines.

In a successful collaboration with the school and, in particular, with teachers Murray Lee and latterly with Eric Cinnamon, the club negotiated a programme using the professional of the day on regular coaching visits to the school. The club used the school 'net' facilities after Christmas each year, to prepare for the forthcoming season and the school teams played their Saturday morning games on the top pitch at The Green. Both Regent House and North Down recognised the importance of a close liaison and worked diligently to maintain it.

THE LEGEND OF RAMAN LAMBA

No player in post-war Ulster cricket made a bigger impact than Raman Lamba. He was a legend in his time and gave the club a huge boost. However it may surprise many people to learn that Raman was fourth choice when he was recruited in 1984. Born on 2nd January, 1960 in Meerut, north of New Delhi, Raman's introduction to North Down and the Comber community became a life changing experience for him and the beginning of a remarkable cricket journey for those who saw him play, and particularly for those who played with him.

RAMAN LAMBA

He was the media's dream, a story always about to 'break' whether as a result of performances on the field or his antics off it.

He was the reason that forced the NCU to defend itself against Cliftonville in the High Court in 1990 and he was the reason why the ICU had to remain on high alert with its rules. His marriage to Kim Crothers brought him great happiness and the birth of Cameron and Jasmine.

He was a totally professional cricketer and from his first half-century against neighbours Donaghadee to his last hundred at The Lawn, he shone like a beacon with his wonderful array of attacking shots, slick footwork and speed between the wickets. His enthusiasm rubbed off on the younger players who took him as their role model, on his own age group with whom he became 'one of the lads,' and on the veterans, some of whom gained a new lease of life when playing with him. His performances brought bigger crowds to matches and they were rarely disappointed. In every sense Raman was a celebrity.

Unforgettable was his 166 not out against Malahide in the Irish Senior Cup at The Green when the team chased 270 to win by two wickets.

His undefeated double century against a bemused Queen's University team in the Senior Challenge Cup underlined the ultimate mismatch of cup cricket, but he admired quality bowling and in that game he treated the economical Paul Stafford with great respect.

He brought great excitement to the Ballymena Sixes, hitting an amazing 76 not out in the 1985 semi-final and 84 in the final. This version of the game seemed made for him with his medium fast bowling, brilliance in the field and his 'showboating' with the bat. What a terrific Twenty20 player he would have been.

He revitalised Ian Shields' career as his veteran opening partner and we established a unique batting relationship that was for a time one of the best in the province. The contrast was stark and the opposition tactics to split us wide-ranging.

Raman's proudest moment in Irish cricket came in 1986 when he walked down the steps at Ormeau with Kris Srikkanth to open the innings for India against Ireland; Mohammad Azharuddin, Sandeep Patil and Ravi Shastri would follow in the batting line-up.

That same year, in the One Day Series against the Australians, he scored a century and two fifties and won the Man-of-the-Series Award.

Raman was arguably the best batsman ever to play at The Green and it was fitting that he was an integral part of the Irish Senior Cup win in 1989 against Donemana, when he batted patiently on a green and damp wicket for 34 runs, that in the opinion of many players and spectators was worth a lot more.

His annual benefit match at Comber was a star-studded affair and when the visiting Indian Gymkhana team brought their 'teas' with them, teams and guests were treated to an Indian gastronomical delight, the cricket almost incidental.

Raman's attendance at the NCU coaching qualification sessions in 1994 may have been compulsory but he added another dimension to it. He was joined by some of the other overseas 'pros' and a few local players at Queen's to complete the course. He was irrepressible and queried long established techniques of batsmanship, frequently interrupted the flow of coaches Ian Johnston and John Solanky, bounced tennis balls off his fellow 'pros' and covertly assisted others whose language skills caused problems with the written examinations. In short, he made the occasion great fun for everyone.

LINDSAY MINOR CUP WINNERS 1988: BACK – D STEEN (CHAIRMAN), T MCBURNEY, W CAMPBELL, K CAMPBELL, P WISHART, K GRAHAM, J HILES, K MCKENNA. FRONT – G MORELAND (SCORER), S GREGG, M O'PREY, R MORELAND (CAPT), C MONTGOMERY, N BECK

Raman was blessed with a superb eye and quick fire reflexes. He liked to give bowlers the charge, and had a flair for improvisation that made for great entertainment. Ironically, his one-day international form for India was patchy after his dream debut, and he failed to fire in his four Test matches. However, he remained a prolific scorer in first-class cricket, with two triple-centuries and an impressive Ranji Trophy average of over 53. He expressed a desire to play for Delhi until the age of 45, but he was only 38 when he died, after being struck on the head while fielding at forward short-leg during a club match in Bangladesh. It was a tragic end for such a wonderful character. Extensive coverage of his death was reported in The Hindu, Dawn, and The Times of India, and many expressions of condolence were received from the cricketing community including the greatest Indian cricketer Sachin Tendulkar, who played alongside Raman in his international debut game against Pakistan. Like everyone else he was stunned by the news of the tragedy. There was also a feeling of disbelief at North Down that their much-loved professional and friend had died and Ian Shields expressed the club's condolences at a memorial service in Belfast.

DIVISION FOUR SECTION 2 WINNERS 1983: BACK – W ALLEN (SNR), N BECK, W ALLEN (JNR), D PATTON, D ORR, J HILES, D STEEN, W MCKIBBIN. FRONT – R MCILVEEN, PJ ARTT (CAPT), J MCKITTRICK.

Raman loved Ireland, he loved Comber, he loved The Green, and he loved the members who made him feel so much a part of their lives. In return he gave us almost a decade of brilliant cricket and many great memories.

IN AND AROUND THE CLUB

North Down was well represented in the inaugural Ulster Cricketer Magazine in 1985 with a front cover depicting Raman Lamba, Robin Haire, David Orr and Simon Corlett at The Green. Ian Shields, Raman Lamba, Robin Haire, Charlie McCrum, Michael Clarke, Andrew White and Taimur Khan, had the honour of being featured on the front cover and Raman and Ian also contributed articles. Rowland White, who also provided North Down with many first-class pictures for the local and national press, brilliantly photographed the front cover photos of White and Khan.

In 1984 the club had an unforgettable tour to the Caribbean in late August/early September featuring 16 members and two guest players.

Prior to the tour the big talking point was Lurgan's refusal to switch the Irish Senior Cup semi-final game, as North Down was going to be without at least half of their team. The match went ahead as scheduled and Lurgan won easily.

During the 16-day tour North Down played five games and had a practice session at the famous Kensington Oval test ground. The opposition was strong and the hot tropical weather was a far cry from Irish conditions, even in the hottest of summers. Four matches were lost, but the playing highlight was a fine victory over the famous Wanderers Club, a game in which tour captain Robin Haire hit a match-winning 84 not out.

The tour fixtures opened on a blistering hot day with a game against the Barbados Workers' Union and in his opening over Clarence Hiles had the commendable figures of two for 12. The home team went on to score 157, which was 49 runs too many for the tourists despite a fine innings from skipper Haire (49).

North Down then played at Wotton where the local team hit 163 and at one stage North Down looked likely to pass it as John Gilliland (72) and Robin Haire (60) were in terrific form. However, much to the delight of the large vocal crowd, both departed in quick succession and the tourists finished, agonizingly, eight runs short of their target. Hospitality off the field was excellent and there were many contenders for the champagne moment, but none to match big Sangster's (Raymond Moreland) magnificent catch on the boundary.

In their third game, North Down faced the powerful Police team who were at the height of their prowess in Barbados club cricket, and with several Barbados national players in their ranks they rattled up 218 for 7. In reply the tourists struggled to 68, although in fairness the Police team would have beaten Ireland at the time, such was their strength.

The fourth game at Wanderers brought the tourists their finest hour and in a thrilling game Robin showed the locals the best of North Down's batting, aided by Peter Artt (23) and a cameo innings from the popular Ivan Connolly (21no). Peter continued his good form into the final game with Queen Elizabeth Hospital, but four days of continuous cricket and a heavy night at the Carlisle nightclub took its toll, as the batting was poor and North Down lost a low scoring game by 32 runs on a 'sticky' wicket. Overall the tour was a resounding success and in addition to many unforgettable social moments, North Down president Jim Barry presented Capt. Peter Short, the president of the Barbados Cricket Association, with a plaque from Oliver Johnson, Mayor of Ards Borough Council as a gesture of goodwill. The tour produced a wealth of stories and much of the off-field camaraderie centred on Denis Artt's unique Cricket Awards and big Raymond Moreland's unforgettable singing, the highlights of every coach ride back to the hotel.

On reflection the tourists didn't pack enough batting strength to support skipper Robin Haire (199 runs ave. 49.7), but cricket tours are not all about cricket and the organization and delivery of a major tour to the Caribbean showed great vision and commitment from the members. Fired with enthusiasm, there were plans to tour Zimbabwe in 1986 but it never came off and the 1984 tour to Barbados remains the major touring highlight amongst many in 150 years of existence.

In the early Eighties, and for the first time in its history, the hockey club put a 5th XI on to the field, made up mostly of cricketers playing social hockey, and under the captaincy of Ian Shields they finished near the top of their league.

But the relationship between the hockey and cricket clubs took a turn for the worse in 1982 when the cricket club, feeling itself under greater financial pressure than usual, asked for an increased contribution from the hockey club for the use of the facilities. The hockey club accepted in principle but the figures were disputed and during protracted negotiations the cricket club entered a hockey team, known as NDCCHC, into the Intermediate League. It was the lowest point in cricket and hockey relations but, gradually, representatives from both clubs met in an attempt to resolve the difficulties and a three-year agreement was signed.

The following years saw positive change, with both clubs generating funds in joint efforts and a pool league and joint golf society in operation. After a couple of years the NDCC hockey team, that had given a good account of itself in the Intermediate league, was dissolved, and most players joined the hockey club. An added bonus was that new hockey players like John Hiles, David Orr, and John Gilliland, went on to play distinguished roles within hockey circles.

By 1986 the co-operation between the clubs went a long way to securing the refurbishment of the clubhouse, just completed in time to welcome visitors for the Easter Hockey tournament in April. Sadly, in the same month, the death of the club president, Sir John (JLO) Andrews, broke the link with the family that was instrumental in the foundation and patronage of the club since 1896.

During this period the new Council artificial pitch came into use, and although a few games were subsequently played at The Green, grass was no longer the main hockey-playing surface.

Profit was uppermost in the minds of the fundraisers who organised the 'Night at the Races' which proved to be excellent entertainment.

One of the best was held on the 21st March, 1980 with Clarence Hiles naming and shaming the horse owners, Miller O'Prey ensuring that the 'Bookies' made a big killing and Ian Shields providing the equipment and showing the American track races.

The committee and members played a full part by selling horses and heading to the venue at 'The Old Crow', an excellent restaurant managed by a former 1st XI captain, Billy Artt and situated beside the Brownlow Arms, which was owned by Jim Burgess, who at one stage was a valuable supporter and 'sponsor'.

The sprinkling of advertisements reflected local support for the event, amongst them Harry McKnight who provided the regular servicing of our cricket machinery and Jim Miskelly who was one of our long time supporters and ran his newsagency from Castle Street. Artt's Honey, Discount Carpets, Erne Tyre Service, Ulster Engraving and Bennett of Comber to name but a few, had placed their advert and contributed to the production of the programme – the Official Race Card.

And so it was at about 7.45 pm the first race was announced – The Ivan Adair Open Chase sponsored by the noted Fish & Poultry Specialists in Castle Street. Ivan, who could be seen regularly at the bar through the haze of his cigarette smoke, passed endless comments on how his syndicate could drive the club forward, but he missed most of the races and the honour of making the presentation to the winners.

A tongue-in-cheek approach by the masterful Hiles showed a tremendous insight into the charactistics of the horse owners, the perceptions of their peers and often their Achilles heels. The newly signed 'Pro' at the club, Michael Reith, had his horse named 'Super Mike' (by Club Coach out of Waringstown) and was ridden by Roy Harrison. Favourite with O'Prey's 'bookies' was Jim Patterson's 'Sent Off' a mare (by Angry Umpire out of Patience) and ridden by N.O.T.

CLARENCE HILES

Cricket. Jim was one of the hockey stalwarts at the club and had recently been given his 'marching orders' in a game!

Another race brought together a few of the club's characters with Denis Artt's 'Money Bags' clear favourite. 'Rivelino' was Don Shields' runner, reflecting his likeness to the great Brazilian soccer star of the time, while Robert Johnston's 'One Too Many' (by Half Stoned Cowboy out of Lots of Bush) reflected wee Rab's favourite tipple and his occasional rendering of the country classic 'Rhinestone Cowboy'.

One of the club's trustees and long-serving cricketers, Wesley Graham, was never allowed to forget his quip after scoring 25 runs in an innings and had his horse named 'Quarter of a Century', a colt (by Alfie's Victim out of Form Often) and ridden by D Star. The reference to Alfie's Victim reflected Wesley's painful experience when hit on the head by Woodvale's pace bowler Alfie Redpath many years previously, and the effect it had on Wesley's development as a batsman.

Wesley was one of the most prolific youth all rounders and continued to make important contributions to the 2nd and 3rd XIs throughout his career. His real strength lay in his ability to 'sell' the club to potential sponsors and, in the process, he raised thousands of pounds. He was a tireless worker behind the scenes and has contributed a lot to the club's prosperity over the years. In his heyday he was a more than useful 'Sixes' exponent. He had all the attributes: available, has car and can bat and bowl!

Jim Barry's mount was aptly named "Wasim Bari" and the hockey club was well represented with Robin Mitchell, Peter Orr, George Harper, Alan Coyle, David Donaldson, Joe Brown and Colin Linter all horse owners.

Well-known cricketers such as former internationals Charlie Corry and Alfie Linehan, were on the card, as was after-dinner speaker and cricketer Colin Barkley from the 'Master Race', Davy Mills of 'The White Horse Inn' in Saintfield, and Sammy Wilson, a former North Down cricketer himself and, ironically, working in the serious horse racing business.

The Artt family had very strong connections with the club with Billy captaining the 1st XI and Peter playing his cavalier cricket on the junior teams. Top wicketkeeper Denis played interpro level and was unlucky not to be capped. Their legacy went far beyond the 'Old Crow Grand Prix', 'The Artt's Honey Champion Stakes' and 'The Artt – Green Gold Cup'.

If Clarence had had a horse of his own it would have been named 'Wrong Foot' (by The Bowler out of The Beamer), The Bowler being his satirical club newsletter hitting hard at all and sundry and the beamer relating to the unpredictable delivery he produced every so often to claim some good wickets!

North Down negotiated a three-year sponsorship deal with Harp Lager in 1982 and in 1985 it was extended for another three years. The sponsorship included the Annual 'Sixes' Competition, individual monthly and annual awards, a two-day coaching course and various internal club competitions. At the launch of the renewal, NCU president Cecil Walker said that the union was extremely pleased that Harp Lager was continuing the very happy relationship with North Down Cricket Club, one of the oldest in Ireland, and who had built up a great tradition in 'Sixes' cricket.

CLARENCE HILES

Although domiciled in Barbados since 1996, Clarence Hiles has remained in close contact with North Down Cricket Club and Irish cricket in general.

His boyhood dreams of emulating the great North Down cricketers of the past were largely 'kept on hold' for most of his cricketing career, as he played mostly in the junior teams until the late Seventies. He was the mastermind behind the 'signing' of Michael Reith from Waringstown in the autumn of 1979, but little did he realise at the time that he would be the bowling partner of Michael when Lawrence Hunter's illness sadly ruled him out of cricket a few months later.

Clarence bowled off the 'wrong foot', wasn't particularly agile in the field, and, by his own admission, wasn't noted for scoring too many runs, although he did register a senior 'fifty' in 1976 against RUC in the first round of the Challenge Cup. On another notable occasion in 1979, when most of the team had feared the worst, he turned a losing Challenge Cup match around at the Demesne in Saintfield and secured a win. His batting aspirations were eventually sacrificed for bowling and under Reith's tutelage he played a huge part in the successful North Down 1st XI side of the early Eighties. He had an uncanny knack of dismissing key opposition batsmen, usually the 'pro', and this alone guaranteed him a regular place in the side. But he was also a great team player, always encouraging and motivating, and to the forefront in defying the odds when faced with adversity.

For such a late developer his bowling record for the 1st XI was impressive, and he reached sixth place in the NCU bowling averages in 1980 and tenth in 1982.

He was a member of the 1981 Senior Challenge Cup winning team, and after he retired from senior cricket he joined his brothers Frank and John in the 2nd XI team that won the Junior Cup and Junior League title in 1986.

He was a great exponent of the 'Sixes' game, and captained North Down teams to victories at the Ballymena 'Sixes' and the RUC 'Sixes' tournaments in the Seventies. He also introduced the North Down 'Sixes' to the club and then brought Harp Lager to the table and for many years the club enjoyed their generous sponsorship. He produced a North Down 'Sixes' programme and with his wit and skill captured the nature of the competitors and almost provocatively predicted the results. In 1978, as the 'Fly on the Wall' editor, he produced a unique North Down newsletter entitled 'The Bowler'. It was an informative satirical magazine designed to reach out to members in the off-season and keep them abreast of happenings in and around the club. It covered such items as tours, AGMs, sponsorship, fixtures for the forthcoming season, pavilion extensions, poems, clubhouse gossip, and profiles on players and officials. It was brilliantly and humourously produced and, even after 30 years, some of the older members still recall its content, some of whom felt its sting on more than one occasion!

In 1985 Clarence produced the much more professional 'Ulster Cricketer' magazine that won praise from virtually every cricket enthusiast in the province. It collated statistics on Irish and Ulster cricket, cricket news items, profiles on cricket personalities, guest articles, and features on umpires, plus an abundance of quality photographs. It was almost compulsory reading for local cricketers and sorely missed when Clarence departed to Barbados in 1996. However, after an eight-year lapse it bounced back with Peter Shields as assistant editor in 2004 for a few years before switching to cyber.

Clarence had a passion for sports journalism and was the main editor of the NCU Centenary Brochure in 1986 which outlined the history of the NCU from its inception. He also produced many cup final and match programmes but his greatest work as a cricket journalist was writing the "History of Senior Cricket in Ulster", a labour of love that took him over 14 years to complete. The work is an encyclopaedia of Ulster cricket, an excellent read, and as a source of local cricket reference is unsurpassable.

Clarence served the club in many roles and was particularly active in fund-raising. He was a born organiser and the driving force behind the club's tour to Barbados in 1984. He was invited into the administration of both the Northern Cricket Union and the Irish Cricket Union in the late Seventies and rose to chairman of the NCU in 1990/1 and, for almost a decade, served collectively as assistant secretary, joint treasurer, NCU delegate and PRO in the Irish Cricket Union. He was chairman of the Ulster Town selectors and in 1995 when he announced his intention to relocate to the Caribbean, the Northern Cricket Union bestowed on him its highest honour when it awarded him an honorary life membership for his services to cricket.

Clarence worked hard for Ulster sport in general, and was a member of the NI Council of Physical Recreation for six years and appointed by the minister to serve on the Sports Council for Northern Ireland from 1993 to 1996. But he has never forgotten his North Down roots and remains as committed to the club today as he was when playing for the Boys' XI almost 50 years ago.

ROBIN HAIRE

Robin Haire may not have emerged from a strong cricketing background, but by the mid-Nineties he had established something of a dynasty at North Down, with sons Ryan and Andrew much to the fore, father Sammy a doyen stalwart and wife Jean and mother Margaret on the ladies committee.

Robin graduated through the Boys' XI and became an outstanding schoolboy cricketer, arguably one of the best ever from Regent House School. He played for Ulster Schools, Irish Schools, Ulster Town Under-19 and toured Canada with Ireland Under-19. At the same time he became an established senior cricketer and benefited greatly from the arrival of Michael Reith and, later, Raman Lamba. When he was appointed 1st XI captain in 1982 he was the youngest skipper in senior cricket and relished the responsibility. He had confidence and maturity beyond his years and, like all great players, an inherent belief in his own ability. He ruffled a few feathers in his early years because of his abrasive and cocky approach, but it was all part of his exuberance and, like a good wine, he matured and

ROBIN HAIRE

mellowed in later years. His graduation as a teenager into the Ulster Town senior interprovincial team was seamless and in 1986 his call-up to the Ireland squad to tour Zimbabwe was the ultimate recognition. He played only three times for Ireland, an appalling reflection of poor selection, but with grit and determination he answered his detractors where it mattered, and over the next 20 years he produced a string of outstanding individual performances that earned him total respect from friend and foe alike.

Robin began his cricket career as a tricky left-arm slow bowler who was also a useful batsman, but he matured into a very sound and focused batsman who could adapt to most situations. He made his senior club debut against Laurelvale at The Green in the Seventies, and although there were high hopes that Robin would become a key player in the team, no one could have predicted the huge contribution he was to make over the next three decades. He won the 1st XI batting award eight times and the bowling award four times. He was a born leader and loved the challenge of captaincy, even when it exposed some frailties in his personality. He demanded 100% commitment on the field but was a warm and outgoing character off it. Over two decades he captained the 1st XI in four spells.

As a player Robin was fiercely competitive and tailor-made for the cut and thrust of cup competition. He led from the front and made his biggest mark as captain when leading North Down to a tremendous 1991 Senior Challenge Cup win over Woodvale, arguably the greatest final of all NCU cup finals. Robin relished every nail-biting finish, although his last ball 'six' off Herbie Parkhill to win the semi-final clash against North of Ireland that same year was the ultimate 'Roy of the Rovers' sensational finish. Or was it? Four years later Robin captained North Down to an epic Irish Senior Cup win over Bready by the narrowest one run margin!

When North Down toured Barbados in 1984 Robin was the inspirational tour captain who played the hero's role in virtually every game. His epic 84 at the famous Wanderers cricket ground to beat the locals was the highlight of the tour and led to long and late celebrations.

But club life wasn't always plain sailing and when a row developed at the club over the importation of players in the late nineties, Robin opted to play for a short time at Downpatrick. Not surprisingly he won the Challenge Cup once again under the leadership of his old friend Jim Patterson. However, North Down 1st XI was relegated but, to his credit, Robin returned to the fold and became the foundation on which a new group of young players would build and reach levels of cricketing excellence that hadn't been seen at The Green for 60 years. With the veteran "Da Haire" providing experience and solidarity to the middle order, North Down enjoyed total supremacy in NCU cricket at the turn of the century and it was a very proud father that joined his two sons in the 2001 Senior Challenge Cup win over North of Ireland, in the last cup final to be staged at Ormeau. As a bonus Ryan hit a century, won the Man-of the-Match Award and ran his dad out! However, Robin's half century in the second innings was every bit as match-winning when the serious questions were asked.

In North Down's special sesquicentenary year Robin still features on the 1st XI after three decades at the top in Ulster cricket. Off the field his contribution to the club has been all embracing and he has served in a wide variety of roles. He remains the lynchpin that fires so much of the club's drive and vision and his work as vice-chairman shows leadership qualities that will benefit the club for many years to come.

TIME TO REFLECT AND TAKE STOCK

It was the end of another era, but one in which the club had made gigantic strides over two decades. North Down Cricket Club had not only moved with the times, it had raised the bar in local cricket with its drive and ambition, it had been successful on and off the field, it had excellent facilities and a strong membership. Indeed much of the success that ensued had been driven from down the club in the early Eighties when a strong social culture developed which enhanced the general atmosphere at the club.

North Down started the Eighties with the shock recruitment of Michael Reith to the club, and played a major part in the cantankerous professionals debate that followed, with arguably the best 'pro' in local cricket and the offer of 'incentives' to attract local players. It didn't endear the club to some critics, but in the cold business world of today success breeds success, and North Down was determined to look after itself and ensure its business was in good shape on and off the field.

Overall this happened very successfully, until a change in strategy in 1997 brought immediate relegation when many key players left.

It was not a disaster but a setback, and it allowed everyone to recharge their batteries and come back all the stronger.

It was therefore no surprise when the 1st XI immediately bounced back, but who could have imagined the success that was to follow?

CHAPTER 10
1998 – 2006 : THE THIRD GOLDEN ERA

"SUNDAY SAW NORTH DOWN CC FROM NORTHERN IRELAND ARRIVE, IF SOMEWHAT BELATEDLY, AT THE MALLORCA CRICKET GROUND. THEY HAD GOT LOST ON THE WAY. NICE GUYS THAT THEY ARE, IT WOULD HAVE PROBABLY BEEN BEST IF THEY HAD FAILED TO ARRIVE AT ALL! MALLORCA CC WOULD CERTAINLY HAVE BEEN SPARED THE EMBARRASSMENT THEY WERE TO SUFFER. NORTH DOWN'S 388 SCORE IN 40 OVERS WILL UNDOUBTEDLY GO DOWN IN MALLORCA CC'S HISTORY AS THE HIGHEST TO BE RECORDED AGAINST THE HOME SIDE. IN TRUE IRISH FASHION THE BOYS FROM NORTH DOWN CC ATTEMPTED, AND I BELIEVE ALMOST SUCCEEDED, IN DRINKING THE BAR DRY! THE SINGING COULD BE HEARD IN PALMA."

WENDY PETERS, MAJORCA DAILY BULLETIN

1999 SENIOR LEAGUE CHAMPIONS: BACK – J Barry (Patron), J Patton (Scorer), I Carser, A O'Prey, A White, W Adams, R Haire, W Dale, D Elliott (Sec), W Wishart (Pres). Front – Robin Haire, M Quinn, P Shields, J Montgomery (Capt), T Khan, M Moreland, P Davidson.

COMBER
IN THE NEW MILLENNIUM

On census day April 2001 the population of Comber stood at 8,933 that meant the town had grown by almost 50% in the previous two decades. Visually it hasn't changed much and while Gillespie and the War Memorial remain the only permanent 'residents' in Comber Square, the gardens surrounding them have been tastefully landscaped with brightly coloured flower-beds and seating. Kane of Comber has disappeared and in its place is town housing, a Tesco supermarket, a restaurant and a beauty parlour. Across the Square there is another restaurant in Mr Kirk's old house, latterly Erskine's, and what used to be Niblock's shop, on the corner opposite Mawhinney's butcher shop, was demolished within a few hours. Further up Castle Street there are several derelict properties, while others have been knocked down and rebuilt. Down Castle Lane close to The Green, a townhouse development has replaced the Albion factory and the old terrace houses opposite the gates are selling for over £180,000.

Jack Drain's beautiful wee house, with the horseshoe porch, was demolished and guess what is going up in its place? Yes, more houses!

Comber attracted many middle-class residents during the Troubles and most of the new housing on the outskirts of the town are private developments to meet the demand. The village culture still remains in the minds of the old residents, but Comber is a dormitory town in every sense, and not only do most people travel to Belfast and Newtownards to work, they also do their shopping there and as a result the commercial heart of the town has diminished. Long gone are the old Andrews' Spinning Mill, the Albion factory, Kane of Comber, the Upper Distillery, the Technical College and 'Hill Sixty' and in their place new property has been built. The town's economic demise has been exacerbated with phase two of the new by-pass linking the Newtownards and Killinchy Roads diverting a lot of traffic from the main streets and bringing further concerns to the town's traders.

On a more positive note the political situation in Ulster has been resolved and everyone is looking to a future devoid of the bomb and the bullet. Just where North Down Cricket Club fits into that future remains to be seen, but it has a unique location in the heart of the town with wonderful sporting memories dating back 150 years.

ULSTER CRICKET
IN THE NEW MILLENNIUM

The old saying that 'there is nothing new under the sun' rang true coming up to the new Millennium when North of Ireland won the Senior Challenge Cup in 1999, Waringstown won the Senior League in 2000 and North Down bounced back up from Section Two, to win the Senior League in 1999 and the Senior Cup in 2000.

The 'Big Three' were back in control of NCU cricket but, alarmingly, not long after, one fell by the wayside.

North Down and North of Ireland met in the last Senior Challenge Cup final to be played at Ormeau in 2001, just as they had contested the first final way back in 1887. But life had significantly changed on the Lower Ormeau Road during the Troubles, and the Belfast club's neighbours now had very different political and demographic aspirations that didn't include cricket and rugby sporting traditions. There were bombs, break-ins, vandalism and intimidation, and the orchestrated campaign had one clear objective, which was to get the club out.

Eventually the North of Ireland club sold out to developers, moved to Collegians and re-invented themselves as Belfast Harlequins. The 'marriage' was a disaster and within a few years the cricket club was forced to move out on its own and it amalgamated with Civil Service to become Civil Service North, based at Stormont.

The Cliftonville club suffered most during the Troubles, but appeared to have come out of the doldrums in the 1990s when they moved to Greenisland and started winning trophies again. However, their new ground came under threat and their future remains uncertain.

Ulster cricket is changing but not everything is negative. The Ulster Cup has brought together the top teams from both northern unions, but when the NCU tried to drive everyone into an All Ireland League the clubs kicked it out as impractical and unworkable.

The game has also changed and there certainly is a greater appetite for more instant cricket and, for a variety of reasons, few people want protracted matches and rearrangements. To accommodate this view the NCU has changed its rules and reduced the overs played in junior and minor league cricket and, in an attempt to avert a backlog of fixtures when the weather is bad, they have permitted the Premier League sides to thrash out a ten overs match to get a result. The Twenty20 version of the game has brought coloured clothing, white balls and musical accompaniment, but for many of the 'old hands' it is simply a more sophisticated version of the old midweek league.

In another concession to change, the Senior Challenge Cup final has been reduced to one innings for a trial period of three years. Many people preferred the two-day format, but others felt it was a dinosaur in the modern game. The fact that only 10 clubs from the 42 affiliated to the NCU have been involved in the two-day final over the previous 30 years may have been a strong influence in their decision-making.

The NCU operate in a technological era when their actions and decisions are openly discussed on website forums and they certainly have their challenges dealing with disciplinary measures, fines for rule breaches, and the potentially contentious issue of registration of players, especially those from overseas.

This led to problems for North Down in the arrangements for the 2002 Senior Challenge Cup final, the rules involving postponements when three players were selected to play for their country, and the corroboration of a mistake in Peter Connell's registration in 2006 that cost the club dearly.

We live in an age when criticism is always an easy option, but when the chips are down and your club comes out worst, then your judgement tends to be affected. Overall the NCU administrators continue to do their job diligently and their hosting of top games in Belfast deservedly won praise as high as the International Cricket Council, but it is the parochial issues that prove to be their Achilles heel.

Ian Shields, Darren Elliott and Robin Haire all served on the NCU executive committee from 2000 to 2006 but in 2007 North Down has no representative at union level for the first time in its history.

ADMINISTRATORS AT NORTH DOWN

Ian Carser started his second year as chairman in 1998 and has continued successfully in this role ever since. Ian's quiet demeanour has made him a popular leader and his focus and vision has taken the club to greater heights than anyone could have predicted.

Gordon Scott passed the secretarial role to Darren Elliott, son of former secretary Sydney. Darren, a successful captain who led the 3rd XI to league championships in 1999 and 2000, and Minor Cup glory in 2002 has an excellent cricket pedigree as uncles Ronnie and George, both played at North Down. Ronnie was a fine opening bowler and useful batsman for the 1st XI who was also capped by Ireland at rugby. George was a batsman on the seconds for a short time before settling back in his home town club Donaghadee. Darren earned the endearing nickname 'Fax' for his wide knowledge on most subjects which he put to good effect when writing his annual secretary's reports. His demanding five-year tenure ended when he resigned in 2004, but Darren has remained a part of the North Down scene.

Sam Magill stepped into the breach and handled the role effectively until

Colin McCaughey was brought on board in 2005. Since then the popular 'Gatch' has carried out his duties admirably and at the same time captained the 4th XI against immense odds. The good news is that he has a vested interest in North Down with his two young sons coming through the ranks, and his proximity to the ground may make it difficult for him to escape!

Over the years the club has been well served by some very diligent treasurers who have carefully managed to balance the books, sometimes in extremely difficult circumstances. Quiet man Tom Mills has occupied this demanding position since 1994 and has shown great skill and tact throughout. He has never hesitated to let the committee know the detail of the

JOHN PATTON, NORTH DOWN'S 1ST XI SCORER

finances through his monthly printouts and has added another dimension to the club's bookkeeping with his ability to budget and plan. He is one of the longest serving treasurers in the club's history and has been honoured with the presidency since 2005.

The third Golden Era at the club has produced much more than playing success, and the treasurer, secretary and chairman have worked well together to ensure North Down is not only a thriving sports club, but also a solid business model.

The formation of several sub committees during this era has greatly enhanced the effective administration of the club. The backup team has slotted naturally into positions of responsibility with Robin Haire and George Harper (Vice Chairmen) Walter Wishart and Cairns Boyd (Bar), Raymond Moreland (Amenities), David Moreland, Alan Stevenson, Colin McCaughey and Paul McLaughlin (Entertainments), Michael

Quinn, Peter Shields, Ryan Haire, (Cricket Development) and Ian Carser, Darren Elliott, Sam Magill (Commercial) heading up sub committees. The '100' Club initiative, begun by Alan Stevenson and carried on by Andrew Frater and Robin Haire, has active support from Raymond Moreland and treasurer Tom Mills and has proved to be a very successful fundraiser. Don Shields remained as Membership secretary and Andrew White, Paul McLaughlin and Marty Moreland took their turn as Fixture Secretary while the North Down CC website, with Ian Shields as Webmaster, took its first tentative steps in 2001 and blossomed under the website professionals, Tibus, with great assistance from Tara Russell. Andrew Haire assisted with contacts at the Ards Borough Council to ensure the smooth running of our nominations for sports awards and such like, and, as the latest arrival on committee, has a lot to offer in the future. The club's administration is arguably better organized and administered than it has ever been.

BILLY DALE WITH LEAGUE TROPHY

CRICKET AT THE GREEN

The third Golden Era is the product of a nucleus of home grown talent sprinkled with a few excellent 'blow-ins' who have not only been talented cricketers, but people with personality and character to match. And success hasn't been solely restricted to the senior team, as the junior teams have played their part in bringing silverware and honour to the club.

Michael Quinn could not have had a more difficult sporting challenge than captaining the 1st XI in 1998 in Section Two, but the arrival of two Ards men was to aid the recovery. The experienced Paul Davidson, a medium pace bowler, had league winner's medals in the First Division Section 4 and Section 3 with Ards. In 1998 he picked up his Section 2 winner's medal and followed this in 1999 with the Section 1 accolade. Paul must be unique in the game to have won all four NCU Division 1 medals - in reverse order.

Young Andrew White, an all rounder, had enormous potential, clearly demonstrated in his school and Colts' performances, but was yet to perform at the top level. After making a substantial contribution over a few seasons, Paul retired and Andrew developed into one of the best young cricketers in the Province. Yes, there was a belief that the club would eventually be stronger for promoting the young guns, but 'Beastie' Quinn must have had some misgivings when they fell at the first hurdle against unfancied Academy at The Green. But Michael was a fighter and rallied his troops with new 'pro' Mohammed Asuaf, and the rapidly maturing talents of the younger players. It was a tough learning curve, but he deservedly took the side straight back into the top flight losing only one other game to Derriaghy. Asuaf, or 'As' as he was known, was a personable Bristolian who weathered the storm of doubters after a series of early 'ducks', to play a few crucial innings when it mattered most and finish with an average of 40. He was enthusiastic, determined and worked well with the younger players to become one of the most popular 'pros' to ever play at The Green. Michael did a great job in 1998 and later became increasingly involved with youth coaching as development officer at the club and, subsequently, within the NCU and ICU.

The 'feel good factor' returned just as quickly as it had disappeared, and the positive effects rippled down through the club. The 2nd XI, well led by Andrew Macrory, won 15 times in 16 outings and won their league trophy, with RJ Montgomery, (Ards' Monty) and Ian Carser in prolific batting form. Marty Moreland scored runs and took wickets while brother David destroyed some bowling attacks with big hitting. Young Aaron Mills and Barry Ireland led a strong attack, and the ever-popular Keith Malone provided great back-up, plenty of experience and tons of encouragement.

The 3rd XI almost produced a hat-trick of league wins, but Raymond Moreland's team ran out of time, having won nine from eleven starts with fine performances from Miller O'Prey, David Moreland, Billy Gordon, Darren Elliott and George Harper, while the inimitable Andrew Frater kept the 4th XI in a secure league position.

Happily our 'prodigal sons' Billy Adams and Robin Haire returned from Downpatrick in early August 1998, and the future looked even brighter with the close season signing of Pakistani all rounder Taimur Khan.

Taimur had been highly recommended by London agent Dr. Mo Aslam, had played for Pakistan Universities, toured New Zealand with the Pakistan 'A'

JONATHAN MONTGOMERY
WITH THE SENIOR LEAGUE TROPHY 1999

team and played domestically for the Allied Bank and the Peshawar Regional side. He had a proven pedigree but, like all overseas players, he had to prove himself again in a strange country with an inclement climate and some fiercely partisan locals!

1999 signalled the beginning of John Gilliland's retirement process. John was an excellent right-hand batsman and occasional bowler who represented Ulster Town on many occasions and, at one stage, was on the verge of Irish selection. The quiet man of the team, he was technically solid, with an inherent ability to play forcefully off the back foot. He had the safest hands in the club and an uncanny knack of hitting the stumps, especially in a 'bowl out.'

Jo Montgomery took over the 1st XI captaincy in 1999 and the side started well, picking up the prestigious Britannia Team of the Month award for May, but no one could have anticipated that by the end of that season a 63-year drought would end when Montgomery held high the Ulster Bank Senior League trophy in early September. In that Senior League winning match, Taimur Khan's four for 15 and Billy Adams' two for 29 helped reduce North of Ireland to a 153 total and an opening partnership of 54 from Alan O'Prey and Andrew White laid the foundation for the historic win. Although it was Ryan Haire who hit the winning run it was a great unbeaten 63 from O'Prey that was the highlight of the North Down innings.

It was a great personal triumph for the 22-year-old Montgomery, who already had a Senior Challenge Cup and an Irish Senior Cup winner's medal. But to bring the Senior League Trophy to The Green for the first time in 63 years and in his first year as captain, was something special. He has now played in seven Challenge Cup finals, two Irish and two Ulster Cup Finals, captained and managed the successful Colts side to two Colts' Cup wins and played in the 2nd XI 'double' winning side in 2006. Is there more to come?

The balance of the side was just right, with the experienced Robin Haire controlling the batting in the middle order and Billy Adams causing opposition batsmen problems at the start of their innings. Paul Davidson, a useful bowler, playing the best cricket of his life, and the ageless Billy Dale, ably supported him.

'Bumper' Dale began his cricket career in the Belfast Cricket League and was 'recruited' by fellow Stranmillis student Ian Shields to play at Comber. It was a long and fruitful association, and Billy became one of the most effective seam bowlers in recent times at The Green. His popularity extended beyond the changing room and the North Down faithful applauded his positive attitude and obvious enjoyment of the game. Arguably, he reached his pinnacle with North Down in that 1999 season, while Michael Quinn had the added satisfaction of seeing his good work the previous year totally fulfilled.

Officially the most improved player in that memorable 1999 season was Marty Moreland, who took many vital wickets, scored important runs and also found time and enthusiasm to captain the midweek team to a Section A title, with victory over Dunmurry.

Taimur Khan finished his first season at The Green with 28 wickets and 886 runs and secretary Darren Elliott stated that he 'completed the jigsaw' in his annual report. But 'Timi' had done much more, he had won the respect and friendship of the North Down members and a bond was established that was to have significant long-term benefits for the club.

There was also disappointment in 1999 when Wayne Horwood's five wickets and Alan Rutherford's 90 runs led to a second round exit from the Challenge Cup against Woodvale, while a heavy first round defeat against Strabane in the Irish Senior Cup ensured the focus would be on league success.

Expectations were high in 2000 and for much of the season the team looked likely to emulate the success of the previous year, but everything went sour one fateful August weekend when the NCU decreed that the team would have to play three weekend games without their three international players. The harsh decision was appealed but to no avail and, when two of the games were lost, the title was surrendered to Waringstown.

It was a bitter pill to swallow, but great teams succeed in the face of adversity and this was a great team. Compensation came with a Senior Challenge Cup win over Woodvale, the first since 1994, after beating Ballymena, Donacloney, Cliftonville and

Waringstown on the way to the final. In the semi-final clash with the Villagers at The Green, Peter Shields (51 no) and Michael Quinn (three for 11) gave the very vocal North Down fans plenty to celebrate in a tense 18 runs win.

The press recorded the cup final as mediocre, but that didn't affect the enjoyment of the large band of North Down supporters who lauded the comfortable

AGGRESSIVE LEFT HANDED BATSMAN RYAN HAIRE HAS HUMBLED MANY OPENING BOWLING ATTACKS

48 runs win. A very proud Jo Montgomery held the Senior Challenge Cup trophy tightly as he was carried shoulder high from the presentation. In the match itself Andrew White's 67 was the only 'fifty' in the game, while Billy Dale's match figures of six for 68 proved the pick of the bowlers.

The Irish Senior Cup produced some exciting games and the regular trips to Dublin took North Down to Phoenix, Pembroke and Merrion. The players experienced opposition and conditions unlike anything they had faced before and acquitted themselves well on and off the pitch.

Paul Davidson restricted Phoenix to 187 with four for 31. Peter Shields (56) and Robin Haire (41) laid the foundation and Ryan Haire with an unbeaten 35 enabled a three wicket win and a return to Pembroke in the next round.

The bowlers did an excellent job to restrict Pembroke to 163 and the game was won with only two balls left with Robin Haire (40 no) after Paul Davidson hit 16 vital runs.

Then it was back to Dublin again and the neat little enclosed ground at Merrion for a third round tie, but after posting a modest 156 total, the rains came and Merrion were happy to come to Comber a fortnight later for the replay.

Robin Haire (66 no) and Peter Shields (64) recovered the situation from a poor start, and the 196 total proved too much for the visitors with Marty Moreland taking four for 35 off his ten overs.

But this cup run came to an abrupt end at the John Hunter Memorial Ground in Limavady, when the home team scored 294, and North Down never got close. More disappointment ensued, when Donemana beat us in the new ClubTurf Ulster Cup.

The inaugural Chris Russell Captain of the Year Award went to Jo Montgomery, and Robin Haire and Billy Dale took the 1st XI batting and bowling honours.

There was also recognition at the highest level of representative cricket.

Andrew White won the first of many Irish caps, scored a century against Denmark in the European Championships and was the North Down Player of the Year. Ryan Haire also made his international debut.

Peter Shields captained the Ireland under 19 team in Sri Lanka and with Ryan Haire, Alan O'Prey and Andrew White brought great credit to the club.

The return of Taimur Khan for his second season was welcomed by all at The Green and along with Andrew White, Billy Adams, Paul Davidson and Billy Dale featured in the top ten in the NCU end-of-year averages.

Overall it was a very good season, but it would get better.

Having tasted success with Senior League and Senior Challenge Cup honours in the previous two years, hopes were high for yet more honours and Peter Shields in his first year as captain delivered a league and cup double in 2001. Not since 1936 had both trophies been displayed at The Green.

The season had a fairytale finish but a terrible start when the first match was lost away to Instonians. But there was a long way to go, and with only two more defeats during the season, the outcome of the championship came down to a mid-September confrontation with title holders Waringstown at The Green. Surprisingly it proved to be a no contest and a huge anti-climax as North Down, with some satisfaction, recaptured the title.

The Senior Challenge Cup campaign started with a nine wickets win at Muckamore when Andrew White

ONE SHOT MORE...FOR THE HONOUR OF DOWN : A HISTORY OF NORTH DOWN CRICKET CLUB 1857 – 2007

SENIOR CHALLENGE CUP WINNERS 2003: BACK – D KENNEDY, J BARRY (PATRON), N RUSSELL, G PATTERSON, M DALZELL, W ADAMS, R HAIRE, T KHAN, I SHIELDS (PRES).
FRONT – A WHITE, ROBIN HAIRE, J MONTGOMERY, P SHIELDS (CAPT), M MORELAND, A HAIRE.

stole the show with 87 not out. In the next round at Bangor he went a little better with a superb 116 in an easy eight wickets win. That set up a semi-final clash with Cliftonville and, after the bowlers restricted them to 184 for nine, Ryan Haire (75 no) and dad Robin (67) completed a comfortable seven wickets win and secured another cup final appearance at Ormeau.

Waiting in the wings was North of Ireland and a nostalgic occasion, as it was the last cup final to be played at this historic venue. Both clubs had shared the same stage in the inaugural final in 1887 and over the years 'headquarters' had witnessed some outstanding performances, but few would have matched the batting partnership of Ryan Haire and Peter Shields in this game. The match was delayed due to rain, and then Ryan took 25 balls to get off the mark, running out his dad Robin in the process. From then on he was a different batsman, as he struck the ball to all quarters of the ground with aggression and precision. From 87 for three, Ryan and Peter added a record 200 runs in a memorable stand that virtually killed off the home team and certainly destroyed their confidence. Ryan hit a superb 109 not out and Peter 75 not out, in a captain's supporting role that allowed his partner to reach his memorable milestone. Robin added a solid half century in the second innings to consolidate the first innings advantage, and there was a little irony in the fact that North's best bowlers were none other than former North Down all rounder Alan O'Prey, who took five wickets, and future North Down all rounder Ralph Coetzee. But Alan had a mountain to climb in this game and, in due course, North Down won by 93 runs.

Peter lifted the Senior Cup and Ryan took the Man of the Match award on a memorable August afternoon. It was one of many highlights for Peter in his first season as skipper because he capped a fine batting record with 88 not out in the crucial league match against Waringstown and then went on to win the Dai Jones wicket-keeping award at the NCU annual dinner for the most dismissals during the season.

Robin Haire, Andrew White, Ryan Haire, Taimur Khan and Jo Montgomery all had good seasons with the bat and Taimur Khan, Marty Moreland, Billy Dale and Andrew White all made major contributions with the ball. The most economical bowler was Billy Adams whose overs cost a miserly 2.9 runs each.

Early exits from the Irish Senior Cup and the Ulster Cup showed some vulnerability, but the club basked in the glory of a unique league and cup double, and the subsequent award of Britannia Team of the Year confirmed what everybody inside and outside The Green had already determined. Anything otherwise would have been a shock, given the fact that monthly awards had already been secured for June, July and August/September.

The team successfully defended the league title in 2002, surprisingly for only the third time, (1898 and 1930 being the others). Only two league games were lost, to Lurgan and Muckamore, and the former inflicted further pain when they won the one innings Senior Challenge Cup final.

Weather played havoc with the arrangements for this final, and the club and the NCU became embroiled in different interpretations of the rules. However, there were no excuses on the day, as North Down underperformed and Lurgan took full advantage.

Peter Shields collected his second league trophy and also retained the Dai Jones wicket-keeping award and was selected for the NCU regional squad alongside Marty Moreland, Andrew White and Ryan Haire. Andrew had a prolific season with 915 runs, including

Ryan Haire (109no) and Peter Shields (70no) complete the 1st Cup Final Innings in the last Ormeau Final in 2001. They had added an unbeaten 200 for the 4th wicket. The match was won by 93 runs.

Andrew White on his way to another big score at The Green

DAVID KENNEDY ONE OF THE TOP BATSMEN IN IRISH CRICKET

a second round cup century against Waringstown, 40 wickets and established himself in the Ireland team with some excellent European Championship performances.

2002 was another good season for the club and another step forward for a maturing 1st XI. Everyone made major contributions, the hallmark of a winning side, with Robin Haire, Taimur Khan and Andrew White leading the way. Billy Adams took 33 wickets at only 15.7 apiece but it was his economy rate at less than three runs per over which stood out.

The history of our club shows that from 1887 to 1898 and from 1924 to 1936 North Down was the premier cricket club in Ulster and, understandably, these periods have become known as 'Golden Eras.' At the end of the 2002 season the 1st XI had enjoyed five seasons of success and a third 'Golden Era' was predicted. They still had a bit to go to win such lofty status, but they were setting high standards and there was every reason to think it was going to continue. The same could be said for the club off the field as there was a strong 'feel-good' factor around the clubhouse and the administration was in good hands. The supporters were building in numbers, with Jim 'Cooperman' Cooper orchestrating a motley entourage home and away, and not short on advice for all and sundry, whether asked or not!

The senior squad was significantly strengthened when Neil Russell and Marty Dalzell joined from Instonians, Ian Cleland from Woodvale and David Kennedy from Ballymena, four players of widely different temperaments, and each very talented in his own right. The 2003 season was therefore eagerly awaited, but before the serious cricket got under way, 19 members of North Down headed for Mallorca for a pre-season tour. From all accounts this was a very enjoyable trip, but apart from a record-breaking score of 388 off 40 overs at Mallorca CC grounds, no other details have surfaced to date. Perhaps a case of 'what goes on tour stays on tour' and all that?

It was however reported that Marty Dalzell's first ball of this tour struck second slip Raymond Moreland on the knee, causing great pain, great hilarity and a new version of Esperanto!

The prime goal in 2003 was to win a hat trick of league titles, a feat that had only been accomplished by the Waringstown side of the late seventies, the Lisburn side of the early fifties and the North of Ireland side at the turn of the previous century. It was a lofty ambition but the team kept a clear focus all season and, with two games still to play, the NCU chairman, Dr. Murray Power, was on hand to present the championship trophy to North Down captain Peter Shields after a victory over Downpatrick at The Green in late August.

The bonus was the addition of the Senior Challenge Cup and victories over Dunmurry (113 runs), Cliftonville (nine wickets) and Belfast Harlequins (ten wickets) set the stage for a shoot-out with habitual old rivals Waringstown.

Cup form had been as good as league form all season and Andrew White led the way with 148 against Dunmurry, 72 against Cliftonville and 81 not out against Belfast Harlequins.

The final was played at Stormont and, in glorious weather, Andrew continued where he left off, with 80 runs, ably supported by Robin Haire (50). Martin Moreland and Marty Dalzell took three wickets each and a telling first innings lead of 47 runs was 'in the bag'. In the second innings 'DK' Kennedy (93 no) was rampant, and for once someone outshone 'Whitey' with the bat, but only just, as he registered another half century. It left the Villagers an imposing target of 258 runs to win and they were never in the hunt, finishing 95 runs short.

Peter Shields collected the Senior Challenge Cup once again, and in the middle of all the celebrations was our oldest member, Jim Barry, the club Patron, who sadly was never to enjoy another celebration, as he passed away during the winter.

No impact was made in either the Irish Senior

Cup or Ulster Cup, the latter demise at the hands of the dreaded 'bowl-out,' but this didn't unduly affect morale with another league and cup double safely secured.

Andrew White was the undoubted Player of the Year, after a dream season when he joined the elite '1,000 Club', players who have scored more than a thousand runs in a season. Oscar Andrews, James Macdonald, Michael Clarke and Raman Lamba were already there from North Down, but Andrew also added the most runs in the NCU, most wickets, and most catches taken. He was the Britannia Player of the Year and became even more established as an international cricketer.

He was at the peak of his cricketing prowess and so was North Down, but when everything in the garden looked rosy, Instonians 'poached' our star player in the close season.

Andrew's departure was a topic of much debate both inside and outside the club, and everyone knew that such a talent would be missed. The club attitude was that, although this was the case, there were other talented players in the team and they would now have the opportunity to step forward and fill the void.

The 2004 defeat by Bangor at the start of the season, not helped by finger surgery for the North Down captain, an ankle injury to Marty Dalzell and a delayed Taimur Khan flight from Pakistan, turned out to be critical. The wait for the 'Gryphons' to stumble en route to the title never happened, and North Down had to settle for a share of second place.

The Senior Challenge Cup defence started at Bangor 12 days after the surprise league defeat, but there was no upset in the cup as Ryan Haire (103 no) and young Gavin McKenna (four for 45) ensured a seven wickets win. Woodvale came to The Green and posted 170 for 6, but Ryan's undefeated 45 was enough to secure a comfortable five wickets win and a semi-final trip to the Meadow in Downpatrick.

David Kennedy stole the show with an innings of 119, but although Downpatrick came within four runs of the 250 target, they succumbed under great North Down pressure.

The final against Belfast Harlequins at Stormont was a great game, 'DK' showing his class once again with an unbeaten first innings century and opener Jo Montgomery hitting 72. Harlequins were 43 runs short at the end of the first day, but North Down's modest 165 for 8 in their second innings left the door open and Harlequins captain Wayne Horwood accepted the challenge.

Wayne batted beautifully and appeared to be comfortably winning the cup, when Peter Shields made a surprise bowling change and brought part-time bowler Kennedy into the action. It proved inspired captaincy, as 'DK' claimed Horwood's wicket with a

NORTH DOWN CAPTAIN PETER SHIELDS STUMPS WARINGSTOWN'S GARFIELD HARRISON
IN THE 2003 SENIOR CHALLENGE CUP FINAL AT STORMONT

'caught and bowled' and took two for four to win the game! It was the first ball of the only over that he bowled all season and he hasn't bowled since! Needless to say there was never any doubt as to who would win the Man of the Match award!

Despite all the successes within Ulster, the Irish Senior Cup was another disappointment following a first round exit at Pembroke.

David Kennedy was awarded the Larry Warke batting trophy at the NCU Dinner and became the first player to win it at two different clubs, having won it at Ballymena in 1998.

Ryan Haire also had a brilliant season and joined the '1,000 Club' with a series of aggressive batting performances. He also played for the NCU and the Irish Development Squad and won the North Down Player of the Year Award, which his grandfather Sam proudly collected on his behalf at the club dinner, as he was in Australia playing cricket and preparing for his participation at the Port Elizabeth Cricket Academy in early 2005.

From a very early age Ryan has made major contributions to North Down, coming through all the youth teams with major input in bowling and batting. Representative honours followed at Regent House School, the NCU and Ireland, and they have been richly deserved. More than any other, he destroyed opposition bowling attacks with his free flowing trademark cover drives. Ryan helped change the team's style of play and with Neil Russell as his opening partner, substantial and rapid opening partnerships demoralised visiting teams to The Green on many occasions, and thrilled the local supporters. Ryan's contribution to North Down goes deeper, and as Development Officer, he has ensured that a conveyor belt of young talent has been established and that the young players have received the specialist coaching that has led to their presence in the Saturday teams.

His loyalty to North Down has been manifest in different ways, none more pertinent than his choice to play for his club, when an Ireland 'A' team place was his for the taking.

Ralph Coetzee joined the club for the 2005 season and what an asset he has turned out to be. He carries the quiet spoken and gentle temperament on to the field of play, but plays with a steely resolve and an abundance of ability and character. A left hand batsman with superb timing and a miserly left arm slow bowler, he has brought a balance and new dimension to the side. He scored 64 not out in the Senior Challenge Cup first round win over Instonians that led to a meeting with Laurelvale and a clash with old friends and former North Down players, Paul and Charlie McCrum.

THE TALENTED ALL ROUNDER RALPH COETZEE

THE POWER AND AGGRESSION OF NEIL RUSSELL

However, 216 runs from the combined efforts of Neil Russell, Gavin Rodgers, David Kennedy and Robin Haire plus four wickets from Ian Cleland saw them off by 63 runs. Almost inevitably it set up another meeting with Waringstown.

The semi-final took place at The Green and it turned out to be another intriguing encounter. North Down opener Neil Russell hit an inspired century, Coetzee a brilliant 61 not out in quick time, and

CHAPTER 10 : 1998 – 2006 : THE THIRD GOLDEN ERA

North Down 2nd XI Junior Cup Winners 2006: Back – A Stevenson, M Campbell, R Galway, I Arthur, R McMillan, G Patterson, W Adams, D Wishart, A Frater (Scorer). Front – I Carser, A Baird, J Montgomery (Capt), D Clarke, A Thakur, D Graham.

Waringstown was set a formidable 292 target to win. They took up the gauntlet in some style and were threatening, when the outcome effectively swung on a magnificent 'caught and bowled' by Marty Moreland to dismiss Kyle McCallan for 79. It was Marty's only wicket but it was a match winner.

A neutral observer might assume that Marty Moreland was an ordinary player in a highflying team. How wrong he would be. For a decade Marty has simply been an outstanding player in a very good 1st XI. He has generally bowled at the heart of the innings against the cream of the opposition batsmen and many, to their cost, have underestimated his casual approach to the wicket and the flighted delivery. Surprisingly overlooked by the representative selectors, Marty has proved over a number of seasons that he earned the right to play at the higher level. He has scored vital runs, held critical catches, and has been instrumental in the success of the 1st XI in this Golden Era.

The 2005 Senior Cup Final returned to Downpatrick for the first time since 1997 when the home team won the right to face North Down.

The evenly contested first innings turned into a North Down bowling blitz in the second, when they dismissed the home side for 108 runs and won by eight wickets.

North County and Strabane put paid to hopes of hardware outside the Province, while the loss of the first two league games meant it was tough going trying to make up lost ground. The team rallied well especially late in the season, and the surge paid off with a share of the title with Waringstown.

The Green provided a natural setting for the inaugural Twenty20 Finals Day after the NCU got it right in their vision and promotion of the competition.

The North Down Titans overcame Bangor Gryphons and the Carrickfergus Eagles to lift the trophy, and the substantial crowd ensured that this competition was here to stay.

Ryan Haire had another terrific season with over 900 runs, and Peter Shields won the NCU Larry Warke batting award with an average of over 70. Neil Russell was denied entry into the '1,000 Club' because 200 of his runs were scored while playing for the 2nd XI but what another great season he had!

Ian Cleland took 43 wickets and Marty Moreland 41, the latter controlling the middle of the innings and the former generally economical at the start of the innings and devastatingly effective in dealing with the tail-enders. It was to be Ian's last of a three year stay with the club, a time marked with personal success and a huge contribution to the pace bowling department.

The loyal supporters, many of whom had agonised in the defeats of the past, basked in the glories of the present without too much thought for the future.

And who could fault them?

In 2006 the close season 'signing' of New Zealander Peter Connell, brought a wave of anticipation to The Green after his registration was completed and accepted by the NCU. Connell soon confirmed his ability with a five-wicket haul at the Lawn and became a formidable opening partner for Taimur Khan, forging the best opening attack in the NCU.

The season was a great success for new captain Ryan Haire, as North Down won the NCU Twenty20 Cup, the NICA-sponsored Ulster Cup and then clinched the Senior League title at Wallace Park at the end of the season with only one defeat.

But then an amazing turnaround took place after Waringstown, in the midst of media speculation, challenged Connell's registration. The NCU initially backed their original decision but then allowed the Waringstown challenge, and after much acrimony between the clubs and legal action on both parts, the NCU awarded the league championship to Waringstown.

The club accepted that they had made a genuine error in their registration papers and the NCU confirmed that it had accepted the error in good faith. North Down felt harshly treated by the outcome and, with most to gain, Waringstown walked off with a league title won in the committee room.

The saga was compounded by the fact that Waringstown had beaten North Down in the semi-final of the Senior Cup at the Lawn and went on to win the trophy thus giving them a league and cup 'double.' However, most observers saw it as a hollow victory, as cricket is played on the field, not the committee room.

The Connell affair detracted considerably from another great season at The Green, and it took a lot of soul searching in the close season to regain focus and bounce back. But 2007 was the club's sesquicentenary season and that was plenty reason for the club to put 2006 behind it and move forward.

For the record, Peter Connell and Marty Moreland each took over 40 wickets, Ryan Haire scored 1,026 runs at an average of 51, David Kennedy averaged over 100 and won the Larry Warke batting award for the fourth time. 'DK', in his fifth season with the club, epitomised everything good about the game, and made a terrific contribution in the 1st XI with batsmanship of international standing and slip fielding second to none. He set a high standard at the club for integrity and sportsmanship, demonstrated in practical terms what the Spirit of the Game means and was recognised by our Umpires and Scorers Association, NIACUS, with their Fair Play award in 2006.

DOWN THE CLUB

Four of our young players were selected for the Ireland Under 19 team to play in the European Colts Championship in July 1998 and it was fitting that Ryan Haire, Alan O'Prey, Peter Shields, and Andrew White played the first match against Holland at The Green. The game was won by seven wickets and was followed by another victory against Denmark at Ballygomartin Road and when the Scotland game was rained off, Ireland had qualified for a place in the under 19 World Cup finals in Sri Lanka, with Shields given the honour of captaining the side.

In January they jetted off to Columbo to represent their club and country and they weren't without support, as Jo Montgomery, Betty and Miller O'Prey jnr., Rowland and Richard White, Raymond and Marty Moreland, David Wishart, Ian Shields and club secretary Darren Elliott all made the unforgettable journey to the beautiful island of Sri Lanka.

The 2nd XI moved up to Division Two Section 1 in 1999 and finished a creditable third and lost in the semi-final of the Junior Cup with Keith Malone at the helm. Ian Carser and RJ Montgomery scored lots of runs, Alan Stevenson and David Moreland played their accustomed and often destructive aggressive cricket and veteran Don Shields kept a tidy wicket and marshalled the lower order. Most promising was the dual opening bowling attack of Michael Dines and Aaron Mills.

In Millennium year, the 2nd XI, captained by the 'Ards Monty', Jonathan Montgomery, finished fifth in the league but unfortunately made an early exit from the Junior Cup. Andrew Haire delivered some excellent bowling figures and the evergreen Roy Keenan kept runs to a minimum. Peter Law, Ian Carser, Darren

Ulster Cup Winners 2006: Back – P Connell, P Shields, N Russell, M Dalzell, G McKenna, J Montgomery, R Coetzee, A Frater (Scorer). Front – M Moreland, R Galway, Ryan Haire (Capt), R Haire, T Khan,

Clarke and Andrew Macrory scored the bulk of the runs with David Moreland recording a fine century at Ormeau, a wonderful memory for any batsman.

Ian Carser, although captain of the 2nd XI in 2001, had a prolonged spell in the 1st XI and the seconds' captaincy was taken over by Peter Law, who faced difficulties with a shortage of players and the team struggled to avoid relegation. Carser played in only five innings, scoring 342 runs at an average of 114, but this and bowler Roy Keenan's economy rate was enough to keep them in Section 1. As always, Ian led by example, and he held the side together with top performances with bat and ball.

Change came in 2005 when new captain Darren Clarke brought a fresh approach and a new confidence. The side won 15 of their 18 league games to lift the Division 2 Section 1 trophy for the first time in the club's history and the following year repeated the achievement, finishing joint winners with Lisburn.

However, there was no sharing of the Junior Cup, with a straightforward first round win against Victoria followed by a nail-biting one run win against Bangor, with veteran Ian Carser taking five for 27. A four-wicket semi-final win against Saintfield led to the Wallace Park shoot-out against Drumaness, when 84 from Jo Montgomery and 37 from Ian Carser set the foundation for a 210 runs first innings total. It was too much for Drumaness who succumbed to the slow bowling of Carser, who took four for 36 and four for 24 in the innings and eight runs victory.

In 1999, Chris Russell's 3rd XI won all 11 matches in the league, with great batting performances from Darren Clarke, Billy Gordon, Darren Elliott, Gary Stewart and the captain himself. On the bowling front the pace of the erratic Barry Ireland served as a foil to the measured line and length of Roy Keenan, and Dessie Savage as wicketkeeper added a threat to the batsmen when they faced Graham Moreland and veteran Syd Elliott.

The club members were stunned when Chris died tragically in a road accident in September. He was a terrific young man, and from no age his father Colin had him at the club where he grew up with his many friends. His was a tragic loss and it was a poignant moment when Darren Elliott received his team's trophy from David Gower at the NCU Dinner.

The following year, Darren Elliott took the 3rd XI to a remarkable run of 13 wins from 13 league games, to take the Division Three Section One league championship again, with the evergreen Billy Gordon and Sydney Elliott the batting and bowling award winners respectively. Billy's all round performances played a big part in keeping the 3rd XI in a mid-league table position for the next couple of years and he was there to collect a Lindsay Minor Cup winner's medal in 2002, when Instonians were beaten by a good all round North Down team performance. Gary Stewart was named the Man of the Match for his 53 runs and Alan Stevenson, Peter Law and Billy Gordon took the wickets to enable the 17 runs win. But the unsung hero was Jim Wilson whose slow left-arm bowling was economy personified. So the thirds won the Lindsay Minor Cup after a 14-year gap and then reached the semi-final in 2004 to go out to Waringstown at the Lawn.

Andrew Frater's 3rd XI finished fourth in the league in 2004, but were relegated into Section Two in 2006.

The 4th XI under Andrew Frater won Division Four Section 2 in 1998, the league-deciding fixture being against Bangor in September, in a season when Jonathan Gamble and Billy Gordon scored centuries, the flamboyant Sri Lankan, PL De Silva destroyed the Carrick bowling and Darren Clarke succumbed to the 'nervous nineties' with 91 again against Carrick.

The enthusiastic Andrew did a tremendous job in the early Millennium introducing new and young players to the game and leading his 4th XI to third place in the league in 2001. A Minor Qualifying Cup final followed in 2002 but two years later there was great pressure to dispense with the 4th XI as player shortage threatened the junior sides. This did not happen, as Graham Moreland, David Moreland and Colin McCaughey ensured that a 4th XI was put in the field.

The midweek competition was revived and between 1999 and 2004 North Down, usually under the leadership of Marty Moreland, appeared in four finals,

2ND XI DIVISION TWO SECTION 1 LEAGUE CHAMPIONS 2005: BACK – P LAW, J GILLILAND, I CLELAND, M QUINN, G MCKENNA, C NAPIER, J NAPIER, A BAIRD, M MORELAND, R HAIRE. FRONT – M CAMPBELL, I CARSER, G PATTERSON, D CLARKE (CAPT) J MONTGOMERY, D SHIELDS, I ARTHUR.

beating Dunmurry in 2001 by two runs at Newforge.

Many clubs rate their success on the performances of the 1st XI and while North Down is no exception there has been great camaraderie up and down the teams in modern times, and the successes at every level, whether individual or team, have been openly celebrated in the clubhouse by everyone.

THE ULSTER CUP IN THE THIRD GOLDEN ERA

Not having qualified for the inaugural Ulster Cup competition in 1999, the following year was the club's first participation. Welcomed by most clubs, it gave players from the top clubs in the NCU and the North West unions the opportunity to play against new opposition in new arenas. It allowed the 'pros' to compete and had the ruling that a result had to be achieved on the day, if necessary through the dreaded 'bowl out'.

It wasn't necessary in our first year as the side crashed out by five wickets at The Holm in Donemana.

In 2001, Taimur Khan and Peter Shields both scored 70s against Limavady at Comber and the side won by eight runs, but couldn't cope with Brigade at Beechgrove where they lost heavily by nine wickets in the next round.

A visit to the competitive teams in the North West was always a challenge, but the first round v2isit to Strabane in 2002 was fruitful, and the comfortable eight wickets win led to a match with Donemana at The Green. Bowlers dominated and chasing 139 was by no means straightforward and not as comfortable as the five wicket win indicated.

The scheduled June final against Downpatrick, abandoned due to the weather, was played in August at The Meadow, with great bowling performances from Andrew White (three for nine) Taimur Khan, Billy Adams and Billy Dale, each with two wickets and the wicketless Marty Moreland who bowled his eight overs for eight runs! The eight wickets win was just reward for a team that had grown in confidence against the oft-feared Northwesters.

In 2003 the 'rub of the green' was with North Down in their bowl out against Donemana, when a strike from Azhar Shafique was 'no balled' and Ian Cleland won the tie with a last ball wicket. In the second round at The Green the home side had plenty of confidence when set a 166 runs target by Limavady. However, and unluckily as it turned out, a deluge caused the game to be abandoned and Kamran Akmal, the Pakistani international wicket keeper, struck twice to help Limavady to a 4-2 'bowl-out' win.

In an expanded 16-team competition in 2004, a win against Bready (by nine wickets) set up a high scoring encounter that saw Taimur Khan and the brilliant Hasan Raza score centuries in the Glendermott game at Comber. North Down won with Billy Adams claiming a 'five-for' and in another thriller at Limavady in the semi final North Down were beaten in an agonising one run defeat.

Strabane won the Ulster Cup in 2005 but were really fortunate to go through to the second round when North Down were 145 for two, chasing 184, when 'the wheels came off' thanks to Bobby Rao's six for 31 and they were beaten by two runs.

The competition continued to bring thrilling finishes, even in atrocious conditions, and when six of the scheduled first round fixtures were reduced to bowl outs in 2006, Brigade and North Down provided a first round nail biter at Comber that included a brilliant Peter Connell catch at deep mid wicket to dismiss Wajhatullah Wasti and three comical run outs that

SRI LANKA BOUND FOR YOUTH WORLD CUP 2000: RYAN HAIRE, ANDREW WHITE, PETER SHIELDS, ALAN O'PREY

brought a one run victory.

A 3-2 'bowl out' win at murky Ballyspallen was a just reward, as the North West side had been bowled out in their innings for 80 runs when the rain arrived, and a great semi-final win over Glendermott at Comber brought two giants together at Upritchard Park, Bangor.

North Down scored 236 in their 40 overs against Limavady with Taimur Khan (89) and Peter Shields (73 not out) laying the foundation for the challenging target and when Marty Dalzell trapped Zeeshan Malik, lbw, and Des Curry fell the same way to Ralph Coetzee, the challenge petered out, leaving North Down winners by 88 runs. It was the second Ulster Cup win.

MILLENNIUM YOUTH

The Regent House side that won the Schools' Cup in 1998 had nine of the team associated with North Down and they had steamrolled Methodist College (by seven wickets), Bangor Grammar (eight wickets), Coleraine AI (141 runs) and RBAI (86 runs) before they met Campbell College at Moylena in the final and won by 114 runs. When they won the Gordon McCullough Memorial Cup, they had achieved a unique double, largely down to the performances of the young North Down players Paul McLaughlin, Aaron Mills, Barry Ireland, and Christopher Fry along with the 'big three' of Shields, Haire and White.

The school expressed its gratitude to the North Down club for facilitating the home games and the hospitality that they received.

Regent House had been supplying their cricketing cream to North Down for years and players like Robin Haire, Ian Shields, Ian Carser, Michael Quinn and Sydney Elliott were all alumni of Regent and all captains of the 1st XI at The Green. There were many others, both players and administrators, too many to mention, who had their cricketing roots in the school. Going further back, Walter Fawcett, former international player and NCU umpire was another 'old boy' and one of the few who, today, can recall keeping wicket to the bowling of the legendary James Macdonald, former Headmaster at the school.

In 2003, and still under the guidance of Murray Lee and Eric Cinnamon, Regent House School had its most successful year since the late nineties with the Napier brothers, Christopher and Jonathan, Richard McMillan, Adam Baird and Matthew Campbell to the fore.

The youngsters were never neglected and with former Club Development Officer Michael Quinn being recognised at the NCU Annual Dinner for his work with the NCU Under 13s and the Irish Under 13s, the coaching proceeded at The Green with Marty Moreland, Ryan Haire, Roy Keenan and Peter Shields all contributing.

The powerful Colts' side that had won the Cup in 1996 repeated the success two years later under Marty

Colts' Cup Winners 2005: Back – A Mayne, J Napier, R Galway, D Graham, S Cummings, G Eynon, M Campbell, G McKenna. Front – S Hamilton, I Arthur, C Napier (Capt), A Baird.

Moreland's leadership. They convincingly beat Woodvale and Armagh before winning the final against Ballymena at the Mall and the young players who had known such success at schools and youth level were about to be tested on the bigger stage.

In 2003, the young players in the Under 15 group reached the Graham Cup final, a rare achievement, but as happened in their NCU league, lost out at the last hurdle.

The youth section in 2004 flourished under the direction of Ryan Haire, and Daniel Graham played for the NCU Under 15s while Iain Arthur played for the Lords Taverners Belfast Under 14 XI.

The youth section continued to impress with the Colts Cup returning to The Green for the first time since 1998 after a thrilling encounter against Instonians at Greenisland. The game was tied and North Down won on the strength of fewer wickets lost.

Gavin McKenna, still in his teens, had played representative cricket in England, Wales, Scotland, South Africa, Denmark, Sri Lanka and Spain and in 2008 was due to play in Malaysia in his second Youth World Cup. Already a Senior Cup, Senior League, and Ulster Cup medal winner, his experience should benefit North Down in the years ahead. Iain Arthur progressed from the Taverners to the NCU under 15s, before becoming a 'double' winner with the North Down 2nd XI in 2006.

Ryan Haire was justly rewarded at the Ards Borough Council Sports Awards evening, when he received the Coach of the Year Award from Northern Ireland football manager Laurie Sanchez, in recognition of the important work that he has put in at youth coaching.

In and around the club

As we approach the end of our story, one very important aspect of the game of cricket in Comber has gone unmentioned. Throughout each era the cricketers have relied on their mothers, wives, partners and girlfriends to provide the sustenance at the half-time interval between innings.

From the earliest days, the teas were provided by a select group of ladies whose servants or maids carried out the more menial tasks of setting the table, pouring the tea and taking the dishes back to the manor or estate to be cleaned.

As times changed, the catering was bought in by the players, and by the 1920s and 30s, Robert James White, known locally as 'Mickey', was the key supplier of the refreshments, aided and assisted by the late Jim Barry.

As we progressed into the fifties, the difficulty of collecting the tea money from each player became apparent, and it wasn't long before the onus fell on the players to produce the sandwiches. The cakes were still provided at a cost to those players not able to provide the sandwiches.

The great organiser of the teas and collector of tea money was none other than Big Willie, who ensured that his favourite jam sandwiches were produced, and that nobody left the ground without paying. It didn't always run smoothly, and the young players in particular found ingenious ways of evading the collector.

Many ladies throughout the years have helped prepare the teas, and in the seventies and early eighties salads were served up for all the teams at The Green. It was at this time, not surprisingly, that the club established a reputation for the excellence of their refreshments, a reputation that is becoming more difficult to maintain as the years go by. The days of the ladies committee have gone, and unfortunately the onus has fallen on the team captains to organise their own teas, a duty that adds considerably to an already demanding role.

However, the ladies have not totally disappeared and there is not a more welcome sight for the cricketer after a gruelling 50 overs in the sun, than that of the 'tea lady', waiting with teapot in hand and a few extra delicacies on the plate.

After the success of winning the Senior League for the first time since 1936, the Annual Dinner at La Mon Hotel in 1999 was a special occasion. Only one survivor of the last North Down team to win the league remained, and Neville Petts, aged 86, was invited to join our celebrations. Neville flew in from Kent with his son David and had a wonderful evening relating stories about matches and personalities from his era and conveyed his feelings on the great work being done, particularly in relation to the development of youth cricket at The Green. He was a gentleman in every sense of the word. On his departure, and with his son remarking that he could now die happy, he received a standing ovation from the assembled players and members. Neville died two weeks after his visit and his memorial seat, placed in front of the pavilion, bears the inscription, 'Last Man Out'.

The success on the field of play and the development of young players under the guidance of Michael Quinn was matched within the executive committee, as the advertising revenue was expanded through major sponsor David Lloyd.

In an effort to encourage the North Down Hockey Club to use the facilities, a new walkway was established between the pavilion and the Leisure Centre. Ards Borough Council, a benefactor to the club over many years, made a major contribution, after great work from George Harper and a presentation to the ABC from Ian Shields. The driving force behind the initiative was former player and current trustee Wesley Graham who, for many years, has been the club's advisor on many legal and planning issues and who, in the eighties, broke all fund raising records with his commercial zeal and expertise.

The tired old 'square' was partially replaced with Surrey loam wickets providing new challenges for the excellent groundsman Raymond Moreland, especially during the so-called summer of 2002.

Walter Wishart stood down from the presidency, but this had no effect on his work-rate about the club. During this era Walter played many roles, organising the bar and helping with the ground to name but two. He was always available and ensured that the essential and often practical aspects of running our club were adhered to. He played through the times when success was limited and enjoys more than most the current successes at all levels.

In February 2002, the Mayor, Councillor Margaret Craig, whose husband John played cricket and hockey for many years at The Green, invited the 1st XI panel and club officers to a celebratory dinner in Roma's Restaurant, in recognition of the achievements of the 2001 'double' season. The treat was repeated when Councillor Jim McBriar, then Mayor and a Comber man of long standing, entertained the club in the Londonderry Room in the Town Hall to celebrate the 2003 league and cup 'double'

The Comber Rotary Club also entertained a number of members at Balloo House, and presented the club with an award for its 'Services to the Community'. In keeping with community spirit, the club held its annual Kwik Cricket competition for primary schools and hosted a musical entertainment and talk on Thomas Andrews for the Belfast Titanic Society.

The opening of the refurbished pavilion was one of the highlights off the field.

The old wooden structure had been knocked down and a brick pavilion established in 1909; a major centenary extension went up in 1957; refurbishment took place in the 1970s and a major extension in the 1990s.

This latest refurbishment was brought about by the endeavours of the excellent executive committee and, under the guidance of Kenny Nelson, himself a former cricketer, some of the club members were in the thick of the demolition and reconstruction. Peter Shields was a virtual Clerk of Works and Raymond Moreland marshalled the squads in the wrecking and rebuilding as the daily routines on some occasions resulted in overnight vigils!

Many new organisations have used the premises for their functions bringing much needed revenue and adding to the community culture of the club.

During the first week in July 2005, The Green hosted three ICC World Cup qualifying games, Ireland against Uganda, Namibia versus Oman and Bermuda against Uganda, the latter falling foul to the abysmal weather. For his part in the organisation of the fixtures, Ian Shields received an award from Ards Borough Council at their Annual Sports Awards evening; but it was a real club effort with the rain making it difficult on a number of fronts.

The club continued to host a wide variety of other matches and these included the Annual White Stick Trophy match between the NCU and Leinster umpires, and a number of games against the MCC.

PETER SHIELDS

The North Down 1st XI captain for the historic 2007 season was Peter Shields and it was fitting that a true cricketing son of Comber was at the helm.

Born into a cricket family with an unrivalled pedigree, Peter's indoctrination was complete when he followed in father Ian's footsteps as skipper in 2001. But in stark contrast to the challenging seventies at the club, his stewardship has been at the highest level of Irish club cricket, and the successes that have ensued have made his old man a very proud father.

In his six years of captaincy Peter has proudly lifted the Senior Challenge Cup five times, the Senior League Championship Trophy four times and the Ulster Cup and Twenty20 Cup once. It is a phenomenal record for a young player who has not only led by example but has won the esteem of his peers inside and outside the club.

Perhaps it was inevitable that Peter would assume

PETER SHIELDS WITH THE
2005 SENIOR CHALLENGE CUP

the reigns of leadership given his background and his progress at Regent House School. He was an outstanding schoolboy cricketer and led a number of school teams to success at various youth levels. He captained the Under 15 team to Ulster Bank Junior Schools Cup and Jubilee Cup wins and as 1st XI skipper he had the honour of leading his side to an historic schools cricket 'double' when they won the McCullough Cup and the Senior Schools Cup in 1998. Three years earlier Peter was a member of North Down's first Graham Cup winning team in 1995, and he added Colts Cup wins in 1996 and 1998. His cricketing CV sits up with the best in local cricket, as do his outstanding individual performances on the way.

His elevation into the North Down 1st XI brought him under Michael Quinn's leadership in Section Two in 1998 and there's no doubt that Michael's strong motivational skills and team ethic played a big part in Peter's cricket education. It was put to good effect the following year when Peter captained the Irish Under

19 team to success in the European Colts Tournament, a World Cup qualifying event held in Northern Ireland.

He was later honoured with the captaincy of the Irish team to go to Sri Lanka for the Under 19 World Cup in January 2000 and had great pride carrying the Irish Cricket Union flag at the opening ceremony before leading the side out to play the hosts in the first match of the tournament in Colombo.

Other honours lay on the horizon and his personal performances as a batting wicketkeeper took him to the top of local club cricket, and the Ireland senior selectors awarded him full international status for his two matches against Scotland at Ayr and Ormeau. He also played for the Irish Development XI and the NCU Interprovincial team.

Peter Shields should have played many times for Ireland but throughout his career the old thorny issue of club or country presented a conflict of interest that was difficult to dispel. There was never any doubt that Peter wanted to play at the highest level, but his cricketing heart and soul was at The Green and that's where his focus has remained since he made his senior cricket debut.

A very talented, if not spectacular, batsman, one of Peter's strongest assets is his ability to read a match, and in much the same way that he assesses and maximizes the attributes of his team members, he can adapt to most situations when he is at the crease. His support of Ryan Haire in the 2001 Challenge Cup final was unselfish and mature, not just because it allowed the aggressive young opener the opportunity to hit an unforgettable century, but because it fostered team spirit and showed his growing qualities as a leader. Such qualities didn't happen overnight but have been inherent in Peter's lifelong high standards of sportsmanship and fair play, qualities that were seen early when he won the Northern Ireland Sportstep Scheme Fairplay Award for his excellent behaviour and sportsmanship during a hockey Coaching Scheme in 1993.

Peter has gone on to be an outstanding senior hockey player with a keen eye for a goal, but cricket has remained his overriding passion. Always the team player, his individual performances have sometimes been overshadowed by the prolific feats of his colleagues in the modern era, but NCU individual awards came his way in 2001, 2002 and 2007, when he won the Dai Jones Trophy for wicket keeping, and in 2005 topped the NCU batting averages to win the Larry Warke Trophy.

These were personal milestones within an exceptional North Down cricket career that has much to offer, because Peter Shields has contributed much more than just playing the game, he remains a committed administrator and committee man who fully appreciates the work and support given by so many people to help North Down succeed.

There could be no better man at the helm in this special year. *(JCH)*

IAN CARSER

As an Ards youth and a sporting enthusiast, it was perhaps inevitable that Ian's Regent House School rugby led to an association with the successful Ards rugby club, and for a time he played at senior level as an effective scrum half. However, his real talent and success found expression in his cricket at The Green.

Ian has been associated with North Down since he was a boy and was another of the Regent House School cricketers to emerge and make a major contribution to the club. At school he played for the 1st XI and had an Ulster Schools trial as a slow bowler. He initially played under Jimmy Boucher for the 3rd XI in 1981 and won the batting cup the following year. It was the start of an illustrious cricket career.

Remarkably he only won the 1st XI bowling cup once, in 1989, with a grand haul of 41 wickets, but he was a frugal bowler who conceded few runs and played a leading part in the 1st XI for almost two decades.

Ian has played for all of the levels within the club on his way to the captaincy of the 1st XI, a position he held for two spells, in 1989/1990 and 1993/1994.

The Irish Senior Cup and NCU Senior Challenge Cups brought him real success and his four wickets for 34 in the semi-final against Carlisle at The Green guaranteed a final at Rathmines against the much fancied Donemana team in 1989 and Ian, after a brilliant two for nine in ten overs, collected the Irish Senior Cup for the first time in the club's history.

In the 1993 campaign he had some outstanding performances in this competition with three for 23 against Clontarf, three for 25 against Strabane and 55 runs against Bready in the semi-final, that led to a great final performance against Brigade when he bowled his 10 overs and took one for 17. He scored a century and took four for 40 against Bready at Magheramason in 1994, winning the Man of the Match award, but his 64 runs and four for 40 didn't save the side from going out of the competition at Ardmore and another MOM award was little compensation.

He also had the distinction of captaining the side in the historic 1994 Senior Challenge Cup final with Lisburn that ended in a tie.

Ian had a peculiar bowling action that looked awkward and prompted some observers to question its legality. He played interprovincial cricket for Ulster Town and recorded figures of five for 79 in a marathon 38 overs spell against Munster in 1992. In the game

The Thomas Andrews North Down XI v The Belfast Titanic Society inaugural match: "This was no normal match and a barbecue was held at half time. It had been agreed that each team would play 20 overs (whatever that means!), with a break at the changeover. Many of those present had no idea how a game of cricket was played and I don't think they were any the wiser when it was over".

THE OFFICIAL JOURNAL OF THE BELFAST TITANIC SOCIETY, SUMMER 2007

IAN CARSER WITH HIS FLIGHTED SPIN

against South Leinster that same year the square leg umpire Robin Glenn controversially refused to call Ian for throwing after Dublin umpire Brian Carpenter questioned his bowling action. Three years later, in a quarter-final Irish Senior Cup game at Railway Union, Ian was 'called' by Dublin umpire Liam Keegan who indicated that he threw his quicker delivery. Ian indicated that he hadn't bowled any quicker deliveries and when he bowled P O'Brien off the last ball of that over, he was tactfully taken out of the attack. The unorthodox Carser action was never seriously questioned and its legality was more a case of perception than reality.

He was a popular cricketer in NCU circles and toured Zimbabwe in 1995 with the Ulster Grasshoppers, and was captain of the tourists to Cyprus the following year. He finished his Grasshoppers tours with an unforgettable South African trip in 1998 and the following year played the second half of the season on the 2nd XI.

By the time that he played for the NCU President's XI against a North of Ireland Select XI in 1999, he was making an enormous contribution to the club's 2nd XI.

He was captain of this side from 2001 to 2004 and saw steady progress each season until business commitments forced him to stand down as skipper, but he remained a key player in their league and cup successes.

Ian succeeded Billy Crawford when he became chairman of the club mid-1996 and it was no surprise that, when the good times returned in 1998, the club's fortunes on the field were matched by his positive leadership off it.

He was the driving force behind the long-term sponsorship contracts, arrangements that have been critical to the club in its drive towards improvement and Ian has worn his commercial hat with great distinction throughout. His drive and enthusiasm played major parts in the pavilion refurbishment, the major work on the ground, the purchase of new machinery, the reorganisation of the sub-committees, and progress towards the use of a Development Officer.

He has brought tremendous personal commitment, vision, and business acumen to chairman's role and those who have misread his quiet disposition have failed to appreciate his steely resolve to get things done. His personal relationships with his fellow club and team members have enhanced his standing within the club and few would argue that he has been a major player on and off the field during the last 20 years.

Ian Carser has been instrumental in establishing and nourishing the third Golden Era.

CHAPTER 11
2007 : THE SESQUICENTENARY YEAR

"WE THANK YOU, O GOD, FOR THE GAME OF CRICKET AND FOR THE OPPORTUNITIES FOR HEALTHY RIVALRY AND SPORTING CAMARADERIE THAT IT PROVIDES. WE THANK YOU FOR THOSE WHO ESTABLISHED THE NORTH DOWN CRICKET CLUB AND FOR ALL THAT HAS BEEN ACHIEVED BOTH ON AND OFF THE FIELD OVER THE PAST 150 YEARS. IN PARTICULAR, TONIGHT, WE THANK YOU FOR THE SUCCESSES OF TEAMS AND INDIVIDUALS IN CUP AND LEAGUE COMPETITIONS OVER THE PAST YEAR. WE THANK YOU FOR THIS OCCASION OF CELEBRATION AND FOR THE PRIVILEGE OF SHARING FELLOWSHIP WITH OUR DISTINGUISHED GUESTS AND REPRESENTATIVES OF OTHER CLUBS."

THE 'GRACE' AT THE GALA DINNER IN LA MON HOTEL, PRONOUNCED BY THE VERY REVEREND HAMILTON LECKEY, FORMER RECTOR OF ST MARY'S PARISH CHURCH, COMBER AND DEAN OF DOWN, 13TH OCTOBER 2007.

WATER UNDER THE BRIDGE

The Peter Connell registration debacle of 2006 didn't do anything to improve relations between the club and the NCU hierarchy and the annual games against Waringstown had Combermen booking their seats early for the fixtures against their fierce rivals.

It was a very determined and harmonious executive committee that met after Christmas 2006 to plan the programme for the sesquicentenary celebrations and although the weather was to be unkind, the events that were finalised became part of an historic anniversary year.

FLOWERS IN THE RAIN

Long time supporter and friend of the club, Alan Foley, arranged with the Ards Borough Council for a commemorative floral display in Comber Square depicting the 150th anniversary. Unfortunately, the proposed official opening by the Mayor of Ards, Councillor Robin Drysdale, did not materialise, as a deluge hit the area and the official opening was cancelled. The display remained in the Square for a number of weeks to remind the townspeople of our historic milestone.

CELEBRATORY GAMES

The game in May against the MCC was uneventful, but enjoyable for those taking part, the highlight being the excellent lunch provided by first class Ballynahinch caterer, Bertie Douglas. David Kennedy played for the victorious MCC and was, in his customary manner, the 'thorn in the side' of the opposition.

The inaugural Belfast Titanic Society match was

NORTH DOWN XI THAT PLAYED THE BELFAST TITANIC SOCIETY XI FOR THE INAUGURAL TITANIC BELL: BACK – HARRY HAWKE, NORMAN WEIR, MERVYN BASSETT, ERIC NESBITT, GEORGE MORROW, ALAN WILSON, ROY BECK. FRONT – MATT WILSON, NORMAN BECK, RAYMOND MORELAND, JIM COOPER, DAVID PATTON, DAVID MCVEIGH.

played between the North Down Supporters XI and the Titanic XI resulting in a great evening's entertainment. Highlight was the barbecue between innings and with the North Down XI winning comfortably, much gloating and exaggeration followed in the clubhouse.

The North Down midweek veterans, as part of the North Down sesquicentenary celebrations, challenged Instonians, celebrating their 75th anniversary.

The match played at The Green turned out to be a thriller, with Instonians posting 110 in their 20 overs and North Down needing one to win off the last ball. The match resulted in a tie and the 'drink out' went into extra time but was eventually won by North Down.

Following on from a competitive match the previous year, the touring team from Rajastan played a North Down Select XI at the end of June and again won the day, this time by 50 runs.

LEAGUE AND CUP SUCCESS

Meanwhile at The Green there was a confidence and belief that the outstanding success since 1998 could be maintained in this special year.

The more serious issue of regaining the Senior Challenge Cup began in May, and Woodvale, Laurelvale and Instonians all perished on our home patch, setting up the final that everyone wanted. The Laurelvale game had provided a 56 ball century from Ryan Haire and the Instonians switched semi final at The Green was not without anxious moments in a nervous run chase.

The final at The Meadow in Downpatrick was the first official one-day final and was, unfortunately, not blessed with decent weather and when Waringstown chose to bat, the North Down pace attack of Peter Connell and Marty Dalzell struck early.

Montgomery, Connell, Dalzell and Shields celebrate Cup Final wicket

New Premier League champions celebrate at The Meadow, Downpatrick 2007: Back – R Haire, T Khan, P Connell, N Russell, M Dalzell, G McKenna, J Patton (Scorer). Front – Robin Haire, M Moreland, P Shields (Capt), D Kennedy, R Coetzee.

An 80 run partnership between Kyle McCallan and James Hall rescued the situation, until a Marty Moreland caught and bowled removed McCallan, and with it the prospect of a big Waringstown total. Hall's wicket, two runs later, brought added grief to the Villagers, and the arrival of rain necessitated a return to the ground the following day.

On resumption on Saturday morning in fine weather, the North Down team was given a great boost by a magnificent diving catch at point by Ryan Haire to dismiss the dangerous Simon Harrison, and thereafter wickets fell at regular intervals until the close, with 188 runs the target for a North Down victory.

Each of the five North Down bowlers had taken wickets, with Moreland finishing on 3 for 40.

After losing the early wicket of Neil Russell, 61 runs were added by Ryan Haire and David Kennedy and when the Haire wicket fell, Kennedy took over. His controlled innings of 80 was a match winner and it was

Under 13 XI Irish Champions after defeating Merrion in Dublin: Back – R Haire (Coach), A Shields (Capt), J Adams, P Carser, P Eakin, R Irwin, M Sandford, A Mitchell, J Hamilton, P Jess, L Dugan, M McIvor, T Khan (Coach). Front – P Knaggs, K Adams, A Malcolm-Bourne, S Irvine.

left to Marty Moreland to provide 'one shot more' to bring off a win that seemed to encapsulate all the emotions of our previous 30 Senior Challenge Cup wins. It wasn't the absorbing contest that the neutral craved, but there weren't many neutrals in the ground and the win was a magnificent anniversary present.

In combination with the League Championship win that was completed at Downpatrick in September, the 1st XI had absorbed the pressure after their league defeat at the Lawn earlier in the year, gained revenge at The Green and underlined what a good side they were.

The Irish Cup run was brief, and after a comfortable win at home against Strabane, the trip to Dublin to play Phoenix proved unsuccessful, and, with the exception of Michael Turkington, who hit a defiant fifty, it was a poor performance. May 2008 will take the side to the lovely ground at Malahide for a first round encounter and who knows what after that!

The successful defence of the Ulster Cup in the sesquicentenary season began at The Green in June with a comfortable 47 run win over visitors Brigade, followed by a devastating 155 run win against Donemana and an equally convincing win against Lisburn at Wallace Park in July. The miserable weather during the month had taken its toll on many grounds, and at the Park, the 131 run North Down total was always going to be enough.

Another final was scheduled for Upritchard Park, Bangor, in August against Instonians, the goal being a unique 'treble'. It wasn't to be, as a total of 206 always looked vulnerable in the 40 over game, and former North Down player, Andrew White and Regan West produced a great a third wicket partnership to deny North Down.

It did not however detract from a brilliant season, the glory and celebrations extending beyond our 1st XI.

Billy Adams' 2nd XI had a terrific season, reaching the final of the Junior Cup and retaining the Division 2 Section 1 championship, to bring about a tremendous hat-trick of titles. This had been the primary goal in the sesquicentennial year and Billy Adams had a powerful squad, added to from the previous year, by the ebullient and talented Michael Turkington, a former Cliftonville player, always popular on his many visits to The Green.

Gary Patterson produced the runs that he had always threatened, and won the 2nd XI batting award for the first time, and the ever-reliable Ian Carser won the club's 2nd XI bowling award for the fourth time in six years. Jo Montgomery and Andrew Haire, both very capable cricketers at the higher level, turned in major performances during the year. Youth was given its chance, with Daniel Graham, Iain Arthur, Simon Cummings, Simon Hamilton, Ryan Galway and

NORTH DOWN PLAYER OF THE YEAR 2007 FLANKED BY PAUL ALLOTT, LEFT AND SIR EVERTON WEEKES

Matthew Knaggs, amongst others, promising much for the future. Richard McMillan delivered big scores in a great season and was called into the senior side on a number of occasions and Billy Adams captained the side with skill, determination and an unshakable belief in the ability of his team.

The 2006 cup success was not repeated in 2007, one of the few disappointments in the year, as North Down won their way through to the final against Lurgan who deservedly won at Wallace Park in the face of a below par performance from North Down.

The 3rd XI under Andrew Frater, Ian Shields and Matthew Campbell stuttered in the league programme, and the aim of returning to the top section was dealt a blow when the first four matches were lost with only the comfort of progress in the Lindsay Minor cup, keeping morale high. The tide turned with a victory over Derriaghy at the end of June and the 3rd XI continued to recover from the early setbacks and went on to finish mid table. The side did well to reach the cup final, but was beaten by a strong Bangor XI, assisted by the poor weather that caused a Monday evening continuation, leaving the team without the unavailable key bowlers, Terry Ritchie and Andrew Frater.

The 4th XI, after struggling in the reconstituted Division 3 Section 4 in 2004, finished 3rd and gained promotion in 2005, stabilised in 2006 and in 2007 finished mid table. It was a great season, fulfilling most of their fixtures and most importantly, under the direction of Graham Moreland and Colin McCaughey, introducing young players to senior cricket.

Development Officer Ryan Haire, with help from club professional Taimur Khan ensured that their young players were recognised and included in the senior teams. For the first time in many years an under 11 side was established, but it was with the older under 13s that real success came when the side won the NCU Banogue Cup for the first time, and followed this with an historic Irish Cup win in Dublin.

The side had all the ingredients for success. Talented young cricketers, nurtured and developed by enthusiastic and capable coaches, with supportive parents assisting where possible.

Sam Russell, Scott Irvine and Paul Ritchie experienced the Belfast Taverners festival of cricket at Arundel and Irvine and Alistair Shields played for the NCU under 13 team. At the other end of the youth spectrum, Gavin McKenna was preparing to jet off to Malaysia in January 2008 for his second Youth World Cup.

ULSTER BANK AWARDS

In an event that reflected the excellent organisational and presentational skills of Robin Walsh, the end of season Ulster Bank awards were presented at the sponsors headquarters in Belfast in October. Gerard Wilson from the Ulster Bank, along with Ivan Anderson the NCU President, handed over awards to Ian Shields, a proxy for Ryan Haire who had won two with centuries against CSN and Derriaghy; two also for David Kennedy for his centuries against Lisburn

GAVIN MCKENNA
AND UMPIRE WALTER MONTGOMERY

and Derriaghy; one for Taimur Khan for his 101 not out against Lurgan; Ralph Coetzee for his Individual North Down Performance of the season, 102 not out against Waringstown and one to the North Down Player of the Year, Marty Moreland for his 6 for 25 against Carrickfergus.

GALA DINNER

The new Sesquicentenary flag flew proudly at La Mon Hotel for the Gala Dinner in October, when Clarence Hiles, who had flown in from Barbados, acted as MC for the evening and opened the proceeding by welcoming the 300 guests.

Sir Everton Weekes, who had accompanied Hiles from the Caribbean, received a warm welcome, and after congratulating the club on a magnificent past and present, stated that the club was on the right path for an equally successful future. He proposed the toast to the North Down Cricket Club.

Former 1st XI cricketer, The Very Reverend Hamilton Leckey, formerly Rector of St Mary's Parish Church in Comber and Dean of Down, pronounced the 'Grace' before the meal.

The club awards were presented by Sir Everton and guest speaker, Paul Allott, former England Test cricketer and Sky Sports broadcaster, the highlight being the award of the Player of the Year to Marty Moreland who featured in many match changing moments, hit the winning runs in the cup final and took 52 wickets during the season.

Two great servants of the club, Sammy Haire and Walter Wishart received framed commemorative prints of The Green from Sir Everton Weekes and Paul Allott and received a resounding applause from the assembled.

The toast to the NCU was delivered by the North Down chairman Ian Carser and responded to by Ivan Anderson, the NCU President, who spoke of the major contribution that the North Down club had made from the earliest days and the continuing success both at 1st XI and youth level.

Tom Mills, the North Down President, proposed the toast to the Irish Cricket Union and this was responded to by Roy Torrens, the Ireland team manager who had many tales to relate of the Irish World Cup success in the West Indies.

The guest speaker Paul Allott was high in praise of the North Down club and its excellent website and told stories of his days in the England and Lancashire teams.

Clarence Hiles with the gavel, ensured that the auction was a major success and it was particularly satisfying that the artist of the original watercolour of The Green was in attendance. James Cooke had played cricket at The Green as a boy and the subsequent auction and purchase of his painting brought him great satisfaction, both personally and on behalf of the club. Ray Browne, President of the North Down

TAIMUR KHAN AND RAYMOND MORELAND

THE ARTIST, JAMES COOKE, HANDS OVER HIS WATERCOLOUR OF 'THE GREEN' TO CHAIRMAN IAN CARSER, LEFT AND PRESIDENT TOM MILLS.

Hockey Club, purchased the painting on behalf of the hockey club and presented it immediately to the cricketers to hang in the club pavilion. A much appreciated gesture.

Norman Mawhinney donated the magnificent framed England cricket shirt signed by 18 England cricket captains. It was appropriately acquired by Charles Beverland, a former cricketer of note with North of Ireland and proprietor of La Mon Hotel.

In late June, Ian Shields visited the Stormont ground as a photographer for the Ulster Cricketer, to take in the practice sessions of the touring Indian and South African teams and along with the photographic equipment, he carried a print of the James Cooke watercolour.

After speaking with Chandu Borde, the Indian manager, and briefing him on the 150th celebrations and the story of our former Indian professional, Raman Lamba, the whole Indian squad willingly signed the print. Rohan Mahajan, deputy sports editor of the Hindustan Times, subsequently carried the story of our club to thousands of Indian readers.

The same successful outcome followed the South African practice the next day with AB de Villiers, the former Carrickfergus 'pro' being photographed holding the second print that all his team had signed.

Both items at auction remained within the club, as Ryan Haire bid successfully for the South African print and Ian Shields, after a family conspiracy and to his delight, acquired the Indian print.

Wes Campbell scooped the bargain of the evening with the West Indian framed shirt donated by Clarence Hiles, and the happy man leaving the room was the club President and treasurer, Tom Mills. He wasn't alone, as it had been a wonderful evening of nostalgia and celebration.

NCU DINNER

The final act of celebration in the sesquicentenary year was the NCU Dinner with three tables reserved for the North Down contingent. David Kennedy collected the Larry Warke batting trophy, the fifth consecutive year that a North Down player has won it and the second in succession for David.

Peter Shields, in addition to the Premier League trophy, lifted the Dai Jones wicket-keeping award and Billy Adams was presented with the Second Division Section 1 trophy as outright winners, having shared it with Lisburn in the previous year.

The 'Newsletter' NCU Team of the Year included Ryan Haire, David Kennedy, Marty Moreland and Peter Connell, a fair reflection of the dominance of the 1st XI during the season.

THE WAY AHEAD

The story so far has verified a well-held belief that history has a habit of repeating itself. Or as stated at the outset, 'what goes around comes around'.

We are fortunate to have ownership of one of the best playing surfaces in the country and continue to have capable and enthusiastic groundsmen to look after it. The early custodians would have marvelled at artificial pitches, covers for the playing surface and a square without the natural aeration of the worm population.

What will the next 50 years bring in the development of the ground? The only sure thing is that every effort will be made to improve and extend the playing and pavilion facilities. Maybe the plans for the original two-storey pavilion of 1909 will be retrieved and looked at again, and a players' veranda finally established.

There will be an edge to the game, but there is respect amongst the players, and I expect it to be hard and fair. In the end, win or lose, we will have a drink afterwards and say well done.

PETER SHIELDS, NORTH DOWN CAPTAIN, COMMENTING IN THE SENIOR CHALLENGE CUP FINAL PROGRAMME, 27TH JULY 2007

NORTH DOWN 2ND XI DIVISION TWO SECTION 1 CHAMPIONS 2007: BACK – S HAIRE (PATRON), M TURKINGTON, J MONTGOMERY, G PATTERSON, D GRAHAM, R MCMILLAN, A STEVENSON, M CAMPBELL, T MILLS (PRESIDENT). FRONT – S HAMILTON, I ARTHUR, W ADAMS (CAPT), I CARSER (CHAIRMAN), A HAIRE. ABSENT – S CUMMINGS, R GALWAY.

Terence Andrews looked at the 'social club' concept in some detail in his 1946 report. Maybe the way ahead will involve bringing more sporting organisations on board, and as we go to print, the North Down Hockey Club, with a proposed cricket based 5th XI, are intending to bring the game back to the grass surface at The Green in 2007.

A further step back into the recycling of history would see dart teams visiting, cycling and athletic events around the perimeter, bowls being played on summer evenings and even football as per 1880s!

The concept of cricket being for the young and unattached doesn't hold, as many of our senior players continue to play in the junior ranks and remain in the game, adding valuable experience on and off the field.

Our supporters have shown how, with success on the field, they can assist with many developments at the club and the hope is that they will continue to remain strong in numbers and voice.

Within the club the recent proliferation of baby girls, leads one to think and hope that ladies cricket at some stage in the future will be played at The Green. It wouldn't be the first time that an attempt has been made, as a North Down ladies team played against Belfast ladies in the seventies. The game flourishes in the South so why not in the NCU?

The third 'Golden Era' will come to an end just as the first did in 1900 and the second in 1939. We don't know when, but it should not be as dramatic as before, with an established network of youth teams.

The future lies with the young players, and the club has for the first time in its history, produced an Irish Cup winning side in the under 13 age group. They have witnessed high standards set by the best senior squad the club has known and have hopefully learned that reaching the top requires dedication and hard work as well as talent. How many of them will celebrate our bicentenary?

The most important aspect by far is enjoyment of the game and this is being instilled into our young players on a weekly basis as they 'rub shoulders with' the veterans who continue to derive great pleasure from the game.

We must look to the future and draw inspiration from the wonderful legacy that is ours. North Down cricketers have always played hard, but fair, and the friendships and camaraderie with other clubs has always been very important to us.

No one can predict what will happen in the future, but while committed and able people, who love the game, give of their time and skills, the future of North Down Cricket Club will be secure and in good hands.

North Down Officials and Guests pre Gala Dinner at La Mon 13th October 2007:
Back – A Stevenson, S Haire (Patron NDCC), S Elliott, W Wishart, C McCaughey (Secretary NDCC), R Moreland, N Russell, P Allot (Guest Speaker), Sir E Weekes (Special Guest), T Mills (President NDCC), I Carser (Chairman NDCC), C Hiles (Master of Ceremonies), C Boyd.
Front – I Shields, Robin Haire, D Shields, A Haire, M Moreland, P Shields, Ryan Haire.

The Premier League and Senior Challenge Cup Winners 2007: Back – T Mills (President), I Carser (Chairman), R Haire, J Montgomery, P Connell, D Kennedy, N Russell, M Dalzell, A Haire, M Turkington, A Frater (Scorer), S Haire (Patron). Front – R Coetzee, T Khan, P Shields (Capt), M Moreland (Vice-Capt), Ryan Haire. Absent – G McKenna (Youth World Cup commitments); J Patton (1st XI Scorer).

APPENDICES

Presidents from 1979 – 2007

1979 – 1987	Jim Barry
1988 – 1994	Eddie Doherty
1995 – 1996	Sammy Haire
1997 – 2001	Walter Wishart
2002 – 2004	Ian Shields
2005 – 2007	Tom Mills

Chairmen from 1900 – 2007

1900 – 1908	WT Graham
1909	Thomas Andrews
1910 – 1920	James Andrews
1921 – 1952	William Andrews
1953 – 1956	James Macdonald
1957 – 1965	William Andrews
1966 – 1978	Jim Barry
1979 – 1981	Edward Doherty
1982 – 1987	Derek Steen
1988 – 1991	Sydney Elliott
1992 – 1996	Billy Crawford
1997 –	Ian Carser

Secretaries from 1869 – 2007

1869 – 1898	WT Graham
1899 – 1900	J Niblock
1900 – 1904	HW Andrews
1905 – 1907	W Andrews & WT Graham
1908 – 1912	DA Gold
1914 – 1918	Diverse
1919	AE Wishart
1920 – 1925	S Davidson
1926 – 1934	JLO Andrews & WE Bates
1935	WE Bates (GW Spence Assistant)
1936	TG Andrews
1937 – 1940	HF Andrews
1941	RT Crosby
1942 – 1944	W Galbraith and R Rowan
1945 – 1946	GW Spence
1947 – 1948	F Hodgkiss
1949 – 1950	J Macdonald & GW Fawcett
1951	J Macdonald & JJ Smyth
1952 – 1959	JJ Smyth
1960	WJ Artt
1961 – 1965	D Nesbitt
1966 – 1971	RF Thompson
1972 – 1982	SC Elliott
1983 – 1993	T Ritchie
1994	SC Elliott
1995 – 1997	G Scott
1998 – 2002	DJ Elliott
2003 – 2004	S Magill
2005 –	C McCaughey

Treasurers from 1900 – 2007

1900 – 1905	JM Andrews
1906 – 1909	J Shean JP
1910 – 1930	John Murray Esq. BA
1931 – 1933	WJ Taylor & WR Morrow
1934	J Macdonald & WR Morrow
1935 – 1939	J Macdonald
1940 – 1946	WR Morrow
1947	AD May
1948	GW Spence & J Macdonald
1949 – 1953	WT Crosby
1954	T Boyd
1955 – 1958	CW Taylor
1959 – 1963	J Boucher
1964 – 1965	RF Thompson
1966 – 1967	A Reid
1968 – 1972	A Thompson
1973	R Crosby
1974 – 1979	W McKibben
1980 – 1981	T McMillan
1982 – 1990	W McKibben
1994 –	T Mills

North Down's 31 Irish Cricketers

		Caps
Albert E Anderson	1926	1
Oscar Andrews	1902	7
W Andrews	1928	1
Ralph T Coetzee	2003	8
Jack Dearden	1922	4
G Walter Fawcett	1956-59	12
Robin S Haire	1986	3
Ryan S Haire	2000	6
J Harris	1924	7
David S Kennedy	2002	1
Raman Lamba	1990	4
James Macdonald	1926	29
Thomas John ('TJ') Macdonald	1928	17
Paul McCrum	1989-97	69
Charles ('Charlie') McCrum	1990-94	22
David GR McKibbin	1937	1
Alfred E ('Fred') McMurray	1939	1
Alfred E ('Eddie') Marks	1953-57	6
Victor A Metcalfe	1936	3
William A Miller	1924	1
David AH Milling	1912	3
Paul D Moore	1992-94	2
Harry R Morgan	1931	12
Stanley M Morgan	1930	1
Michael S Reith	1969-80	44
Adrian R Semple	1989	2
E Donald R Shearer	1932-52	32
I Peter Shields	1999	2
David R Taylor	1924	1
Willie Vint	1879-92	10
Andrew R White	2002-	92

The North Down Professionals 1884 – 2007

1884-1885	A Clay
1886-1887	Patton
1894	Brown
1895	Baines
1896	Millership
1897	Watmore
1904-1905	Patton
1906-1910	CJ Lowings
1911	Millership/ AC Johns
1912	Chambers
1913	Millership
1914	Harling
1915	WG Watmore
1919	Coates
1920	WG Watmore
1921-1922	JW Case
1923-1924	JW Kingston
1925-1926	HL Mabbott
1927-1928	GJ Harris
1929	A Dodson
1930	W Lee
1931-1933	T Pearson
1934-1935	Preece
1936	R Patton
1937	Riddington
1938-1939	R Patton
1940	Lee
1941-1942	R Patton
1943-1944	T Maxwell
1945-1946	R Patton
1947	T Maxwell
1948	R Patton
1949-1979	No Professionals
1980-1982	M Reith
1983	Javed Mohammed
1984-1985	Raman Lamba
1986	Asjit Jayaprakasham
1987-1989	Raman Lamba
1990	Asjit Jayaprakasham
1991	Michael Clarke
1992	Milund Gungal
1993-1996	Raman Lamba
1997	Gregg Smith
1998	Asuaf Mohammed
1999-	Taimur Khan

North Down 1st XI Captains 1857 – 2007

1857 – 60	Robert Braithwaite (Co – Founder)
1861 – 68	Robert Withers
1869 – 70	RJ Braithwaite (Son of the Founder)
1871 – 75	J Frame
1876 – 91	John Andrews Jnr
1892	T J Andrews
1893 – 01	John Andrews Jnr
1902 – 07	James Andrews
1908	DR Taylor
1909	James Andrews
1910 – 46	W Andrews
1947	ND Murphy
1948 – 49	W Andrews
1950	JCB Irwin
1951 – 52	GW Spence
1953	WT Watt DFC
1954 – 60	W Dempster
1961 – 62	P Craig
1963	WJ Artt
1964 – 65	W Dempster
1966 – 67	P Craig

1968 – 71	WJ Artt
1972	M Campbell
1973 – 75	WI Shields
1976 – 78	L Hunter
1979 – 80	S Elliott
1981 – 82	MS Reith
1983 – 84	RS Haire
1985	WI Shields
1986 – 88	RS Haire
1989 – 90	IP Carser
1991 – 92	RS Haire
1993 – 94	IP Carser
1995 – 96	RS Haire
1997 – 98	M Quinn
1999 – 00	JHS Montgomery
2001 – 05	IP Shields
2006	Ryan S Haire
2007 –	IP Shields

NCU Individual Awards (Inaugurated 1989)

Larry Warke Batting Trophy:
2003	Andrew White
2004	David Kennedy
2005	Peter Shields
2006	David Kennedy
2007	David Kennedy

Jack Bowden All Rounder Trophy:
1991	Charlie McCrum
1993	Charlie McCrum
1994	Charlie McCrum
2002	Andrew White
2003	Andrew White
2004	Andrew White

Dai Jones Wicket Keeping Trophy:
1993	Paul Moore
1994	Paul Moore
2001	Peter Shields
2002	Peter Shields
2007	Peter Shields

Maultsaid Challenge Cup Batting Award:
2001	Andrew White

Maultsaid Challenge Cup Bowling Award:
2000	Billy Dale

Hasley Under 15 Trophy:
1996	Ryan Haire

Honours 1st XI Senior Challenge Cup Winners

Senior Challenge Cup: 1887, 1888, 1890, 1891, 1892, 1893, 1894, 1897, 1898, 1908, 1913, 1919, 1920, 1924, 1926, 1927, 1928, 1931, 1932, 1934, 1936, 1981, 1991, 1994*, 2000, 2001, 2003, 2004, 2005, 2007
Irish Senior Cup: 1989, 1993, 1995
Ulster Cup: 2002, 2006
Twenty20 Cup: 2005, 2006# *Shared #Voided by NCU

Honours 1st XI Senior League Winners

Premier League Winners: 2006*, 2007
Senior League Winners: 1896 (Shared), 1897, 1898, 1906, 1910, 1919, 1921, 1927, 1929, 1930, 1932, 1934, 1936, 1999, 2001, 2002, 2003, 2005 (Shared)
Senior League Section 2 Winners: 1971, 1973, 1977, 1979, 1998
Senior Qualifying League Winners: 1949, 1955
*Title awarded to Waringstown

Junior Team Honours in Cup and League

2nd XI Honours
Junior Cup: 1894, 1897, 1904, 1926, 1981, 1986, 2006
Division Two Section 1 Winners: 2005, 2006 (Shared), 2007
Division Two Section 2 Winners: 1986, 1995, 1998
Second Division Section B: 1960, 1973
Second Division Section C: 1956
Second Division: 1925

3rd XI Honours
Intermediate Cup: 1980
Lindsay Minor Cup: 1988, 2002
Division Three Section 1: 1978, 2000
Division Three Section 2: 1989, 1999
Division Three Section 3: 1996
Third Division Section A: 1975
Third Division Section B: 1974
Second Division Section F: 1973
Second Division Section G: 1967

4th XI Honours
Minor Qualifying Cup: 1987
Division Four Sect. 1 League Winners: 2001
Division Four Sect. 2 League Winners: 1983, 1987, 1999

Midweek XI Honours
Midweek Cup: 1999, 2001
Midweek League: 1973, 1974, 1975, 1976, 1977, 1981

Youth Section
Colts' Cup: 1996, 1998, 2005
Graham Cup: 1995
Banogue Cup (Under 13): 2007
Irish Cup (Under 13): 2007

North Down '1000' Club

Timed Cricket (All Matches)

		RUNS	AVERAGE
1897	Oscar Andrews	1112	38.34
1927	James Macdonald	1072	48.73
1930	James Macdonald	1349	61.32
1932	James Macdonald	1058	40.62

Limited Overs Cricket since 1966

1987	Raman Lamba	1266	60.30
1988	Raman Lamba	1368	65.10
1991	Michael Clarke	1211	55.00
1994	Raman Lamba	1127	80.50
2003	Andrew White	1025	51.25
2004	Ryan S Haire	1005	45.70
2006	Ryan S Haire	1026	51.30
2007	Taimur Khan	1028	51.40

North Down 'Golden Wickets'

Timed Cricket (All Matches)

		WICKETS	AVERAGE
1897	Tommy Graham	107	7.8
1920	Tommy Maxwell	103	11.3
1926	James Macdonald	106	6.3
1927	James Macdonald	109	8.5
1931	James Macdonald	115	7.8

Limited Overs Cricket since 1966

1979	Lawrence Hunter	55	7.6
1980	Michael Reith	51	17.6
1993	Charlie McCrum	50	14.3
1994	Paul McCrum	50	16.7
2007	Marty Moreland	52	15.9

Senior Challenge Cup Finals Won 1887 – 2007

1887

Final of the Inaugural Senior Challenge Cup v North at Ormeau

1st Innings
North 47 (S Turner 5 for 25)
North Down 159 (Patton 34, J Andrews Jnr 30)
2nd Innings
North 107
North Down won by an innings and 5 runs
Team: J Andrews Jnr. (Capt.), TJ Andrew, AA De Wind, WT Graham, FM Harris, EB Killen, DAH Milling, R Milling, R Patton, S Turner, WS Turner

1888

Senior Challenge Cup Final v Ulster at Ormeau
1st Innings
Ulster 85 (W Turner 2 for 22)
North Down 47 (McGowan 5 for 21, Reid 5 for 24)
2nd Innings
Ulster 38 (W Turner 6 for 6)
North Down 77 for 5 (J Andrews 40 not out)
North Down won by 5 wickets
Team: J Andrews Jnr. (Capt.), TJ Andrews, WT Graham, EB Killen, DAH Milling, R Milling, R Patton, S Turner, WS Turner, HW Andrews, W Barbour

1890

According to the Belfast Telegraph when North Down and Armagh had reached the Final, Armagh lodged a protest and the final was not played on the date arranged. At the meeting of the NCU at which the protest was considered, it was decided that the Armagh Club had acted under a misapprehension, but as the North Down Club were unable to arrange another date for the match, the cup was withheld. According to the NCU official statistics, North Down was awarded the cup

1891

Final v North of Ireland at Ormeau on Aug 7th & 8th
1st Innings
North of Ireland 176 (Hughes 38; W Turner 4 for 53)
North Down 157 (JC Lindsay 75 not out; Hughes 5 for 60)
2nd Innings
North of Ireland 82 (Cuming 38; W Turner 7 for 31)
North Down 102 for 8 (Couper 6 for 49)
North Down won by 2 wickets
Team: J Andrews Jnr. (Capt.), TJ Andrews, WT Graham, EB Killen, DAH Milling, R Patton, S Turner, WS Turner, G Combe, D Brown, JC Lindsay

1892

Senior Challenge Cup Final v Ballymoney at Ormeau 12th & 13th August
1st Innings
North Down 282 (G Combe 93, HW Andrews 56, H Milling 27, W Turner 21;
Ballymoney 36 (W Boyle 12 not out; WT Graham 6 for 21, W Turner 4 for 14)
2nd Innings

Ballymoney 67 (W White 29 not out, RS Young 15)
North Down won by an innings and 179 runs – this was our largest Cup Final winning margin.
Team: TJ Andrews (Capt.), WT Graham, DAH Milling, R Patton, S Turner, WS Turner, G Combe, D Brown, JC Lindsay, RP Hamilton, HW Andrews

1893
Senior Challenge Cup Final v Ulster at Ormeau on 18th and 19th August
1st Innings
Ulster 76 (J Reid 24, J Young 11; W Turner 4 for 25, EB Killen 3 for 27, R Patton 2 for 10)
North Down 198 (H Milling 46, G Combe 38, J Andrews Jnr. 27, JC Lindsay 26; J Reid 6 for 52)
2nd Innings
Ulster 89 (F Ballantine 22, J Reid 14, J Watson 14; W Turner 4 for 35, EB Killen 4 for 36, R Patton 1 for 13)
North Down won by an innings and 33 runs
Team: J Andrews Jnr. (Capt.), TJ Andrews, DAH Milling, R Patton, S Turner, WS Turner, G Combe, EB Killen, JC Lindsay, O Andrews, HW Andrews

1894
Senior Challenge Cup Final v Holywood on 10th & 11th August at Ballynafeigh
1st Innings
North Down 87 (DAH Milling 22, JC Lindsay (I) 17
Holywood 62 (S Beggs 20, J Campbell 12 not out; W Turner 5 for 28
2nd Innings
North Down 30 (JC Lindsay 10; S Beggs 7 for 13, E Hughes 3 for 15
Holywood 33 (D McGonigal 10; W Turner 6 for 12, O Andrews 4 for 13
North Down won by 22 runs – five Cup wins in a row and recorded their lowest total in a Cup Final innings.
Team: J Andrews Jnr. (Capt.), TJ Andrews, DAH Milling, R Patton, S Turner, WS Turner, G Combe, JC Lindsay, O Andrews, HW Andrews, WT Graham

1897
Senior Challenge Cup Final v North of Ireland at Ormeau
1st Innings
North Down 176 (O Andrews 73; C Gillespie 7 for 73)
North of Ireland 112 (FB Newett 58; W Turner 6 for 44)
2nd Innings
North Down 229 (O Andrews 100)
North of Ireland 119 (W Turner 6 for 35)
North Down won by 174 runs
Team: J Andrews Jnr. (Capt.), RP Hamilton, DAH Milling, EL Macnaghten, J Niblock, WS Turner, S Davidson, JC Lindsay, O Andrews, Jas. Andrews, WT Graham

1898
Senior Challenge Cup Final v Ulster at Ormeau
1st Innings
North Down 225 (DAH Milling 80, DR Taylor 61; J Reid 6 for 69)
Ulster 52 (WT Graham 8 for 22)
2nd Innings
Ulster 97 (J Niblock 6 for 20, WT Graham 3 for 35)
North Down won by an innings and 76 runs and WT Graham took 8 for 22 a record for the Club in the Senior Cup – this after being a late call up due to Oscar Andrews being detained in Dublin. WT hadn't played since the end of June!!
Team: J Andrews Jnr. (Capt.), RP Hamilton, DR Taylor, Jas. Andrews, WS Turner, J Niblock, DAH Milling, Jas. Ritchie, S Davidson, AM Andrews, WT Graham

1908
Senior Challenge Cup Final v Cliftonville at Ormeau
1st Innings
North Down 250 (J McDonald 45, W Coulter 45 not out; J Moore 4 for 58)
Cliftonville 76 (WT Graham 5 for 32, AM Crawford 5 for 43)
2nd Innings
Cliftonville 204 (HE Wood 58; WT Graham 4 for 82)
North Down 35 for 2
North Down won by 8 wickets
Team: DR Taylor (Capt.), W Coulter, Jas. Andrews, AE Anderson, Joe Macdonald, RP Houston, AM Crawford, S Davidson, AS Taylor, W Andrews, WT Graham

1913
Senior Challenge Cup Final v Waringstown at Ormeau on 8th & 9th August
1st Innings
North Down 423 (W Andrews 111, AE Anderson 80, Jas Andrews 41, W Coulter 36, DR Taylor 35, WG Abernethy 34, J Dearden 30;

Williamson took 5 wickets
Waringstown 156 (T Anderson 49; W Coulter 4 for 37)
2nd Innings
Waringstown 170 (R Scott 49, J Hampton 46; J Taylor 4 for 46, W Coulter 3 for 63
North Down won by an innings and 97 runs and recorded their highest innings total.
Team: W Andrews (Capt.), W Coulter, Jas. Andrews, AE Anderson, J Dearden, HB Hanna, J Taylor, DR Taylor, DR Wheeler, V Benson, WG Abernethy

1919

Senior Challenge Cup Final v North of Ireland at Ballynafeigh on 15th & 16th August
1st Innings
North Down 175 (DR Wheeler 35, W Coulter 32, WG Abernethy 24, T Maxwell 22; W Pollock 4 for 44, AW McClinton 3 for 43, F Gardiner 2 for 5)
North of Ireland 201 (AW McClinton 96 not out, W Pollock 22, F Gardiner 21, WL Millan 20)
2nd Innings
North Down 202 (W Andrews 48, AE Anderson 43, W Coulter 29; AN McClinton 3 for 36, O Andrews 3 for 58, W Pollock 2 for 59)
North of Ireland 107 (O Andrews 20; HB Hanna 3 for 20, T Maxwell 3 for 33, W Coulter 3 for 39)
North Down won by 69 runs
Team: W Andrews (Capt.), W Coulter, CE Bebe, AE Anderson, J Dearden, HB Hanna, J Taylor, DR Taylor, DR Wheeler, T Maxwell, WG Abernethy

1920

Senior Challenge Cup Final v Cliftonville at Ormeau on 6th & 7th August
1st Innings
Cliftonville 60 (LM Murphy 23; W Lea 5 for 26, T Maxwell 4 for 14)
North Down 108 (W Andrews 39 not out, WA Miller 26; WS Haydock 5 for 31, SJ Stevenson 4 for 28)
2nd Innings
Cliftonville 102 (WS Haydock 34, JH Dunn 16; T Maxwell 5 for 44, W Lea 5 for 48)
North Down 60 for 0 (DR Taylor 31 not out, WA Miller 28 not out)
North Down won by 10 wickets
Team: W Andrews (Capt.), WH Silk, CE Bebe, AE Anderson, J Dearden, WA Miller, FW Willis, DR Taylor, DR Wheeler, T Maxwell, W Lea

1924

Senior Challenge Cup Final v Waringstown at Ormeau on 25th & 26th July
1st Innings
Waringstown 78 (J Williamson 18 not out, J Hampton 15; J Shields 4 for 8, CPR Johnston 4 for 33, B Hill 1 for 8, Jas Macdonald 1 for 17)
North Down 70 (RJE Cadogan 22, CE Bebe 19; J Williamson 6 for 36, T McKenzie 3 for 33, H McKenzie 1 for 1)
2nd Innings
Waringstown 130 (R Scott 37, R Harwood 27; CPR Johnston 3 for 11, RJE Cadogan 3 for 47, J Shields 1 for 18, B Hill 1 for 27)
North Down 139 (AE Anderson 42, WA Miller 21, Jas Macdonald 17; J Williamson 3 for 53, T McKenzie 3 for 53, H McKenzie 2 for 21)
North Down won by 1 wicket. This was the narrowest Cup Final victory.
Team: W Andrews (Capt.), B Hill, CE Bebe, AE Anderson, J Dearden, WA Miller, Jas Macdonald, DR Taylor, RJE Cadogan, CPR Johnston, J Shields

1926

Senior Challenge Cup Final v North of Ireland at Ormeau on 3rd, 4th, 6th and 7th September
1st Innings
North Down 337 (Jas Macdonald 80, DR Taylor, 55 not out, WA Miller 39, CE Bebe 34, AE Anderson 30, J Dearden 25, W Andrews 22, G Spence 20; EA Barry 3 for 69, WR Sproule 3 for 102, AC Douglas 2 for 79, AF Bendall 1 for 24)
Holywood 157 (RJG Grainger 31, EA Barry 27, RA Douglas 26; J Shields 5 for 51, TJ Macdonald 2 for 15, Jas Macdonald 2 for 38)
2nd Innings
North Down 240 for 9 (Jas Macdonald 57, J Shields 51 not out, WA Miller 35, J Dearden 32, G Spence 32; HP Menary 3 for 32, W Sproule 3 for 44, EA Barry 3 for 113)
Holywood 150 (W Sproule 35, AF Bendall 33, EA Barry 31; Jas Macdonald 5 for 41, TJ Macdonald 2 for 43, B Hill 1 for 13)
North Down won by 270 runs
Team: W Andrews (Capt.), B Hill, CE Bebe, AE Anderson, J Dearden, WA Miller, Jas Macdonald, DR Taylor, G Spence, TJ Macdonald, J Shields

1927

SENIOR CHALLENGE CUP FINAL V HOLYWOOD
AT ORMEAU ON 26TH & 27TH AUGUST
1st Innings
HOLYWOOD 99 (CW WELCH 26, CS ANDERSON 18;
JAS MACDONALD 4 FOR 27, TJ MACDONALD 3 FOR 35,
J SHIELDS 2 FOR 22)
NORTH DOWN 169 (AE ANDERSON 33, W ANDREWS
32, CE BEBE 30, JAS MACDONALD 26; CS ANDERSON
4 FOR 48, TG PARSONS 4 FOR 53, WP MCDONOUGH
1 FOR 18)
2nd Innings
HOLYWOOD 59 (CS ANDERSON 24; JAS MACDONALD
8 FOR 18, J SHIELDS 2 FOR 29)
North Down won by an innings and 11 runs
TEAM: W ANDREWS (CAPT.), J HALLIDAY, CE BEBE,
AE ANDERSON, J DEARDEN, WA MILLER,
JAS MACDONALD, DR TAYLOR, G SPENCE,
TJ MACDONALD, J SHIELDS

1928

SENIOR CHALLENGE CUP FINAL V NORTH OF
IRELAND AT BALLYNAFEIGH ON 24TH, 25TH AND 29TH
AUGUST
1st Innings
NORTH OF IRELAND 177 (GW MCCANCE 35, JW ORR
32, RJG GRAINGER 29 NOT OUT, AC DOUGLAS 25;
J SHIELDS 6 FOR 30, J HALLIDAY 3 FOR 30,
B HILL 1 FOR 29)
NORTH DOWN 221 (TJ MACDONALD 60, CE BEBE 35,
JAS MACDONALD 30, 21; J VINT 5 FOR 52,
AC DOUGLAS 4 FOR 51, ADB COCKS 1 FOR 30)
2nd Innings
NORTH OF IRELAND 101 (WGR LOUGHREY (5) 19,
RJG GRAINGER (6) 19; JAS MACDONALD 4 FOR 40,
J SHIELDS 3 FOR 32, J HALLIDAY 1 FOR 4)
NORTH DOWN 59 FOR 3 (TJ MACDONALD (1) 22 NOT
OUT; AC DOUGLAS 2 FOR 24, J VINT 1 FOR 20)
North Down won by 7 wickets. Three Cup wins in a row.
TEAM: W ANDREWS (CAPT.), J HALLIDAY, CE BEBE,
AE ANDERSON, J DEARDEN, B HILL,
JAS MACDONALD, DR TAYLOR, G SPENCE,
TJ MACDONALD, J SHIELDS

1931

SENIOR CHALLENGE CUP FINAL V ULSTER
AT ORMEAU ON 7TH, 8TH AND 11TH AUGUST
1st Innings
NORTH DOWN 119 (HC GRAHAM 40 NOT OUT,
J SHIELDS 22; H MORGAN 4 FOR 38, W MCCLEERY 4
FOR 44)
ULSTER 74 (F JACKSON 15, CT KERR 15;
JAS MACDONALD 8 FOR 26, J SHIELDS 2 FOR 37,
TJ MACDONALD 1 FOR 8)
2nd Innings
NORTH DOWN 256 (TJ MACDONALD 108,
W ANDREWS 37, N PETTS 37, JAS MACDONALD 36;
W MCCLEERY 4 FOR 86, H MORGAN 3 FOR 66,
N TEGART 1 FOR 13
ULSTER 155 (H JACKSON 70, WGR LOUGHRY 20;
JAS MACDONALD 5 FOR 53, J SHIELDS 3 FOR 58,
GA MACDONALD 1 FOR 5)
North Down won by 146 runs
TEAM: W ANDREWS (CAPT.), N PETTS, CE BEBE,
AE ANDERSON, J DEARDEN, MC GRAHAM,
JAS MACDONALD, DR TAYLOR, GA MACDONALD,
TJ MACDONALD, J SHIELDS

1932

SENIOR CHALLENGE CUP FINAL V ARMAGH
AT ORMEAU ON 5TH & 6TH AUGUST
1st Innings
ARMAGH 121 (RJ BARNES 40, G LIVINGSTONE 26;
TJ MACDONALD 4 FOR 12, H MORGAN 3 FOR 41,
J SHIELDS 1 FOR 22)
NORTH DOWN 137 (JAS MACDONALD 28, J DEARDEN
18, AE ANDERSON 17, CE BEBE 17; RJ BARNES 7 FOR
49, W MCKINLEY 1 FOR 18, R MCKINLEY 1 FOR 19,
A ALLEN 1 FOR 27)
2nd Innings
ARMAGH 118 (G LIVINGSTONE 63, W MCKINLEY 12;
H MORGAN 5 FOR 50, JAS MACDONALD 4 FOR 39)
NORTH DOWN 107 FOR 5 (TJ MACDONALD 39 NOT
OUT, JAS MACDONALD 31; A ALLEN 3 FOR 18,
JW MCMAHON 2 FOR 21)
North Down won by 5 wickets
TEAM: W ANDREWS (CAPT.), HR MORGAN,
CE BEBE, AE ANDERSON, J DEARDEN, HC GRAHAM,
JAS MACDONALD, DGR MCKIBBIN, PE MCI CLARKE,
TJ MACDONALD, J SHIELDS

1934

SENIOR CHALLENGE CUP FINAL V WOODVALE
AT ORMEAU ON 11TH, 13TH, 14TH, 16TH AND 17TH
AUGUST
1st Innings
NORTH DOWN 238 (TJ MACDONALD 66, DGR
MCKIBBEN 42, JAS MACDONALD 40; W MCCLEERY
6 FOR 66, CW BILLINGSLEY 2 FOR 30, G WILSON
1 FOR 50, A ARMSTRONG 1 FOR 61)
WOODVALE 157 (R CARROLL 22, R MCCUTCHEON 22,
W MCCLEERY 21 NOT OUT, CW BILLINGSLEY 20,
R MATIER 20; JAS MACDONALD 5 FOR 48,
TJ MACDONALD 2 FOR 33, FH MILLS 2 FOR 39
DR PE CLARKE 1 FOR 22)
2nd Innings
NORTH DOWN 147 (DGR MCKIBBIN 27,
JAS MACDONALD 22, VA METCALFE 21;

CW Billingsley 6 for 48, A Armstrong 3 for 28, W McCleery 1 for 38)
Woodvale 97 (W McCleery 22, G Wilson 18; J Shields 6 for 13, Jas Macdonald 3 for 38, Dr PE Clarke 1 for 21)
North Down won by 131 runs
Team: W Andrews (Capt.), FH Mills, VA Metcalfe, AE Anderson, J Dearden, N Petts, Jas Macdonald, DGR McKibbin, PE McI Clarke, TJ Macdonald, J Shields

1935
Senior Challenge Cup Final v NICC
at Ormeau on 8th, 9th and 14th August
1st Innings
North Down 303 (Jas Macdonald 159 not out, W Andrews 50, J Shields 37; W Johnston 3 for 72, WH Fee 3 for 90, JH Bennett 2 for 33, GWB Gailey 2 for 66)
North of Ireland 114 (JK Wilson 24, WH Fee 21; J Shields 3 for 13, PE McI Clarke 3 for 29, Jas Macdonald 3 for 32)
2nd Innings
North of Ireland 183 (JK Wilson 65, JS Shaw 41, JH Bennett 21; Jas Macdonald 5 for 61, J Shields 4 for 32, PE Clarke 1 for 33)
North Down won by an innings and 6 runs
Team: W Andrews (Capt.), FH Mills, VA Metcalfe, WA Miller, J Dearden, N Petts, Jas Macdonald, DGR McKibbin, PE McI Clarke, H Donnan, J Shields.

1936
Senior Challenge Cup Final v Woodvale
at Cliftonville on 7th & 8th August
1st Innings

Woodvale 82 (CE Posnett 35, R Matier 24; PE Clarke 6 for 33, TJ Macdonald 2 for 7, Jas Macdonald 2 for 30)
North Down 112 (TJ Macdonald 35; AE Armstrong 3 for 28, CW Billingsley 3 for 32, G Wilson 2 for 13, W McCleery 2 for 23)
2nd Innings
Woodvale 77 (W McCleery 27 not out; PE Clarke 7 for 36, Jas Macdonald 3 for 47)
North Down 49 for 6 (N Petts 14 not out; AE Armstrong 4 for 17, G Wilson 2 for 19)
North Down won by 4 wickets. Three Cup wins in a row.
Team: W Andrews (Capt.), FH Mills, VA Metcalfe, W Shields, J Dearden, N Petts, Jas Macdonald, DGR McKibbin, PE McI Clarke, G Spence, J Shields

1981
Senior Challenge Cup Final v Ballymena
at Ormeau on 7th & 8th August
1st Innings
North Down 149 (G Dempster 19, D Artt 18 not out, D Shields 16, J Gilliland 16, M Reith, G Mowat and I Dempster all scored 14; Y Singh 5 for 37, D Kane 4 for 62, N Neill 1 for 18)
Ballymena 149 (G McKenzie 41 not out, D Kane 45; M Reith 6 for 50, W Dale 4 for 41)
2nd Innings
North Down 165 for 8 (J Gilliland 51, G Mowat 31, D Artt 17, JC Hiles 15 not out; N Neill 4 for 59, D Kane 2 for 49)
Ballymena 127 (V Singh 48, W Ridge 36; M Reith 6 for 53, R Haire 1 for 37)
North Down won by 38 runs
Team: M Reith (Capt.), D Artt, W Dale, G Dempster, I Dempster, J Galway, R Haire, C Hiles, G Mowat, D Shields, J Gilliland

1991
Senior Challenge Cup Final v Woodvale
at Downpatrick on 2nd & 3rd August
1st Innings
North Down 251 for 3 (M Clark 111, C McCrum 60, J Gilliland 35 not out, R Haire 23 not out; P Lowry 2 for 48, S Redpath 1 for 70)
Woodvale 242 for 8 (A Raza 146 not out, I Warke 29, G Dempster 21; J Gilliland 3 for 58, C McCrum 2 for 42, M O'Prey 1 for 22, W Adams 1 for 46)
2nd Innings
North Down 235 for 7 (C McCrum (2) 65, M Clark (1) 50, J Gilliland (3) 51, L Semple (5) 27, M Quinn (6) 25; A Raza 4 for 46, P Lowry 1 for 42)
Woodvale 237 (A Raza 67, S Redpath 47, S Warke 36, G Dempster 31; W Adams 4 for 44, I Carser 2 for 53, C McCrum 1 for 26, R Haire 1 for 27, L Semple 1 for 39)
North Down won by 7 runs. 'Pros' banned after this final.
Team: R Haire (Capt.), M Clarke, C McCrum, J Gilliland, M Quinn, I Shields, P Moore, I Carser, L Semple, M O'Prey, W Adams

1994
Senior Challenge Cup Final v Lisburn
at The Meadow on 5th and 6th August
1st Innings
North Down 160 for 9 (C McCrum 58, P McCrum 38; D Heasley 4 for 37, N Doak 1 for 17, D McDowell 1 for 31, U Graham 1 for 31)

Lisburn 158 for 8 (D Heasley 46, R Wiseman 30, M Topping 25; A Semple 3 for 28, P McCrum 2 for 29, C McCrum 1 for 23, R Haire 1 for 23)
2nd Innings
North Down 203 for 7 (A Semple 61 not out, M Quinn 27, R Haire 19; D McDowell 3 for 43, N Doak 2 for 22, H McAuley 1 for 22, D Heasley 1 for 60)
Lisburn 205 (M Blair 57, T McKeown 52, N Doak 18; R Haire 4 for 50, C McCrum 3 for 32, I Carser 1 for 19, A Semple 1 for 54)
Match Tied. Cup Shared for the only time in 120 years of the competition.
Team: I Carser (Capt.), C McCrum, P McCrum, R Haire, J Gilliland, A Semple, M Quinn, P Moore, D Wishart, JHS Montgomery, J Wilson

2000

Senior Challenge Cup Final v Woodvale at Ormeau on 3rd & 4th August
1st Innings
North Down 171 (A White 67, P Shields 32 not out, D Moreland 20; D Cardwell 3 for 18, S Donnelly 2 for 31, R Warnock 1 for 35, R Coetzee 1 for 55)
Woodvale 130 for 9 (R Coetzee 26, G Dempster 22, S Donnelly 22; W Dale 3 for 42, W Adams 2 for 20, P Davidson 2 for 24)
2nd Innings
North Down 116 (Ryan Haire 27, P Shields 18, Robin Haire 16; S Donnelly 4 for 21, D Cardwell 1 for 14, R Coetzee 1 for 15, R Warnock 1 for 28, M McKeown 1 for 30)
Woodvale 109 (S Warke 18, D Scott 17, R Warnock 17; W Dale 3 for 26, P Davidson 3 for 30, A White 2 for 14, M Moreland 2 for 20)
North Down won by 48 runs
Team: JHS Montgomery (Capt.), Robin Haire, Ryan Haire, I Carser, P Shields, M Moreland, D Moreland, P Davidson, W Adams, W Dale, A White

2001

Senior Challenge Cup Final v North of Ireland at Ormeau (The Last Ormeau Final) on 3rd & 4th August
1st Innings
North Down 287 for 3 (Ryan Haire 109 not out, P Shields 76 not out, A White 31, J Montgomery 27; R Coetzee 1 for 14, D Finlay 1 for 58)
North of Ireland 203 (R Coetzee 77, S Redpath 34, W Horwood 28; W Adams 3 for 40, W Dale 3 for 43, A White 2 for 30, Robin Haire 1 for 40, M Moreland 1 for 45)
2nd Innings
North Down 167 (Robin Haire 54, Ryan Haire 30 P Shields 20; A O'Prey 5 for 39, D Finlay 3 for 29, R Coetzee 1 for 16, S Redpath 1 for 28)
North of Ireland 158 (W Horwood 22, S Dyer 19, R Coetzee 19, P Reid 19; A White 3 for 32, M Moreland 2 for 22, W Adams 2 for 34, Robin Haire 1 for 16, W Dale 1 for 23)
North Down won by 93 runs
Team: P Shields (Capt.), Robin Haire, Ryan Haire, A White, G Rodgers, M Moreland, I Carser, W Adams, A Haire, W Dale, JHS Montgomery

2003

Senior Challenge Cup Final v Waringstown at Stormont on 7th & 8th August
1st Innings
North Down 214 for 8 (A White 80, Robin Haire 50, J Montgomery 24; S Kidd 4 for 10, G Harrison 1 for 34, G Kidd 1 for 44, K Morrison 1 for 36)
Waringstown 167 (J Bushe 56, P Hanna 35, A Cousins 21; M Moreland 3 for 39, M Dalzell 3 for 42, W Adams 2 for 26, A White 1 for 28)
2nd Innings
North Down 210 for 5 (D Kennedy 93 not out, A White 54; K Morrison 1 for 20, S Harrison 1 for 26, G Harrison 1 for 28)
Waringstown 163 (S Kidd 29, A Cousins 23; A White 3 for 31, A Haire 2 for 5, M Dalzell 2 for 24, M Moreland 2 for 29, Robin Haire 1 for 32)
North Down won by 95 runs
Team: P Shields (Capt.), JHS Montgomery, A White, Ryan Haire, Robin Haire, A Haire, W Adams, M Moreland, D Kennedy, M Dalzell, N Russell

2004

Senior Challenge Cup Final v Belfast Harlequins at Stormont on 30th & 31st July
1st Innings
North Down 242 for 4 (D Kennedy 105 not out, J Montgomery 72, P Shields 24; W Horwood 2 for 30, N Black 1 for 55)
Belfast Harlequins 199 (C Martin 68, G Wilson 49; I Cleland 2 for 28, Ryan Haire 2 for 36, G McKenna 2 for 40)
2nd Innings

North Down 165 for 8 (D Kennedy 68, P Shields 34; J Patterson 2 for 21, N Black 2 for 25, R Coetzee 1 for 25, A Coulter 1 for 25, W Horwood 1 for 40)
Belfast Harlequins 189 (W Horwood 77, S Dunlop 27, R Coetzee 21; D Kennedy 2 for 4, W Adams 2 for 35, I Cleland 2 for 37, G McKenna 2 for 53, M Moreland 1 for 19)
North Down won by 19 runs
Team: P Shields (Capt.) N Russell, M Moreland, Robin Haire, JHS Montgomery, Ryan Haire, W Adams, D Kennedy, I Cleland, G McKenna, A Haire

2005

Senior Challenge Cup Final v Downpatrick at The Meadow on 4th & 5th August
1st Innings
Downpatrick 208 for 9 (G Ferguson 57, D Mullan 47, N Gelston 34, J Magowan (3) 34; W Adams 3 for 32, R Coetzee 2 for 23, M Dalzell 1 for 35, I Cleland 1 for 65)
North Down 217 for 5 (R Coetzee 51 not out, N Russell 51, P Shields 36; D Mullan 2 for 48, N Gelston 1 for 25, J Cunningham 1 for 37, P Tate 1 for 45
2nd Innings
Downpatrick 108 (D Mullan 23, G Ringland 20; M Moreland 3 for 26, R Coetzee 2 for 16, M Dalzell 1 for 12, W Adams 1 for 26, I Cleland 1 for 27)
North Down 100 for 1 (D Kennedy 52 not out, Ryan Haire 31; J Cunningham 1 for 22)
North Down won by 9 wickets. Three Cup wins in a row.
Team: P Shields (Capt.), D Kennedy, Robin Haire, Ryan Haire, M Moreland, D Moreland, W Adams, M Dalzell, I Cleland, N Russell, R Coetzee

2007

Senior Cup Final v Waringstown at Downpatrick on Friday 27th July
(The first official One Day final)
Waringstown 187 (J Hall 47, K McCallan 34, P Hanna 34; M Moreland 3 for 40, M Dalzell 2 for 34, G McKenna 2 for 35)
North Down 189 for 6 (D Kennedy 80, Ry Haire 32; S Kidd 3 for 35)
North Down won by 4 wickets
Team: P Shields (Capt.), Ryan Haire, N Russell, D Kennedy, R Coetzee, JHS Montgomery, Robin Haire, P Connell, M Moreland, G McKenna, M Dalzell

Irish Senior Cup Finals Won 1982 – 2007

1989

Irish Senior Cup Final v Donemana at Rathmines
Donemana 101 (Alan Dunn 30, R Mitchell 24 not out; R Lamba 3 for 12, W Adams 3 for 34, I Carser 2 for 9, J Gilliland 1 for 1, G Benson 1 for 12)
North Down 102 for 6 (R Lamba 35, M Quinn 21 not out, W Docherty 13 not out; R McBrine 3 for 17, J McBrine 2 for 23, A McBrine 1 for 12)
North Down won by 4 wickets
Team: I Carser (Capt.), R Lamba, I Shields, J Gilliland, R Haire, G Benson, W Docherty, M Quinn, G Mowat, I Connolly, W Adams

1993

Irish Senior Cup Final v Brigade at Rathmines
Brigade 155 (M Kilgore 47, A Rutherford 35, S Smyth 20; A Semple 2 for 34, I Carser 1 for 17, R Haire 1 for 29, M Quinn 1 for 30, C McCrum 1 for 36)
North Down 156 for 3 (C McCrum 87, J Gilliland 32; M Simpson 2 for 34, I Nicholl 1 for 31)
North Down won by 7 wickets
Team: I Carser (Capt.), C McCrum, J Gilliland, R Haire, A Semple, RJ Montgomery, M Quinn, JHS Montgomery, G Benson, P Moore, A Stevenson

1995

Irish Senior Cup Final at The Green, Comber
North Down 227 for 3 (P McCrum 100 not out, R Haire 64 not out, G Rodgers 43; J Long 2 for 53)
Bready 226 (A Rutherford 70, L Jack 41, B Doherty 28, S McConnell 23, D Leckey 21; I Carser 2 for 35, P McCrum 2 for 42, C McCrum 2 for 43, M Quinn 2 for 67)
North Down won by 1 run
Team: R Haire (Capt.), C McCrum, P McCrum, G Rodgers, J Gilliland, A Semple, I Carser, A Macrory, D Moreland, M Quinn, P Moore

Ulster Cup Finals Won 1999 – 2007

2002
ULSTER CUP FINAL AT V DOWNPATRICK
AT THE MEADOW, DOWNPATRICK 25TH AUGUST
DOWNPATRICK 75 (R SHILLIDAY 20; A WHITE
3 FOR 9, W ADAMS 2 FOR 18, T KHAN 2 FOR 21)
NORTH DOWN 79 FOR 2 (A WHITE 36 NOT OUT,
T KHAN 19 NOT OUT; P LENNON 1 FOR 4,
J MAGOWAN 1 FOR 24)
North Down won by 8 wickets
TEAM: P SHIELDS (CAPT.), J MONTGOMERY,
A WHITE, ROBIN HAIRE, T KHAN, RYAN HAIRE,
M MORELAND, D MORELAND, A HAIRE, W ADAMS,
W DALE

2006
ULSTER CUP FINAL V LIMAVADY
AT UPRITCHARD PARK, BANGOR 13TH AUGUST
NORTH DOWN 236 FOR 7 (T KHAN 89, P SHIELDS
73NO, N RUSSELL 21; A RIDDLES 4 FOR 42, C MOORE
1 FOR 27, DES CURRY 1 FOR 48)
LIMAVADY 148 (S SMYTH 45, M MCDAID 36:
M DALZELL 3 FOR 31, P CONNELL 2 FOR 14,
R COETZEE 2 FOR 39, T KHAN 1 FOR 19,
M MORELAND 1 FOR 30)
North Down won by 88 runs
TEAM: RYAN HAIRE (CAPT.), P SHIELDS, N RUSSELL,
T KHAN, R COETZEE, P CONNELL, ROBIN HAIRE,
J MONTGOMERY, M MORELAND, G MCKENNA,
M DALZELL

North Down 1st XI Batting and Bowling Cup Winners (1895 – 2007)

Year	Batsman	Bowler
1895	WS TURNER	WS TURNER
1896	JC LINDSAY	WS TURNER
1897	O ANDREWS	WT GRAHAM
1898	S DAVIDSON	WS TURNER
1899	O ANDREWS	WT GRAHAM
1900	S DAVIDSON	WT GRAHAM
1901	RP HOUSTON	R PATTON
1902	S DAVIDSON	WT GRAHAM
1903	DR TAYLOR	R PATTON
1904	JAS. ANDREWS	JAS. NIBLOCK
1905	DR TAYLOR	WT GRAHAM
1906	JAS. ANDREWS	JAS. NIBLOCK
1907	DR TAYLOR	JAS. NIBLOCK
1908	W ANDREWS	WT GRAHAM
1909	W COULTER	W COULTER
1910	W ANDREWS	RP HOUSTON
1911	W ANDREWS	WG ABERNETHY
1912	W ANDREWS	WG ABERNETHY
1913	W ANDREWS	V BENSON
1914	W ANDREWS	HB HANNA
1915	W ANDREWS	GBT STORY
1916	JH BYERS	JH BYERS
1917	NOT RECORDED	NOT RECORDED
1918	NOT RECORDED	NOT RECORDED
1919	W COULTER	W COULTER
1920	CE BEBE	T MAXWELL
1921	AE ANDERSON	W LEA
1922	W ANDREWS	RJE CADOGAN
1923	W ANDREWS	B HILL
1924	W ANDREWS	JAS. MACDONALD
1925	AE ANDERSON	JAS. MACDONALD
1926	JAS. MACDONALD	JAS. MACDONALD
1927	JAS. MACDONALD	JAS. MACDONALD
1928	TJ MACDONALD	JAS. MACDONALD
1929	TJ MACDONALD	JAS. MACDONALD
1930	JAS. MACDONALD	JAS. MACDONALD
1931	TJ MACDONALD	JAS. MACDONALD
1932	JAS. MACDONALD	JAS. MACDONALD
1933	JAS. MACDONALD	JAS. MACDONALD
1934	JAS. MACDONALD	JAS. MACDONALD
1935	JAS. MACDONALD	JAS. MACDONALD
1936	JAS. MACDONALD	JAS. MACDONALD
1937	JAS. MACDONALD	JAS. MACDONALD
1938	JAS. MACDONALD	JAS. MACDONALD
1939	JAS. MACDONALD	JAS. MACDONALD
1940	DGR MCKIBBIN	N MURPHY
1941	GW SPENCE	W DEMPSTER
1942	GW SPENCE	W DEMPSTER
1943	DGR MCKIBBIN	W DEMPSTER
1944	DGR MCKIBBIN	W DEMPSTER
1945	DGR MCKIBBIN	W DEMPSTER
1946	DGR MCKIBBIN	W DEMPSTER
1947	ND MURPHY	W DEMPSTER
1948	D MURRAY	W DEMPSTER
1949	GW FAWCETT	W DEMPSTER
1950	DGR MCKIBBIN	W DEMPSTER
1951	DGR MCKIBBIN	W DEMPSTER
1952	W WISHART	W DEMPSTER
1953	W DEMPSTER	W DEMPSTER
1954	W DEMPSTER	W DEMPSTER
1955	JW BOYCE	W DEMPSTER
1956	J MCBURNEY	J MCBURNEY
1957	J MCBURNEY	RM TODD
1958	JW BOYCE	RM TODD
1959	W DEMPSTER	W DEMPSTER
1960	W DALZELL	J DALZELL
1961	W DALZELL	J DALZELL
1962	W DALZELL	J DALZELL

Year			Year		
1963	J McBurney	W Dempster	1999	RS Haire	AR White
1964	J McBurney	W Dempster	2000	RS Haire	W Dale
1965	A Thompson	J Dalzell	2001	RS Haire	M Moreland
1966	M Campbell	J Dalzell	2002	AR White	AR White
1967	WI Shields	W Dempster	2003	AR White	AR White
1968	M Campbell	W Wishart	2004	Ryan S Haire	RI Cleland
1969	M Campbell	W Dempster	2005	Ryan S Haire	RI Cleland
1970	WI Shields	W Dempster	2006	Ryan S Haire	P Connell
1971	M Campbell	L Hunter	2007	Ryan S Haire	M Moreland
1972	M Campbell	W Wishart			
1973	WI Shields	W Wishart			
1974	WI Shields	L Hunter			
1975	DC Artt	L Hunter			
1976	WI Shields	L Hunter			
1977	WG Dempster	L Hunter			
1978	WI Shields	L Hunter			
1979	WI Shields	L Hunter			
1980	WI Shields	MS Reith			
1981	MS Reith	MS Reith			
1982	MS Reith	MS Reith			
1983	WI Shields	JC Hiles			
1984	WI Shields	RS Haire			
1985	RS Haire	K Copeland			
1986	WI Shields	RS Haire			
1987	RS Haire	RS Haire			
1988	WI Shields	RS Haire			
1989	J Gilliland	IP Carser			
1990	RS Haire	C McCrum			
1991	C McCrum	L Semple			
1992	RS Haire	C McCrum			
1993	C McCrum	C McCrum			
1994	C McCrum	P McCrum			
1995	C McCrum	P McCrum			
1996	RS Haire	W Adams			
1997	G Rodgers	W Dale			
1998	IP Shields	W Dale			

INDEX

ADAMS W 6,114,119/21,132,135/40,143,147,156/7, 159,170/4
ANDERSON AE 31/5,55/61,66,85,164,167/70,173
ANDREWS JAS 23/4,32/3,36/7,41/2,52,77,163/4
ANDREWS JM 18,23/4,36,45,78
ANDREWS J JNR 12/6,18/21,33,164
ANDREWS O 15,23,25,27/8,31,41,50,52,57,141,164, 166/7
ANDREWS T 18,20,24,28,31,35,38/9
ANDREWS TJ 12/4,19/20,25,31,33,37/8,167
ANDREWS W 5, 41/2, 52/61,70/2,83/4,109,113,163/4,167/70, 173
ARMSTRONG J 100, 106,117
ARTHUR I 143,146,148/9,156
ARTT D 4,90,98/9,101,103,107/9,117/8,127/8, 170,174
ARTT P 6,100,104,106,122,126/7
ARTT W 6, 84,88,90/1,96,98,101/2,106,127,163/5
BAIRD A 143, 146,148
BARKER W 101,105/6
BARRY S 6,102/3,106,121/2
BARRY J 24 65,88 91,93/5,97/100,108,113/4,116/7,120,127/8, 132,138,140,149,163
BAXTER J 44,76/7
BECK N 90,122,125/6,154,162
BECK R 104,154
BENSON G 93,114/5,172
BOUCHER J 4, 84 87/91, 98,100/1,104/6,122/3, 151,163
BOUCHER K 6,117,122,
BOYCE W 86/7,89,92,173
BOYD C 6,134,161
BOYD FJ 61,64
BRUCE GJ 9,35,44,48/50,52,82
CAMPBELL J 6,90,101,104,106,122
CAMPBELL K 6,90,99,102,122/3,125
CAMPBELL MAL 88/9,91,96,98/9,101/2,165,174
CAMPBELL MATT 143,146,148,157
CAMPBELL W 6,90,101,104,106,108,122,125,159
CARSER IP 6,114/5,118,120/1,132,134/5,143,145/6, 148,151/2, 156,158/161,163,165,170/2,174

CLARKE D 143,145/6
CLARKE M 119/120,126,141,164,166
CLELAND I 140,142,144,146/7,171/2,174
COETZEE R 139,142,145,147,155,158,162,164,171/3
COEY W (ARTIE) 87,91
COMBE G 23,25,166
CONNELL P 134,144/5,147,154/5,159/162,172/4
CONNOLLY I 114,120,127,172
COPELAND K 117,123,174
COULTER W 31/5,45,47,167/8,173
CRAIG J 88/9,104,108
CRAIG P (REV) 84 91,164
CRAWFORD W 114,118,152,163
CROSBY R 55 64,77,86/7,89,91/2,98,104,107,117,163
CUMMINGS S 148,156
DALE W 101/2,106/8,117,119,121,123,132,134, 136/7,139,165, 170/1,173/4
DALZELL J 84,89/92,173/4
DALZELL M 138,140/1,145,147,155,162,172/3
DALZELL W 84,91,173
DAVIDSON P 6,132,135/7
DAVIDSON S 23/4,26,28,31 52/3,64,163
DE WIND E 9,19,48/9,52 82
DEARDEN J 32,52,54/9, 61,67,70, 85, 164,167/170
DEMPSTER G 90,99,101,103/4,108,117/8,170/1
DEMPSTER I 104/5,117,122
DEMPSTER W 55,77,79/80,84,86/7,89,91/2,96,98/9,103,112, 117,164,173/4
DOHERTY E 93,99,108,114,117,120,163
DONALDSON A 117, 122
DONALDSON D 108,128
ELLIOTT DJ 6,122,132,134/6,145/6,163
ELLIOTT SC 6,90,98/100,102/5,107,114,117,121/2,146,148,161, 163,165
FAWCETT W 83,86/7,92,148,163/4,173
FOLEY A 6,154
FRATER A 135,143,145/146,157,162

GALWAY J 97,99/100,102/3,105/8,117,121/2, 170
GALWAY R 143,145,148,156
GAMBLE JD 6, 114,146
GILLILAND 99,102,114,117,118/123,126/7,136, 146,170/2,174
GLOVER R 117, 122
GLOVER S 6 88/9,107/8
GRAHAM D 143,148,156
GRAHAM JJW 6,98,101,104,106/7,128,149
GRAHAM K 122,125
GRAHAM WT 13/6,19,21/2, 25/6,31,34,36,38,41, 49,64,163, 166/7,173
GREAT WAR 31,36,41/50,52/3,72,74,93
GREGG A 87/9
GREGG S 122,125
HAIRE A 5,123,135,138,145,156,160/1,171/3
HAIRE ROBIN 99,102/3,106,113/4,117/20,123,126/7, 129/30,132,135/40,142,145/6,148,155,161/2,164/5,170/4
HAIRE RYAN 123/4,132,135/9,141,144/5,147/9,151,155/7, 159/61,164/5,171/4
HAIRE S 93,104,114,118,120,158,161/12,163
HAMILTON S 148,156,160
HARPER G 107,122,128,134/5,149
HASLETT G 122
HILES F 122
HILES J 6,107,121/12,125/7
HILES JC 2,3,6,52,101/4,106/8,113/4,116/8, 122/3,126/8, 158/9,161,170,174
HILL B 57/9,61
HUNTER L 99,101/3,106/9,115,128,165/6,174
IRELAND B 146,148
IRVINE S 155/7
IRWIN JCB 86/7
JOHNSTON B 99, 102
KENNEDY D 138,140/2,144,154/5,157,160,162, 164/5,171/2
KILLEN EB 9,19,22/3,166/7
KIRK D 61,63/4,85,89,100/1,104
LAMBA R 4,110,113/5,121,123/4,126,129,141,159,164,166,172

LAW P 124,145/6
LECKEY H (REV) 91,96,98,114,153,158
LINDSAY JC 23,33,41,166/7,173
LOWINGS C 64,164
MABBOTT HL 59,63,65/6,164
MACDONALD J 53/5,57/61,63/4,67/71,75,77,79/80,83,85,87,93, 96,98,109,113,141,148,163/4,166,168/70,173
MACDONALD TJ 36,45,50,54/5,60/1,63,67,69, 168/70,173
MACRORY A 118,135,145,172
MAGILL S 6,134/5,163
MAGINNIS AJL 97,101,104/6,121
MALONE K 135,145
MAXWELL J 86,88/9,92
MAXWELL T 56/7,64/5,85,164,166,168,173
MCBURNEY J 87/8,91, 173/4
MCCAUGHEY C 117,122,134,146,157
MCCRACKEN D 90,100,102,104,106/7
MCCRUM C 115,118/21,126,142,164/6,170/2,174
MCCRUM P 115,118,120,142,164,166,170/2,174
MCILVEEN R 91,105/7,122,126
MCKENNA G 141,145/6,148/9,155/7,171/3
MCKIBBIN DGR 57,60/1,64,70,77,86,122,164, 169/70,173
MCKIBBIN W 3,90/1,100,114,123,126
MCKITTRICK J 101,104/6,126
MCLAUGHLIN P 6,124,134/5,148
MCLEOD N 104,106,122
MCMILLAN J 99/100,102,104/5,108,117,119
MCMILLAN R 143,148,157,160
MCMILLAN T 90,104/5,114,117,121,163
MCVEIGH D 6,90,100,104/8,154
MCVEIGH R 100/1,104,108
MILLING DAH 19,22,33,40,164,166/7
MILLS FH 61,63,70,169/70
MILLS H 98,104
MILLS T 6,114,134/5,158/63
MITCHELL R 4,6,104,128
MOHAMMED A 'AS' 135,164
MONTGOMERY C 117,122,125
MONTGOMERY J 6,55,63/4,75/6,85,123

MONTGOMERY JHS 6,118,121,124,132,136/9,141,143, 145/6,155/6,160,162,165,171/3
MONTGOMERY RJ 120,135,145,172
MONTGOMERY W 91,98,100/2,104,107
MOORE P 118,120/1,164/5170/2
MORELAND D 115,118,134/5,145/6,171/3
MORELAND G 125, 146, 157
MORELAND J 3,90,123
MORELAND M 121,123/4,132,135/40,144/8,155/6,158,160/2, 171/4
MORELAND R 6,116/7,122/3,125/7,134/5, 140, 149/50,154, 158,161
MOWAT G 99,102,114,117,170,100
MURPHY N 77,83,164,173
MURRAY D 86,88/9,173
MURRAY J 36,53/4,163
NAPIER C 6, 146, 148
NAPIER J 6, 146, 148
NIBLOCK J 24,28,34/5,41,163,167,173
NORRIS 91, 96, 98
O'PREY A 121,123,132,136/7,139,145,147,171
O'PREY D 88/9,92
O'PREY J 57,61,63/4,88
O'PREY M (JNR) 2,88,90,98,101,106/8,116,119/20,122,125,127, 135,145
O'PREY M (SNR) 86,88/9,91
ORR D 122/3,126/7
PATTERSON G 6, 138, 143, 146,156,160
PATTON B 99, 122
PATTON D 122, 126, 154
PATTON J 6,91,98/9,114,117/8, 120,132,134,155,162
PETTS N 60/1,64,67,70,85,92,149,169/70
QUINN M 6,114/5,118/21,123,132,135/7, 146, 148/50,165,170/2
REITH M 109,112/3,115,117/9,123,127/30, 164/6,170,174
RICHARDSON C 88, 104
RITCHIE T 6,101,114,117,122,150,
RODGERS G 6,115,118,120/1,142
RUSSELL C 137, 146
RUSSELL N 6,123/4,138,140,142,144/5, 155, 161/2,171/3
SAVAGE D 117,121/2,146

SAVAGE T 9,90
SCOTT G 114,134,163,
SEMPLE A 118,121,164,171/2
SEMPLE L 120, 170, 174
SHIELDS D 6,84,89/91,98,101,103,108/9,117/8, 121,123,128,135,145/6,161,170
SHIELDS I 24,71,91,93,96/9,101/2,105/10,113/4,117, 120,125/7,134/6,138,145,148/50,157/65,170,172,174
SHIELDS IP 6,21,121,123/4,129,132,135,137/41, 144/5,147/8,150/1,155,159/61,164/5,171/4
SHIELDS J 55,57/61,63,70,85,168/9,170
SHIELDS W 61, 63/4,70, 91,123,170
SPENCE GW 60/1,64,70,77/9,83,85/6,91, 98,163/4,168/70,173
STEEN D 97,101,104/7,114,122,125/6,163
STEVENSON A 6,134/5,143,145/6,161,172
TAIMUR KHAN 126,132,135/41,144/5,147,155/8, 162,164,166,173
TAYLOR DR 24,28,31/2,34/5,37,41/2,47,56/8,61, 64,85,164,167/9,173
THOMPSON A 90/1,98,101,103,106,121/2,163
THOMPSON L 6,86,88/9
THOMPSON R 4,96,98,104,106,122,163
TODD R 63, 86/7 92,108,173
TURKINGTON M 156, 162
TURNER S 19,21/3,41,113,166/7
TURNER WS 15,19,21,25/7,33,41,166/7,173
WATT W 4, 64,76,86/9,91,98,164
WEEKES SIR E 2, 115,158,161
WHITE AR 124,126,132,135/41,145,147/8,156
WILSON J 117,122,146,171
WILSON S 91,102,104,128
WILSON W 96,100,104,106,121
WISHART D 121/2,143,145,171
WISHART P 122,125,
WISHART W 78,86/93,96,98,101/2,105,121,132, 134,149,158,161,163,173/4